S0-BON-706

Śrī Caitanya-caritāmṛta

BOOKS by
His Divine Grace A.C. Bhaktivedanta Swami Prabhupāda

Bhagavad-gītā As It Is
Śrīmad-Bhāgavatam, Cantos 1-5 (15 Vols.)
Śrī Caitanya-caritāmṛta (17 Vols.)
Teachings of Lord Caitanya
The Nectar of Devotion
Śrī Īśopaniṣad
Easy Journey to Other Planets
Kṛṣṇa Consciousness: The Topmost Yoga System
Kṛṣṇa, The Supreme Personality of Godhead (3 Vols.)
Transcendental Teachings of Prahlād Mahārāja
Kṛṣṇa, the Reservoir of Pleasure
The Perfection of Yoga
Beyond Birth and Death
On the Way to Kṛṣṇa
Rāja-vidyā: The King of Knowledge
Elevation to Kṛṣṇa Consciousness
Kṛṣṇa Consciousness: The Matchless Gift
Back to Godhead Magazine (Founder)

A complete catalogue is available upon request

International Society for Krishna Consciousness
3764 Watseka Avenue
Los Angeles, California 90034

All Glory to Śrī Guru and Gaurāṅga

Kṛshnadāsa Kavirāja, b. 1518 or 19.

Śrī Caitanya-caritāmṛta

of Kṛṣṇadāsa Kavirāja Gosvāmī

Antya-līlā
Volume Three

"The Ecstasy of the Lord and His Devotees"

with the original Bengali text, Roman transliterations, synonyms, translation and elaborate purports

by

HIS DIVINE GRACE

A.C. Bhaktivedanta Swami Prabhupāda

Founder-Ācārya of the International Society for Krishna Consciousness

MIDDLEBURY COLLEGE LIBRARY

THE BHAKTIVEDANTA BOOK TRUST
New York · Los Angeles · London · Bombay

BL
1245
V36
K7713
1973
pt. 3
v. 3

6/1977
Rel. Cont.

Readers interested in the subject matter of this book
are invited by the International Society for Krishna Consciousness
to correspond with its Secretary.

International Society for Krishna Consciousness
3764 Watseka Avenue
Los Angeles, California 90034

© 1975 Bhaktivedanta Book Trust

All Rights Reserved

Library of Congress Catalogue Card Number: 73-93206
International Standard Book Number: 0-912776-74-9

First printing, 1975: 20,000 copies

Printed in the United States of America

Contents

Introduction

Śrī Caitanya-caritāmṛta is the principal work on the life and teachings of Śrī Kṛṣṇa Caitanya. Śrī Caitanya is the pioneer of a great social and religious movement which began in India a little less than five hundred years ago and which has directly and indirectly influenced the subsequent course of religious and philosophical thinking not only in India but in the recent West as well.

Caitanya Mahāprabhu is regarded as a figure of great historical significance. However, our conventional method of historical analysis—that of seeing a man as a product of his times—fails here. Śrī Caitanya is a personality who transcends the limited scope of historical settings.

At a time when, in the West, man was directing his explorative spirit toward studying the structure of the physical universe and circumnavigating the world in search of new oceans and continents, Śrī Kṛṣṇa Caitanya, in the East, was inaugurating and masterminding a revolution directed inward, toward a scientific understanding of the highest knowledge of man's spiritual nature.

The chief historical sources for the life of Śrī Kṛṣṇa Caitanya are the *kaḍacās* (diaries) kept by Murāri Gupta and Svarūpa Dāmodara Gosvāmī. Murāri Gupta, a physician and close associate of Śrī Caitanya's, recorded extensive notes on the first twenty-four years of Śrī Caitanya's life, culminating in his initiation into the renounced order, *sannyāsa*. The events of the rest of Caitanya Mahāprabhu's forty-eight years are recorded in the diary of Svarūpa Dāmodora Gosvāmī, another of Caitanya Mahāprabhu's intimate associates.

Śrī Caitanya-caritāmṛta is divided into three sections called *līlās,* which literally means "pastimes"—*Ādi-līlā* (the early period), *Madhya-līlā* (the middle period) and *Antya-līlā* (the final period). The notes of Murāri Gupta form the basis of the *Ādi-līlā,* and Svarūpa Dāmodara's diary provides the details for the *Madhya-* and *Antya-līlās.*

The first twelve of the seventeen chapters of *Ādi-līlā* constitute the preface for the entire work. By referring to Vedic scriptural evidence, this preface establishes Śrī Caitanya as the *avatāra* (incarnation) of Kṛṣṇa (God) for the age of Kali—the current epoch, beginning five thousand years ago and characterized by materialism, hypocrisy and dissension. In these descriptions, Caitanya Mahāprabhu, who is identical with Lord Kṛṣṇa, descends to liberally grant pure love of God to the fallen souls of this degraded age by propagating *saṅkīrtana*—literally, "congregational glorification of God"—especially by organizing massive public chanting of the *mahā-mantra* (Great Chant for Deliverance). The esoteric purpose of Lord Caitanya's appearance in the world is revealed, his co-*avatāras* and principal devotees are described and his teachings are summarized. The remaining portion of *Ādi-līlā,* chapters thirteen through seventeen, briefly recounts his divine birth and his life until he accepted the renounced order. This includes his childhood miracles, schooling, marriage and early philosophical confrontations, as well as his organization of a widespread *saṅkīrtana* movement and his civil disobedience against the repression of the Mohammedan government.

The subject of *Madhya-līlā,* the longest of the three divisions, is a detailed narration of Lord Caitanya's extensive and eventful travels throughout India as a renounced mendicant, teacher, philosopher, spiritual preceptor and mystic. During this period of six years, Śrī Caitanya transmits his teachings to his principal disciples. He debates and converts many of the most renowned philosophers and theologians of his time, including Śaṅkarites, Buddhists and Muslims, and incorporates their many thousands of followers and disciples into his own burgeoning numbers. A dramatic account of Caitanya Mahāprabhu's miraculous activities at the giant Jagannātha Cart Festival in Orissa is also included in this section.

Antya-līlā concerns the last eighteen years of Śrī Caitanya's manifest presence, spent in semiseclusion near the famous Jagannātha temple at Jagannātha Purī in Orissa. During these final years, Śrī Caitanya drifted deeper and deeper into trances of spiritual ecstasy unparalleled in all of religious and literary history, Eastern or Western. Śrī Caitanya's perpetual and ever-increasing religious beatitude, graphically described in the eyewitness accounts of Svarūpa Dāmodara Gosvāmī, his constant companion during this period, clearly defy the investigative and descriptive abilities of modern psychologists and phenomenologists of religious experience.

The author of this great classic, Kṛṣṇadāsa Kavirāja Gosvāmī, born in the year 1507, was a disciple of Raghunātha dāsa Gosvāmī, a confidential follower of Caitanya Mahāprabhu. Raghunātha dāsa, a renowned ascetic saint, heard and memorized all the activities of Caitanya Mahāprabhu told to him by Svarūpa Dāmodara. After the passing away of Śrī Caitanya and Svarūpa Dāmodara, Raghunātha dāsa, unable to bear the pain of separation from these objects of his complete devotion, traveled to Vṛndāvana, intending to commit suicide by jumping from Govardhana Hill. In Vṛndāvana, however, he encountered Rūpa Gosvāmī and Sanātana Gosvāmī, the most confidential disciples of Caitanya Mahāprabhu. They convinced him to give up his plan of suicide and impelled him to reveal to them the spiritually inspiring events of Lord Caitanya's later life. Kṛṣṇadāsa Kavirāja Gosvāmī was also residing in Vṛndāvana at this time, and Raghunātha dāsa Gosvāmī endowed him with a full comprehension of the transcendental life of Śrī Caitanya.

By this time, several biographical works had already been written on the life of Śrī Caitanya by contemporary and near-contemporary scholars and devotees. These included *Śrī Caitanya-carita* by Murāri Gupta, *Caitanya-maṅgala* by Locana dāsa Ṭhākura and *Caitanya-bhāgavata.* This latter text, a work by Vṛndāvana dāsa Ṭhākura, who was then considered the principal authority on Śrī Caitanya's life, was highly revered. While composing his important work, Vṛndāvana dāsa, fearing that it would become too voluminous, avoided elaborately describing many of the events of Śrī Caitanya's life, particulary the later ones. Anxious to hear of these later pastimes, the devotees of Vṛndāvana requested Kṛṣṇadāsa Kavirāja Gosvāmī, whom they respected as a great saint, to compose a book to narrate these episodes in detail. Upon this request, and with the permission and blessings of the Madana-mohana Deity of Vṛndāvana, he began compiling *Śrī Caitanya-caritāmṛta,* which, due to its biographical excellence and thorough exposition of Lord Caitanya's profound philosophy and teachings, is regarded as the most significant of biographical works on Śrī Caitanya.

He commenced work on the text while in his late nineties and in failing health, as he vividly describes in the text itself: "I have now become too old and disturbed in invalidity. While writing, my hands tremble. I cannot remember anything, nor can I see or hear properly. Still I write, and this is a great wonder." That he nevertheless completed, under such debilitating conditions, the greatest literary gem of medieval India is surely one of the wonders of literary history.

This English translation and commentary is the work of His Divine Grace A. C. Bhaktivedanta Swami Prabhupāda, the world's most distinguished teacher of Indian religious and philosophical thought. His commentary is based upon two Bengali commentaries, one by his teacher Śrīla Bhaktisiddhānta Sarasvatī Gosvāmī, the eminent Vedic scholar who predicted, "The time will come when the people of the world will learn Bengali to read *Śrī Caitanya-caritāmṛta,"* and the other by Śrīla Bhaktisiddhānta's father, Bhaktivinoda Ṭhākura.

His Divine Grace A. C. Bhaktivedanta Swami Prabhupāda is himself a disciplic descendant of Śrī Caitanya Mahāprabhu, and he is the first scholar to execute systematic English translations of the major works of Śrī Caitanya's followers. His consummate Bengali and Sanskrit scholarship and intimate familiarity with the precepts of Śrī Kṛṣṇa Caitanya are a fitting combination that eminently qualifies him to present this important classic to the English-speaking world. The ease and clarity with which he expounds upon difficult philosophical concepts lures even a reader totally unfamiliar with Indian religious tradition into a genuine understanding and appreciation of this profound and monumental work.

The entire text, with commentary, presented in seventeen lavishly illustrated volumes by the Bhaktivedanta Book Trust, represents a contribution of major importance to the intellectual, cultural and spiritual life of contemporary man.

—The Publishers

His Divine Grace
A. C. Bhaktivedanta Swami Prabhupāda
Founder-Ācārya of the International Society for Krishna Consciousness

The temple of Jagannātha Purī in Orissa, where Śrī Caitanya Mahāprabhu resided during the last eighteen years of His manifest presence in this world.

Narendra-sarovara, the celebrated lake in the garden near Jagannātha Purī, where Lord Govinda performed His water pastimes with all the devotees. (*p.221*)

The gate to the Guṇḍicā temple, where the goddess of fortune arrests the servants of Lord Jagannātha during the Herā-pañcamī festival.

LEFT: The *samādhi* tomb of Śrīla Narottama dāsa Ṭhākura, the successor of Kṛṣṇadāsa Kavirāja Gosvāmī and a famous Vaisnava poet. RIGHT: The *samādhi* tomb of Śrīla Viśvanātha Cakravartī Ṭhākura, the successor of Narottama dāsa Ṭhākura and the author of many important commentaries on Vaiṣṇava literature.

The *bhajana-kuṭī* of Śrīla Raghunātha dāsa Gosvāmī at Śrī Rādhā-kuṇḍa in Vṛndāvana.

The original Deities and *samādhi* tomb of Śrīla Rāghava Paṇḍita in the village of Pānihāṭi, West Bengal.

PLATE ONE

"When Uddhava was sent by Kṛṣṇa to see the condition of the *gopīs* in Vṛndāvana, he stayed there for a few months in their association and always talked with them about Kṛṣṇa. Although this greatly pleased the *gopīs* and other residents of Vrajabhūmi, Vṛndāvana, Uddhava saw that the *gopīs* were severely afflicted by their separation from Kṛṣṇa. Their hearts were so disturbed that their minds were sometimes deranged. Observing the unalloyed devotion and love of the *gopīs* for Kṛṣṇa, Uddhava desired to become a creeper, a blade of grass or an herb in Vṛndāvana so that sometimes the *gopīs* would trample him and he would receive the dust of their lotus feet on his head." (*pp.26-27*)

PLATE TWO

"One day Rāmacandra Purī came in the morning to the abode of Śrī Caitanya Mahāprabhu. Seeing many ants, he said something to criticize the Lord. 'Last night there was sugar candy here,' he said. 'Therefore ants are wandering about. Alas, this renounced *sannyāsī* is attached to such sense gratification.' After speaking in this way, he got up and left. Śrī Caitanya Mahāprabhu had heard rumors about Rāmacandra Purī's blasphemy. Now He directly heard his fanciful accusations. Ants generally crawl about here, there and everywhere, but Rāmacandra Purī, looking for imaginary faults, criticized Śrī Caitanya Mahāprabhu by alleging that there had been sweetmeats in His room." (*pp.106-107*)

PLATE THREE

"Boarding a boat in the waters of Narendra-sarovara, Lord Govinda performed His water pastimes with all the devotees. Then Śrī Caitanya Mahāprabhu arrived with His personal associates to see the jubilant pastimes of Lord Jagannātha in the Narendra-sarovara. At the same time, all the devotees from Bengal arrived at the lake and had a great meeting with the Lord. Because of the pastimes in the water, there was great jubilation on the shore, with music, singing, chanting, dancing and tumultuous crying. The chanting and crying of the Gauḍīya Vaiṣṇavas mixed and created a tumultuous sound vibration that filled the entire universe. Śrī Caitanya Mahāprabhu entered the water with His devotees and began His pastimes with them in great jubilation." (*pp.221-224*)

PLATE FOUR

"After performing *kīrtana* with His personal associates, Śrī Caitanya Mahāprabhu took *prasāda* with all of them and then asked them to return to their dwellings and take rest." (*pp.238*)

The details of the Lord's picnic (as given in *Madhya-līlā,* Chapter 12, verses 152-202) are as follows: "In the garden, Śrī Caitanya Mahāprabhu sat down with the other devotees. Vāṇīnātha Rāya then came in and brought all kinds of *mahā-prasāda.* Both Kāśī Miśra and Tulasī, the superintendent of the Guṇḍicā temple, brought as much *prasāda* as five hundred men could eat. Seeing the large quantity of *prasāda,* which consisted of rice, cakes, sweet rice and a variety of vegetables, Śrī Caitanya Mahāprabhu was very satisfied. Since Lord Śrī Caitanya Mahāprabhu is omniscient, He knew that type of preparation each person liked. He therefore had Svarūpa Dāmodara deliver these preparations to their full satisfaction. There is no one within these three worlds—save for Śrī Caitanya Mahāprabhu—who is always so willing to increase the glories of the devotees and give them satisfaction. Śrī Advaita Ācārya and Nityānanda Prabhu sat side by side, and when *prasāda* was being distributed, They both engaged in a type of mock fighting."

PLATE FIVE

"The chanting made a tumultuous roar that filled the sky. All the inhabitants of Jagannātha Purī came to see the *kīrtana*. Due to the forceful vibration of *kīrtana*, the entire world began trembling. When everyone chanted the holy name, they made a tumultuous sound. In this way the Lord had congregational chanting performed for some time, and then He Himself desired to dance. The seven groups began chanting and beating their drums in seven directions, and Śrī Caitanya Mahāprabhu began dancing in the center in great ecstatic love. People all around Him floated in the water of His tears. Raising His two arms, the Lord said, 'Chant! Chant!' Floating in transcendental bliss, the people responded by chanting the holy name of Hari." (*pp.230-233*)

PLATE SIX

"It was a steady, long-standing rule that Śrī Caitanya Mahāprabhu would lie down to rest after lunch and Govinda would come to massage His legs. Then Govinda would honor the remnants of food left by Śrī Caitanya Mahāprabhu. This time when the Lord lay down, He occupied the entire doorway. Govinda could not enter the room, and therefore he made the following request. 'Kindly turn on one side. Let me pass to enter the room.' However, the Lord replied, 'I don't have the strength to move My body.' Govinda made his request again and again, but the Lord replied, 'I cannot move My body.' Govinda repeatedly requested, 'I want to massage Your legs,' but the Lord said, 'Do it or don't do it. It depends upon your mind.' Then Govinda spread the Lord's wrapper over the Lord's body and in this way entered the room by crossing over Him." (*pp.239-241*)

PLATE SEVEN

"Accompanied by His personal associates, Śrī Caitanya Mahāprabhu washed and swept the Guṇḍicā temple, cleansing it as usual. The Lord danced and chanted and then enjoyed a picnic in the garden as He had done before. As previously, He danced in front of the Jagannātha car and observed the festival of Herā-pañcamī." (*pp.247-248*)

The details of the Herā-pañcamī festival (as given in *Madhya-līlā,* Chapter 14, verses 106-135) are as follows: "The Herā-pañcamī festival takes place five days after the Ratha-yātrā festival. Lord Jagannātha has left His wife, the goddess of fortune, and gone to Vṛndāvana, which is the Guṇḍicā temple. Due to separation from the Lord, the goddess of fortune arrives at the main gate of the temple accompanied by many members of her family, all of whom exhibit uncommon opulence. When the procession arrives, the maidservants of the goddess of fortune begin to arrest all the principal servants of Lord Jagannātha. The maidservants bind the servants of Jagannātha, handcuff them, and make them fall down at the lotus feet of the goddess of fortune. When the servants fall down before the lotus feet of the goddess of fortune, they almost fall unconscious. They are chastised and made the butt of jokes and loose language."

PLATE EIGHT

"Govinda kept accumulating the food, and soon it filled a corner of the room. There was quite enough to feed at least a hundred people. All the devotees asked Govinda with great eagerness, 'Have you given Śrī Caitanya Mahāprabhu the *prasāda* brought to me?' When the devotees questioned Govinda, he had to tell them lies. Therefore one day he spoke to the Lord in disappointment, 'Many respectable devotees, headed by Advaita Ācārya, make a great endeavor to entrust me with varieties of food for You. You do not eat it, but they ask me again and again. How long shall I go on cheating them? How shall I be freed from this responsibility?' Śrī Caitanya Mahāprabhu replied, 'Why are you so foolishly unhappy? Bring here to Me whatever they have given you.' Śrī Caitanya Mahāprabhu sat down to eat. Then Govinda offered Him the preparations one after another, and as he did so he spoke the name of the person who had given each one. In this way, Govinda gave everyone's name as he put the food before the Lord. Being very satisfied, the Lord began to eat it all. The hard sweets made of coconut, *mukutā nārikela,* the sweetballs, the many kinds of sweet drinks and all the other preparations were at least a month old, but although they were old, they had not become tasteless or stale. Indeed, they had all stayed fresh. That is the mercy of Śrī Caitanya Mahāprabhu. Within a very short time, Śrī Caitanya Mahāprabhu ate enough for a hundred people. Then He asked Govinda, 'Is there anything more left?' Govinda replied, 'Now there are only the bags of Rāghava.' The Lord said, 'Let them remain today. I shall see them later.' The next day, while taking His lunch in a secluded place, Śrī Caitanya Mahāprabhu opened the bags of Rāghava and inspected their contents one after another. He tasted a little of everything they contained and praised it for all its flavor and aroma." (*pp.250-259*)

CHAPTER 7

The Meeting of Śrī Caitanya Mahāprabhu and Vallabha Bhaṭṭa

The following summary of Chapter Seven is given by Śrīla Bhaktivinoda Ṭhākura in his *Amṛta-pravāha-bhāṣya.* In this chapter, Lord Śrī Caitanya Mahāprabhu's meeting with Vallabha Bhaṭṭa is described. There was some joking behavior between these two personalities, and finally Śrī Caitanya Mahāprabhu corrected Vallabha Bhaṭṭa and sympathetically accepted an invitation from him. Before this, Śrī Caitanya Mahāprabhu saw that Vallabha Bhaṭṭa was greatly attached to Gadādhara Paṇḍita. Therefore He acted as if displeased with Gadādhara Paṇḍita. Later, when Vallabha Bhaṭṭa became intimately connected with the Lord, the Lord advised him to take instructions from Gadādhara Paṇḍita. Thus the Lord expressed His feelings of love for Gadādhara Paṇḍita.

TEXT 1

চৈতন্যচরণাম্ভোজমকরন্দলিহো ভজে ।
যেষাং প্রসাদমাত্রেণ পামরোঽপ্যমরো ভবেৎ ॥১॥

caitanya-caraṇāmbhoja-
makaranda-liho bhaje
yeṣāṁ prasāda-mātreṇa
pāmaro 'py amaro bhavet

SYNONYMS

caitanya—of Śrī Caitanya Mahāprabhu; *caraṇa-ambhoja*—at the lotus feet; *makaranda*—the honey; *lihaḥ*—unto those engaged in licking; *bhaje*—I offer my obeisances; *yeṣām*—of whom; *prasāda-mātreṇa*—simply by the mercy; *pāmaraḥ*—a fallen soul; *api*—even; *amaraḥ*—liberated; *bhavet*—becomes.

TRANSLATION

Let me offer my respectful obeisances unto the devotees of Śrī Caitanya Mahāprabhu. Simply by the causeless mercy of the devotees engaged in licking honey from His lotus feet, even a fallen soul becomes eternally liberated.

TEXT 2

জয় জয় শ্রীচৈতন্য জয় নিত্যানন্দ ।
জয়াদ্বৈতচন্দ্র জয় গৌরভক্তবৃন্দ ॥ ২ ॥

jaya jaya śrī-caitanya jaya nityānanda
jayādvaita-candra jaya gaura-bhakta-vṛnda

SYNONYMS

jaya jaya —all glories; *śrī-caitanya*—to Śrī Caitanya Mahāprabhu; *jaya*—all glories; *nityānanda*—to Nityānanda Prabhu; *jaya*—all glories; *advaita-candra*—to Advaita Ācārya; *jaya*—all glories; *gaura-bhakta-vṛnda*—to the devotees of Śrī Caitanya Mahāprabhu.

TRANSLATION

All glories to Śrī Caitanya Mahāprabhu! All glories to Nityānanda Prabhu! All glories to Advaitacandra! And all glories to the devotees of Lord Śrī Caitanya Mahāprabhu!

TEXT 3

বর্ষান্তরে যত গৌড়ের ভক্তগণ আইলা ।
পূর্ববৎ মহাপ্রভু সবারে মিলিলা ॥ ৩ ॥

varṣāntare yata gauḍera bhakta-gaṇa āilā
pūrvavat mahāprabhu sabāre mililā

SYNONYMS

varṣa-antare—the next year; *yata*—all; *gauḍera*—of Bengal; *bhakta-gaṇa*—devotees; *āilā*—came; *pūrva-vat*—as previously; *mahāprabhu*—Śrī Caitanya Mahāprabhu; *sabāre mililā*—met every one of them.

TRANSLATION

The next year, all the devotees of Bengal went to visit Śrī Caitanya Mahāprabhu, and as previously, the Lord met each and every one of them.

TEXT 4

এইমত বিলাস প্রভুর ভক্তগণ লঞা ।
হেনকালে বল্লভ-ভট্ট মিলিল আসিয়া ॥ ৪ ॥

ei-mata vilāsa prabhura bhakta-gaṇa lañā
hena-kāle vallabha-bhaṭṭa milila āsiyā

SYNONYMS

ei-mata—in this way; *vilāsa*—pastimes; *prabhura*—of Śrī Caitanya Mahāprabhu; *bhakta-gaṇa lañā*—with His devotees; *hena-kāle*—at this time; *vallabha-bhaṭṭa*—the greatly learned scholar named Vallabha Bhaṭṭa; *milila*—met; *āsiyā*—coming.

TRANSLATION

Thus Śrī Caitanya Mahāprabhu performed His pastimes with His devotees. Then a learned scholar named Vallabha Bhaṭṭa went to Jagannātha Purī to meet the Lord.

PURPORT

For a description of Vallabha Bhaṭṭa, one may refer to the *Madhya-līlā,* Chapter Nineteen, text 61.

TEXT 5

আসিয়া বন্দিল ভট্ট প্রভুর চরণে ।
প্রভু 'ভাগবতবুদ্ধ্যে' কৈলা আলিঙ্গনে ॥ ৫ ॥

āsiyā vandila bhaṭṭa prabhura caraṇe
prabhu 'bhāgavata-buddhye' kailā āliṅgane

SYNONYMS

āsiyā—coming; *vandila*—offered obeisances; *bhaṭṭa*—Vallabha Bhaṭṭa; *prabhura caraṇe*—at the lotus feet of Śrī Caitanya Mahāprabhu; *prabhu*—Śrī Caitanya Mahāprabhu; *bhāgavata-buddhye*—accepting him as a great devotee; *kailā āliṅgane*—embraced.

TRANSLATION

When Vallabha Bhaṭṭa arrived, he offered his obeisances at the lotus feet of the Lord. Accepting him as a great devotee, the Lord embraced him.

TEXT 6

মান্য করি' প্রভু তারে নিকটে বসাইলা ।
বিনয় করিয়া ভট্ট কহিতে লাগিলা ॥ ৬ ॥

mānya kari' prabhu tāre nikaṭe vasāilā
vinaya kariyā bhaṭṭa kahite lāgilā

SYNONYMS

mānya kari'—with great respect; *prabhu*—Śrī Caitanya Mahāprabhu; *tāre*—him; *nikaṭe*—near; *vasāilā*—seated; *vinaya kariyā*—with great humility; *bhaṭṭa*—Vallabha Bhaṭṭa; *kahite lāgilā*—began to speak.

TRANSLATION

With great respect, Śrī Caitanya Mahāprabhu seated Vallabha Bhaṭṭa near Him. Then Vallabha Bhaṭṭa very humbly began to speak.

TEXT 7

"বহুদিন মনোরথ তোমা' দেখিবারে ।
জগন্নাথ পূর্ণ কৈলা, দেখিলুঁ তোমারে ॥ ৭ ॥

"bahu-dina manoratha tomā' dekhibāre
jagannātha pūrṇa kailā, dekhiluṅ tomāre

SYNONYMS

bahu-dina—for a long time; *manoratha*—my desire; *tomā' dekhibāre*—to see You; *jagannātha*—Lord Jagannātha; *pūrṇa kailā*—has fulfilled; *dekhiluṅ tomāre*—I have seen You.

TRANSLATION

"For a long time," he said, "I have desired to see You, my Lord. Now Lord Jagannātha has fulfilled this desire; therefore I am seeing You.

TEXT 8

তোমার দর্শন যে পায় সেই ভাগ্যবান্ ।
তোমাকে দেখিয়ে,—যেন সাক্ষাৎ ভগবান্ ॥ ৮ ॥

tomāra darśana ye pāya sei bhāgyavān
tomāke dekhiye, ——yena sākṣāt bhagavān

SYNONYMS

tomāra darśana—Your audience; *ye pāya*—anyone who gets; *sei*—he; *bhāgyavān*—very fortunate; *tomāke dekhiye*—I see You; *yena*—as if; *sākṣāt bhagavān*—directly the Supreme Personality of Godhead.

TRANSLATION

"One who receives Your audience is fortunate indeed, for You are the Supreme Personality of Godhead Himself.

TEXT 9

তোমারে যে স্মরণ করে, সে হয় পবিত্র।
দর্শনে পবিত্র হবে,—ইথে কি বিচিত্র ? ॥ ৯ ॥

tomāre ye smaraṇa kare, se haya pavitra
darśane pavitra habe, ——ithe ki vicitra?

SYNONYMS

tomāre—You; *ye*—anyone who; *smaraṇa kahe*—remembers; *se*—he; *haya*—becomes; *pavitra*—purified; *darśane*—by seeing; *pavitra*—purified; *habe*—will be; *ithe*—in this; *ki vicitra*—what astonishment.

TRANSLATION

"Since one who remembers You is purified, why should it be astonishing that one becomes purified by seeing You?

TEXT 10

যেষাং সংস্মরণাৎ পুংসাং সদ্যঃ শুধ্যন্তি বৈ গৃহাঃ।
কিং পুনর্দর্শনস্পর্শপাদশৌচাসনাদিভিঃ ॥ ১০ ॥

yeṣāṁ saṁsmaraṇāt puṁsāṁ
sadyaḥ śuddhyanti vai gṛhāḥ
kiṁ punar darśana-sparśa-
pāda-śaucāsanādibhiḥ

SYNONYMS

yeṣām—of whom; *saṁsmaraṇāt*—by remembrance; *puṁsām*—of persons; *sadyaḥ*—immediately; *śuddhyanti*—become purified; *vai*—certainly; *gṛhāḥ*—the houses; *kim punaḥ*—what to speak of; *darśana*—by seeing; *sparśa*—touching; *pāda-śauca*—washing the feet; *āsana-ādibhiḥ*—by offering a seat and so on.

TRANSLATION

" 'One can immediately purify his entire house simply by remembering exalted personalities, to say nothing of directly seeing them, touching their lotus feet, washing their feet or offering them places to sit.'

PURPORT

This is a quotation from *Śrīmad-Bhāgavatam* (1.19.33).

TEXT 11

কলিকালের ধর্ম—কৃষ্ণনাম-সঙ্কীর্তন।
কৃষ্ণ-শক্তি বিনা নহে তার প্রবর্তন ॥ ১১ ॥

kali-kālera dharma——kṛṣṇa-nāma-saṅkīrtana
kṛṣṇa-śakti vinā nahe tāra pravartana

SYNONYMS

kali-kālera—of this age of Kali; *dharma*—the duty; *kṛṣṇa-nāma-saṅkīrtana*—chanting the holy name of Lord Kṛṣṇa; *kṛṣṇa-śakti vinā*—without being empowered by Lord Kṛṣṇa; *nahe*—is not; *tāra*—of that; *pravartana*—propagation.

TRANSLATION

"The fundamental religious system in the age of Kali is the chanting of the holy name of Kṛṣṇa. Unless empowered by Kṛṣṇa, one cannot propagate the saṅkīrtana movement.

TEXT 12

তাহা প্রবর্তাইলা তুমি,—এই ত 'প্রমাণ'।
কৃষ্ণশক্তি ধর তুমি,—ইথে নাহি আন ॥ ১২ ॥

tāhā pravartāilā tumi, ——ei ta 'pramāṇa'
kṛṣṇa-śakti dhara tumi, ——ithe nāhi āna

SYNONYMS

tāhā—that; *pravartāilā*—have propagated; *tumi*—You; *ei*—this; *ta* —certainly; *pramāṇa*—evidence; *kṛṣṇa-śakti*—the energy of Kṛṣṇa; *dhara*—bear; *tumi*—You; *ithe nāhi āna*—there is no question about it.

TRANSLATION

"You have spread the saṅkīrtana movement of Kṛṣṇa consciousness. Therefore it is evident that You have been empowered by Lord Kṛṣṇa. There is no question about it.

PURPORT

Śrī Madhvācārya has brought our attention to this quotation from the *Nārāyaṇa-saṁhitā:*

dvāparīyair janair viṣṇuḥ
pañcarātraiś ca kevalaiḥ
kalau tu nāma-mātreṇa
pūjyate bhagavān hariḥ

"In the Dvāpara-yuga one could satisfy Kṛṣṇa or Viṣṇu only by worshiping opulently according to the *pāñcarātrikī* system, but in the age of Kali one can satisfy and worship the Supreme Personality of Godhead Hari simply by chanting His holy name." Śrīla Bhaktisiddhānta Sarasvatī Ṭhākura explains that unless one is directly empowered by the causeless mercy of Kṛṣṇa, one cannot become the spiritual master of the entire world (*jagad-guru*). One cannot become an *ācārya* simply by mental speculation. The true *ācārya* presents Kṛṣṇa to everyone by preaching the holy name of the Lord throughout the world. Thus the conditioned souls, purified by chanting the holy name, are liberated from the blazing fire of material existence. In this way, spiritual benefit grows increasingly full, like the waxing moon in the sky. The true *ācārya,* the spiritual master of the entire world, must be considered an incarnation of Kṛṣṇa's mercy. Indeed, he is personally embracing Kṛṣṇa. He is therefore the spiritual master of all the *varṇas* (*brāhmaṇa, kṣatriya, vaiśya* and *śūdra*) and all the *āśramas* (*brahmacarya, gṛhastha, vānaprastha* and *sannyāsa*). Since he is understood to be the most advanced devotee, he is called *paramahaṁsa-ṭhākura. Ṭhākura* is a title of honor offered to the *paramahaṁsa.* Therefore one who acts as an *ācārya,* directly presenting Lord Kṛṣṇa by spreading His name and fame, is also to be called *paramahaṁsa-ṭhākura.*

TEXT 13

জগতে করিলা তুমি কৃষ্ণনাম প্রকাশে ।
যেই তোমা দেখে, সেই কৃষ্ণপ্রেমে ভাসে ॥ ১৩ ॥

jagate karilā tumi kṛṣṇa-nāma prakāśe
yei tomā dekhe, sei kṛṣṇa-preme bhāse

SYNONYMS

jagate—throughout the entire world; *karilā*—have done; *tumi*—You; *kṛṣṇa-nāma prakāśe*—manifestation of the holy name of Lord Kṛṣṇa; *yei*—anyone who; *tomā dekhe*—sees You; *sei*—he; *kṛṣṇa-preme*—in ecstatic love of Kṛṣṇa; *bhāse*—floats.

TRANSLATION

"You have manifested the holy name of Kṛṣṇa throughout the entire world. Anyone who sees You is immediately absorbed in ecstatic love of Kṛṣṇa.

TEXT 14

প্রেম-পরকাশ নহে কৃষ্ণশক্তি বিনে ।
'কৃষ্ণ'– এক প্রেমদাতা, শাস্ত্র-প্রমাণে ॥ ১৪ ॥

prema-parakāśa nahe kṛṣṇa-śakti vine
'kṛṣṇa'——eka prema-dātā, śāstra-pramāṇe

SYNONYMS

prema—of ecstatic love of Kṛṣṇa; *parakāśa*—manifestation; *nahe*—cannot be; *kṛṣṇa-śakti vine*—without the power of Kṛṣṇa; *kṛṣṇa*—Lord Kṛṣṇa; *eka*—the only one; *prema-dātā*—giver of *prema; śāstra-pramāṇe*—the verdict of all revealed scriptures.

TRANSLATION

"Without being especially empowered by Kṛṣṇa, one cannot manifest ecstatic love of Kṛṣṇa, for Kṛṣṇa is the only one who gives ecstatic love. That is the verdict of all revealed scriptures.

TEXT 15

সন্ত্ববতারা বহবঃ পুষ্করনাভস্য সর্বতোভদ্রাঃ ।
কৃষ্ণাদন্যঃ কো বা লতাস্বপি প্রেমদো ভবতি ॥" ১৫ ॥

santv avatārā bahavaḥ
puṣkara-nābhasya sarvato-bhadrāḥ
kṛṣṇād anyaḥ ko vā latāsv
api premado bhavati"

SYNONYMS

santu—let there be; *avatārāḥ*—incarnations; *bahavaḥ*—many; *puṣkara-nābhasya*—of the Lord, from whose navel grows a lotus flower; *sarvataḥ-bhadrāḥ*—completely auspicious; *kṛṣṇāt*—than Lord Kṛṣṇa; *anyaḥ*—other; *kaḥ vā*—who possibly; *latāsu*—on the surrendered souls; *api*—also; *prema-daḥ*—the bestower of love; *bhavati*—is.

TRANSLATION

" 'There may be many all-auspicious incarnations of the Personality of Godhead, but who other than Lord Śrī Kṛṣṇa can bestow love of God upon the surrendered souls?' "

PURPORT

This is a verse written by Bilvamaṅgala Ṭhākura. It is found in the *Laghu-bhāgavatāmṛta* (1.5.37).

TEXT 16

মহাপ্রভু কহে—"শুন, ভট্ট মহামতি ।
মায়াবাদী সন্ন্যাসী আমি, না জানি কৃষ্ণভক্তি ॥ ১৬ ॥

mahāprabhu kahe——"śuna, bhaṭṭa mahā-mati
māyāvādī sannyāsī āmi, nā jāni kṛṣṇa-bhakti

SYNONYMS

mahāprabhu kahe—Śrī Caitanya Mahāprabhu replied; *śuna*—please hear; *bhaṭṭa*—My dear Vallabha Bhaṭṭa; *mahā-mati*—learned scholar; *māyāvādī*—in the Māyāvāda school; *sannyāsī—sannyāsī; āmi*—I; *nā jāni*—I do not know; *kṛṣṇa-bhakti*—devotional service to Kṛṣṇa.

TRANSLATION

Śrī Caitanya Mahāprabhu replied, "My dear Vallabha Bhaṭṭa, you are a learned scholar. Kindly listen to Me. I am a sannyāsī of the Māyāvāda school. Therefore I have no chance of knowing what kṛṣṇa-bhakti is.

TEXT 17

অদ্বৈতাচার্য-গোসাঞি —'সাক্ষাৎ ঈশ্বর' ।
তাঁর সঙ্গে আমার মন হইল নির্মল ॥ ১৭ ॥

advaitācārya-gosāñi——'sākṣāt īśvara'
tāṅra saṅge āmāra mana ha-ila nirmala

SYNONYMS

advaita-ācārya-gosāñi—Advaita Ācārya; *sākṣāt īśvara*—directly the Supreme Personality of Godhead; *tāṅra saṅge*—by His association; *āmāra*—My; *mana*—mind; *ha-ila*—has become; *nirmala*—purified.

TRANSLATION

"Nevertheless, My mind has become purified because I have associated with Advaita Ācārya, who is directly the Supreme Personality of Godhead.

TEXT 18

সর্বশাস্ত্রে কৃষ্ণভক্ত্যে নাহি যাঁর সম ।
অতএব 'অদ্বৈত-আচার্য' তাঁর নাম ॥ ১৮ ॥

sarva-śāstre kṛṣṇa-bhaktye nāhi yāṅra sama
ataeva 'advaita-ācārya' tāṅra nāma

SYNONYMS

sarva-śāstre—in all revealed scriptures; *kṛṣṇa-bhaktye*—in the devotional service of Lord Kṛṣṇa; *nāhi*—is not; *yāṅra*—of whom; *sama*—equal; *ataeva*—therefore; *advaita*—without a competitor; *ācārya*—*ācārya; tāṅra nāma*—His name.

TRANSLATION

"He is unparalleled in His understanding of all the revealed scriptures and the devotional service of Lord Kṛṣṇa. Therefore He is called Advaita Ācārya.

TEXT 19

যাঁহার কৃপাতে ম্লেচ্ছের হয় কৃষ্ণভক্তি ।
কে কহিতে পারে তাঁর বৈষ্ণবতা-শক্তি ? ১৯ ॥

yāṅhāra kṛpāte mlecchera haya kṛṣṇa-bhakti
ke kahite pāre tāṅra vaiṣṇavatā-śakti?

SYNONYMS

yāṅhāra—whose; *kṛpāte*—by mercy; *mlecchera*—of *mlecchas; haya*—is; *kṛṣṇa-bhakti*—devotional service to Kṛṣṇa; *ke*—who; *kahite pāre*—can describe; *tāṅra*—His; *vaiṣṇavatā-śakti*—power of Vaiṣṇavism.

TRANSLATION

"He is such a great personality that by His mercy He can convert even the meateaters [mlecchas] to the devotional service of Kṛṣṇa. Who, therefore, can estimate the power of His Vaiṣṇavism?

PURPORT

It is extremely difficult to convert a *mleccha,* or meateater, into a devotee of Lord Kṛṣṇa. Therefore anyone who can do so is situated on the highest level of Vaiṣṇavism.

TEXT 20

নিত্যানন্দ-অবধূত—'সাক্ষাৎ ঈশ্বর'।
ভাবোন্মাদে মত্ত কৃষ্ণপ্রেমের সাগর ॥ ২০ ॥

nityānanda-avadhūta—'sākṣāt īśvara'
bhāvonmāde matta kṛṣṇa-premera sāgara

SYNONYMS

nityānanda—Lord Nityānanda; *avadhūta*—*paramahaṁsa; sākṣāt īśvara*—directly the Supreme Personality of Godhead; *bhāva-unmāde*—by the madness of ecstatic love; *matta*—overwhelmed, intoxicated; *kṛṣṇa-premera*—of love of Kṛṣṇa; *sāgara*—the ocean.

TRANSLATION

"Lord Nityānanda Prabhu, the avadhūta, is also directly the Supreme Personality of Godhead. He is always intoxicated with the madness of ecstatic love. Indeed, He is an ocean of love of Kṛṣṇa.

TEXT 21

ষড়্‌দর্শন-বেত্তা ভট্টাচার্য-সার্বভৌম।
ষড়্‌দর্শনে জগদ্‌গুরু ভাগবতোত্তম ॥ ২১ ॥

ṣaḍ-darśana-vettā bhaṭṭācārya-sārvabhauma
ṣaḍ-darśane jagad-guru bhāgavatottama

SYNONYMS

ṣaṭ-darśana—of the six philosophical theses; *vettā*—the knower; *bhaṭṭācārya-sārvabhauma*—Sārvabhauma Bhaṭṭācārya; *ṣaṭ-darśane*—in six philosophical theses; *jagat-guru*—the spiritual master of the entire world; *bhāgavata-uttama*—the best of the devotees.

TRANSLATION

"Sārvabhauma Bhaṭṭācārya perfectly knows the six philosophical theses. He is therefore the spiritual master of the entire world in the six paths of philosophy. He is the best of devotees.

TEXT 22

তেঁহ দেখাইলা মোরে ভক্তিযোগ-পার।
তাঁর প্রসাদে জানিলুঁ 'কৃষ্ণভক্তিযোগ' সার ॥ ২২ ॥

teṅha dekhāilā more bhakti-yoga-pāra
tāṅra prasāde jāniluṅ 'kṛṣṇa-bhakti-yoga' sāra

SYNONYMS

teṅha—he; *dekhāilā*—has shown; *more*—to Me; *bhakti-yoga*—of devotional service; *pāra*—the limit; *tāṅra prasāde*—by his mercy; *jāniluṅ*—I have understood; *kṛṣṇa-bhakti*—of devotional service to Lord Kṛṣṇa; *yoga*—of the *yoga* system; *sāra*—the essence.

TRANSLATION

"Sārvabhauma Bhaṭṭācārya has shown Me the limit of devotional service. Only by his mercy have I understood that devotional service to Kṛṣṇa is the essence of all mystic yoga.

TEXT 23

রামানন্দ-রায় কৃষ্ণ-রসের 'নিধান' ।
তেঁহ জানাইলা—কৃষ্ণ —স্বয়ং ভগবান্ ॥ ২৩ ॥

rāmānanda-rāya kṛṣṇa-rasera 'nidhāna'
teṅha jānāilā——kṛṣṇa——svayaṁ bhagavān

SYNONYMS

rāmānanda-rāya—Śrīla Rāmānanda Rāya; *kṛṣṇa-rasera*—of the transcendental mellow of Kṛṣṇa's devotional service; *nidhāna*—the mine; *teṅha*—he; *jānāilā*—has given instruction; *kṛṣṇa*—Lord Kṛṣṇa; *svayam*—Himself; *bhagavān*—the Supreme Personality of Godhead.

TRANSLATION

"Śrīla Rāmānanda Rāya is the ultimate knower of the transcendental mellows of Lord Kṛṣṇa's devotional service. He has instructed Me that Lord Kṛṣṇa is the Supreme Personality of Godhead.

TEXT 24

তাতে প্রেমভক্তি —'পুরুষার্থ-শিরোমণি' ।
রাগমার্গে প্রেমভক্তি 'সর্বাধিক' জানি ॥ ২৪ ॥

tāte prema-bhakti——'puruṣārtha-śiromaṇi'
rāga-mārge prema-bhakti 'sarvādhika' jāni

SYNONYMS

tāte—therefore; *prema-bhakti*—devotional service in ecstatic love; *puruṣa-artha*—of all goals of human life; *śiromaṇi*—the crown jewel; *rāga-mārge*—on the path of spontaneous love; *prema-bhakti*—love of Kṛṣṇa; *sarva-adhika*—the highest of all; *jāni*—I can understand.

TRANSLATION

"Through the mercy of Rāmānanda Rāya, I have understood that ecstatic love of Kṛṣṇa is the highest goal of life and that spontaneous love of Kṛṣṇa is the highest perfection.

PURPORT

Puruṣārtha ("the goal of life") generally refers to religion, economic development, satisfaction of the senses and, finally, liberation. However, above these four kinds of *puruṣārthas,* love of Godhead stands supreme. It is called *parama-puruṣārtha* (the supreme goal of life) or *puruṣārtha-śiromaṇi* (the most exalted of all *puruṣārthas*). Lord Kṛṣṇa is worshiped by regulative devotional service, but the highest perfection of devotional service is spontaneous love of Godhead.

TEXT 25

দাস্য, সখ্য, বাৎসল্য, আর যে শৃঙ্গার ।
দাস, সখা, গুরু, কান্তা,—'আশ্রয়' যাহার ॥ ২৫ ॥

dāsya, sakhya, vātsalya, āra ye śṛṅgāra
dāsa, sakhā, guru, kāntā, ——'āśraya' yāhāra

SYNONYMS

dāsya—servitude; *sakhya*—friendship; *vātsalya*—paternal love; *āra*—and; *ye*—that; *śṛṅgāra*—conjugal love; *dāsa*—the servant; *sakhā*—friend; *guru*—superior; *kāntā*—lover; *āśraya*—the shelter; *yāhāra*—of which.

TRANSLATION

"The servant, friend, superior and conjugal lover are the shelters of the transcendental mellows called dāsya, sakhya, vātsalya and śṛṅgāra.

TEXT 26

'ঐশ্বর্যজ্ঞানযুক্ত', 'কেবল'-ভাব আর ।
ঐশ্বর্য-জ্ঞানে না পাই ব্রজেন্দ্রকুমার ॥ ২৬ ॥

'aiśvarya-jñāna-yukta', 'kevala'-bhāva āra
aiśvarya-jñāne nā pāi vrajendra-kumāra

SYNONYMS

aiśvarya-jñāna-yukta—with understanding of the opulences; *kevala*—pure; *bhāva*—emotion; *āra*—also; *aiśvarya-jñāne*—by understanding of the opulences; *nā pāi*—one does not get; *vrajendra-kumāra*—the son of Nanda Mahārāja.

TRANSLATION

"There are two kinds of emotion [bhāva]. Emotion with an understanding of the Lord's full opulences is called aiśvarya-jñāna-yukta, and pure, uncontaminated emotion is called kevala. One cannot achieve shelter at the lotus feet of Kṛṣṇa, the son of Mahārāja Nanda, simply by knowing His opulences.

PURPORT

Vide *Madhya-līlā,* Chapter Nineteen, text 192.

TEXT 27

নায়ং সুখাপো ভগবান্ দেহিনাং গোপিকাসুতঃ ।
জ্ঞানিনাঞ্চাত্মভূতানাং যথা ভক্তিমতামিহ ॥ ২৭ ॥

nāyaṁ sukhāpo bhagavān
dehināṁ gopikā-sutaḥ
jñānināṁ cātma-bhūtānāṁ
yathā bhakti-matām iha

SYNONYMS

na—not; *ayam*—this Lord Śrī Kṛṣṇa; *sukha-āpaḥ*—easily available; *bhagavān*—the Supreme Personality of Godhead; *dehinām*—for materialistic persons who have accepted the body as the self; *gopikā-sutaḥ*—the son of mother Yaśodā; *jñāninām*—for persons addicted to mental speculation; *ca*—and; *ātma-bhūtānām*—for persons performing severe austerities and penances or for personal associates; *yathā*—as; *bhakti-matām*—for persons engaged in spontaneous devotional service; *iha*—in this world.

TRANSLATION

" 'The Supreme Personality of Godhead, Kṛṣṇa, the son of mother Yaśodā, is accessible to those devotees engaged in spontaneous loving service, but He is not as easily accessible to mental speculators, to those striving for self-

realization by severe austerities and penances, or to those who consider the body the same as the self.'

PURPORT

This verse is from *Śrīmad-Bhāgavatam* (10.9.21).

TEXT 28

'আত্মভূত'-শব্দে কহে 'পারিষদগণ' ।
ঐশ্বর্য-জ্ঞানে লক্ষ্মী না পাইলা ব্রজেন্দ্রনন্দন ॥ ২৮ ॥

'ātma-bhūta'-śabde kahe 'pāriṣada-gaṇa'
aiśvarya-jñāne lakṣmī nā pāilā vrajendra-nandana

SYNONYMS

ātma-bhūta-śabde—the word *ātma-bhūta; kahe*—means; *pāriṣada-gaṇa*—personal associates; *aiśvarya-jñāne*—in the understanding of opulence; *lakṣmī*—the goddess of fortune; *nā pāilā*—could not get; *vrajendra-nandana*—the shelter of Kṛṣṇa, the son of Nanda Mahārāja.

TRANSLATION

"The word 'ātma-bhūta' means 'personal associates.' Through the understanding of opulence, the goddess of fortune could not receive the shelter of Kṛṣṇa, the son of Nanda Mahārāja.

PURPORT

Lakṣmī, the goddess of fortune, has complete knowledge of Kṛṣṇa's opulences, but she could not achieve the association of Kṛṣṇa by dint of such knowledge. The devotees in Vṛndāvana, however, actually enjoy the association of Kṛṣṇa.

TEXT 29

নায়ং শ্রিয়োঽঙ্গ উ নিতান্তরতেঃ প্রসাদঃ
স্বর্যোষিতাং নলিনগন্ধরুচাং কুতোঽন্যাঃ ।
রাসোৎসবেঽস্য ভুজদণ্ডগৃহীতকণ্ঠ-
লব্ধাশিষাং য উদগাদ্‌ব্রজসুন্দরীণাম্ ॥ ২৯ ॥

nāyaṁ śriyo 'ṅga u nitānta-rateḥ prasādaḥ
svar-yoṣitāṁ nalina-gandha-rucāṁ kuto 'nyāḥ

rāsotsave 'sya bhuja-daṇḍa-gṛhīta-kaṇṭha-
labdhāśiṣāṁ ya udagād vraja-sundarīṇām

SYNONYMS

na—not; *ayam*—this; *śriyaḥ*—of the goddess of fortune; *aṅge*—on the chest; *u*—alas; *nitānta-rateḥ*—who is very intimately related; *prasādaḥ*—the favor; *svaḥ*—of the heavenly planets; *yoṣitām*—of women; *nalina*—of the lotus flower; *gandha*—having the aroma; *rucām*—and bodily luster; *kutaḥ*—much less; *anyāḥ*—others; *rāsa-utsave*—in the festival of the *rāsa* dance; *asya*—of Lord Śrī Kṛṣṇa; *bhuja-daṇḍa*—by the arms; *gṛhīta*—embraced; *kaṇṭha*—their necks; *labdha-āśiṣām*—who achieved such a blessing; *yaḥ*—which; *udagāt*—became manifest; *vraja-sundarīṇām*—of the beautiful *gopīs,* the transcendental girls of Vrajabhūmi.

TRANSLATION

" 'When Lord Śrī Kṛṣṇa was dancing with the gopīs in the rāsa-līlā, the gopīs were embraced by the arms of the Lord. This transcendental favor was never bestowed upon the goddess of fortune or the other consorts in the spiritual world. Indeed, never was such a favor even imagined by the most beautiful girls in the heavenly planets, whose bodily luster and aroma resemble those of lotus flowers. And what to speak of worldly women who are very beautiful according to the material estimation?'

PURPORT

This is a verse from *Śrīmad-Bhāgavatam* (10.47.60).

TEXT 30

শুদ্ধভাবে সখা করে স্কন্ধে আরোহণ ।
শুদ্ধভাবে ব্রজেশ্বরী করেন বন্ধন ॥ ৩০ ॥

śuddha-bhāve sakhā kare skandhe ārohaṇa
śuddha-bhāve vrajeśvarī karena bandhana

SYNONYMS

śuddha-bhāve—in pure consciousness; *sakhā*—friend; *kare*—does; *skandhe*—on the shoulder; *ārohaṇa*—rising; *śuddha-bhāve*—in pure consciousness; *vraja-īśvarī*—the Queen of Vraja; *karena bandhana*—binds.

TRANSLATION

"In pure Kṛṣṇa consciousness, a friend mounts the shoulder of Kṛṣṇa, and mother Yaśodā binds the Lord.

PURPORT

Śuddha-bhāva, pure consciousness, is not dependent on an understanding of the Lord's opulences. Even without such opulences, the devotee in *śuddha-bhāva* is inclined to love Kṛṣṇa as a friend or son.

TEXT 31

'মোর সখা', 'মোর পুত্র',— এই 'শুদ্ধ' মন।
অতএব শুক-ব্যাস করে প্রশংসন ॥ ৩১ ॥

'mora sakhā,' 'mora putra,'——ei 'śuddha' mana
ataeva śuka-vyāsa kare praśaṁsana

SYNONYMS

mora sakhā—my friend; *mora putra*—my son; *ei*—this; *śuddha*—pure; *mana*—consciousness; *ataeva*—therefore; *śuka-vyāsa*—Śukadeva Gosvāmī and Vyāsadeva; *kare praśaṁsana*—praise.

TRANSLATION

"In pure Kṛṣṇa consciousness, without knowledge of the Lord's opulences, a devotee considers Kṛṣṇa his friend or son. Therefore this devotional attitude is praised even by Śukadeva Gosvāmī and Vyāsadeva, the supreme authority.

TEXT 32

ইত্থং সতাং ব্রহ্মসুখানুভূত্যা
দাস্যং গতানাং পরদৈবতেন।
মায়াশ্রিতানাং নরদারকেণ
সাকং বিজহ্রুঃ কৃতপুণ্যপুঞ্জাঃ ॥ ৩২ ॥

itthaṁ satāṁ brahma-sukhānubhūtyā
dāsyaṁ gatānāṁ para-daivatena
māyāśritānāṁ nara-dārakeṇa
sākaṁ vijahruḥ kṛta-puṇya-puñjāḥ

SYNONYMS

ittham—in this way; *satām*—of persons who prefer the impersonal feature of the Lord; *brahma*—of the impersonal effulgence; *sukha*—by the happiness; *anubhūtyā*—who is realized; *dāsyam*—the mode of servitude; *gatānām*—of those who have accepted; *para-daivatena*—who is the supreme worshipable

Deity; *māyā-āśritānām*—for ordinary persons under the clutches of external energy; *nara-dārakeṇa*—with He who is like a boy of this material world; *sākam*—in friendship; *vijahruḥ*—played; *kṛta-puṇya-puñjāḥ*—those who have accumulated volumes of pious activities.

TRANSLATION

" 'Those who are engaged in self-realization, appreciating the Brahman effulgence of the Lord, and those engaged in devotional service, accepting the Supreme Personality of Godhead as master, as well as those who are under the clutches of māyā, thinking the Lord an ordinary person, cannot understand that certain exalted personalities—after accumulating volumes of pious activities—are now playing with the Lord in friendship as cowherd boys.'

PURPORT

This verse is from the *Śrīmad-Bhāgavatam* (10.12.11).

TEXT 33

ত্রয্যা চোপনিষদ্ভিশ্চ সাংখ্যযোগৈশ্চ সাত্বতৈঃ ।
উপগীয়মানমাহাত্ম্যং হরিং সাঽমন্যতাত্মজম্ ॥ ৩৩ ॥

trayyā copaniṣadbhiś ca
sāṅkhya-yogaiś ca sātvataiḥ
upagīyamāna-māhātmyaṁ
hariṁ sāmanyatātmajam

SYNONYMS

trayyā—by followers of the three *Vedas* who perform great sacrifices like Indra and other demigods; *ca*—also; *upaniṣadbhiḥ*—by the followers of the *Upaniṣads,* the topmost portion of Vedic knowledge; *ca*—also; *sāṅkhya*—by the philosophers who analytically study the universe; *yogaiḥ*—by mystic *yogīs; ca*—and; *sātvataiḥ*—by devotees who follow the method of worship mentioned in the *Pañcarātra* and other Vedic literatures; *upagīyamāna*—being sung; *māhātmyam*—whose glories; *harim*—unto the Supreme Personality of Godhead; *sā*—she, mother Yaśodā; *amanyata*—considered; *ātma-jam*—her own son, born out of her body.

TRANSLATION

" 'When mother Yaśodā saw all the universes within the mouth of Kṛṣṇa, she was certainly astonished for the time being. Nevertheless, she still considered the Lord her own son, although He is worshiped by great personalities who

offer him sacrifices, great saints who understand the greatness of the Lord by studying the Upaniṣads, great philosophers who analytically study the universe, great yogīs who know him as the all-pervading Supersoul, and even devotees who accept the Lord as the Supreme Personality of Godhead.'

PURPORT

This verse is from *Śrīmad-Bhāgavatam* (10.8.45).

TEXT 34

নন্দঃ কিমকরোদ্‌ব্রহ্মন্ শ্রেয় এবং মহোদয়ম্ ।
যশোদা বা মহাভাগা পপৌ যস্যাঃ স্তনং হরিঃ ॥ ৩৪ ॥

nandaḥ kim akarod brahman
śreya evaṁ mahodayam
yaśodā vā mahā-bhāgā
papau yasyāḥ stanaṁ hariḥ

SYNONYMS

nandaḥ—Nanda Mahārāja; *kim*—what; *akarot*—has performed; *brahman*—O *brāhmaṇa; śreyaḥ*—auspicious activities; *evam*—thus; *mahā-udayam*—rising to such an exalted position as the father of Kṛṣṇa; *yaśodā*—mother Yaśodā; *vā*—or; *mahā-bhāgā*—most fortunate; *papau*—drank; *yasyāḥ*—of whom; *stanam*—the breasts; *hariḥ*—the Supreme Personality of Godhead.

TRANSLATION

" 'O brāhmaṇa, what pious activities did Nanda Mahārāja perform to receive the Supreme Personality of Godhead Kṛṣṇa as his son? And what pious activities did mother Yaśodā perform that made the Absolute Supreme Personality of Godhead Kṛṣṇa call her "mother" and suck her breasts?'

PURPORT

This verse is from *Śrīmad-Bhāgavatam* (10.8.46).

TEXT 35

ঐশ্বর্য দেখিলেহ 'শুদ্ধের' নহে ঐশ্বর্য জ্ঞান ।
অতএব ঐশ্বর্য হইতে 'কেবল'-ভাব প্রধান ॥ ৩৫ ॥

aiśvarya dekhileha 'śuddhera' nahe aiśvarya-jñāna
ataeva aiśvarya ha-ite 'kevala'-bhāva pradhāna

SYNONYMS

aiśvarya—opulence; *dekhileha*—even after seeing; *śuddhera*—of a pure devotee; *nahe*—is not; *aiśvarya-jñāna*—knowledge of opulence; *ataeva*—therefore; *aiśvarya ha-ite*—than the understanding of opulence; *kevala-bhāva*—pure emotion; *pradhāna*—more eminent.

TRANSLATION

"Even if a pure devotee sees the opulence of Kṛṣṇa, he does not accept it. Therefore pure consciousness is more exalted than consciousness of the Lord's opulence.

TEXT 36

এ সব শিখাইলা মোরে রায়-রামানন্দ ।
অনর্গল রসবেত্তা প্রেমসুখানন্দ ॥ ৩৬ ॥

e saba śikhāilā more rāya-rāmānanda
anargala rasa-vettā prema-sukhānanda

SYNONYMS

e saba—all this; *śikhāilā*—instructed; *more*—unto Me; *rāya-rāmānanda*—Rāmānanda Rāya; *anargala*—incessantly; *rasa-vettā*—one who understands transcendental mellows; *prema-sukha-ānanda*—absorbed in the happiness of ecstatic love of Kṛṣṇa.

TRANSLATION

"Rāmānanda Rāya is extremely aware of transcendental mellows. He is incessantly absorbed in the happiness of ecstatic love of Kṛṣṇa. It is he who has instructed Me all this.

TEXT 37

কহন না যায় রামানন্দের প্রভাব ।
রায়-প্রসাদে জানিলুঁ ব্রজের 'শুদ্ধ' ভাব ॥ ৩৭ ॥

kahana nā yāya rāmānandera prabhāva
rāya-prasāde jāniluṅ vrajera 'śuddha' bhāva

SYNONYMS

kahana nā yāya—cannot be described; *rāmānandera prabhāva*—the influence of Rāmānanda Rāya; *rāya*—of Rāmānanda Rāya; *prasāde*—by the mercy;

jāniluṅ—I have understood; *vrajera*—of the inhabitants of Vraja; *śuddha bhāva*—unalloyed love.

TRANSLATION

"It is impossible to describe the influence and knowledge of Rāmānanda Rāya, for only by his mercy have I understood the unalloyed love of the residents of Vṛndāvana.

TEXT 38

দামোদর-স্বরূপ—'প্রেমরস' মূর্তিমান্।
যাঁর সঙ্গে হৈল ব্রজ-মধুর-রস-জ্ঞান ॥ ৩৮ ॥

dāmodara-svarūpa——'prema-rasa' mūrtimān
yāṅra saṅge haila vraja-madhura-rasa-jñāna

SYNONYMS

dāmodara-svarūpa—Svarūpa Dāmodara Gosvāmī; *prema-rasa*—the transcendental mellows of ecstatic love; *mūrtimān*—personified; *yāṅra saṅge*—by whose association; *haila*—there was; *vraja*—of Vraja; *madhura-rasa*—of the mellow of conjugal love; *jñāna*—knowledge.

TRANSLATION

"The transcendental mellow of ecstatic love is personified by Svarūpa Dāmodara. By his association I have understood Vṛndāvana's transcendental mellow of conjugal love.

TEXT 39

'শুদ্ধপ্রেম' ব্রজদেবীর—কামগন্ধহীন।
'কৃষ্ণসুখতাৎপর্য',—এই তার চিহ্ন ॥ ৩৯ ॥

'śuddha-prema' vraja-devīra——kāma-gandha-hīna
'kṛṣṇa-sukha-tātparya', ——ei tāra cihna

SYNONYMS

śuddha-prema—unalloyed love; *vraja-devīra*—of the *gopīs* or Śrīmatī Rādhārāṇī; *kāma-gandha-hīna*—without a scent of material lust; *kṛṣṇa*—of Kṛṣṇa; *sukha*—happiness; *tātparya*—the purpose; *ei*—this; *tāra*—of that; *cihna*—the symptom.

TRANSLATION

"The unalloyed love of the gopīs and Śrīmatī Rādhārāṇī is without any trace of material lust. The criterion of such transcendental love is that its only purpose is to satisfy Kṛṣṇa.

TEXT 40

যত্তে সুজাতচরণাম্বুরুহং স্তনেষু
ভীতাঃ শনৈঃ প্রিয় দধীমহি কর্কশেষু ।
তেনাটবীমটসি তদ্ব্যথতে ন কিং স্বিৎ
কূর্পাদিভির্ভ্রমতি ধীর্ভবদায়ুষাং নঃ ॥ ৪০ ॥

yat te sujāta-caraṇāmburuhaṁ staneṣu
bhītāḥ śanaiḥ priya dadhīmahi karkaśeṣu
tenāṭavīm aṭasi tad vyathate na kiṁ svit
kūrpādibhir bhramati dhīr bhavad-āyuṣāṁ naḥ

SYNONYMS

yat—which; *te*—Your; *sujāta*—very fine; *caraṇa-ambu-ruham*—lotus feet; *staneṣu*—on the breasts; *bhītāḥ*—being afraid; *śanaiḥ*—gently; *priya*—O dear one; *dadhīmahi*—we place; *karkaśeṣu*—rough; *tena*—with them; *aṭavīm*—the path; *aṭasi*—You roam; *tat*—they; *vyathate*—are distressed; *na*—not; *kim svit*—we wonder; *kūrpa-ādibhiḥ*—by small stones and so on; *bhramati*—flutters; *dhīḥ*—the mind; *bhavat-āyuṣām*—of those of whom Your Lordship is the very life; *naḥ*—of us.

TRANSLATION

" 'O dearly beloved! Your lotus feet are so soft that we place them gently on our breasts, fearing that Your feet will be hurt. Our lives rest only in You. Our minds, therefore, are filled with anxiety that Your tender feet might be wounded by pebbles as You roam about on the forest path.'

PURPORT

This verse is spoken by the *gopīs* in *Śrīmad-Bhāgavatam* (10.31.19).

TEXT 41

গোপীগণের শুদ্ধপ্রেম ঐশ্বর্যজ্ঞানহীন ।
প্রেমেতে ভর্ৎসনা করে এই তার চিহ্ন ॥ ৪১ ॥

gopī-gaṇera śuddha-prema aiśvarya-jñāna-hīna
premete bhartsanā kare ei tāra cihna

SYNONYMS

gopī-gaṇera—of the *gopīs; śuddha-prema*—unalloyed love; *aiśvarya-jñāna-hīna*—devoid of knowledge of opulences; *premete*—of pure love; *bhartsanā*—chastisement; *kare*—do; *ei*—this; *tāra*—of that; *cihna*—the symptom.

TRANSLATION

"Obsessed with pure love, without knowledge of opulences, the gopīs sometimes chastised Kṛṣṇa. That is a symptom of pure ecstatic love.

TEXT 42

পতিসুতান্বয়ভ্রাতৃবান্ধবা-
নতিবিলঙ্ঘ্য তেঽন্ত্যচ্যুতাগতাঃ ।
গতিবিদস্তবোদ্গীতমোহিতাঃ
কিতব যোষিতঃ কস্ত্যজেন্নিশি ॥ ৪২ ॥

pati-sutānvaya-bhrātṛ-bāndhavān
ativilaṅghya te 'nty acyutāgatāḥ
gati-vidas tavodgīta-mohitāḥ
kitava yoṣitaḥ kas tyajen niśi

SYNONYMS

pati—husbands; *suta*—sons; *anvaya*—family; *bhrātṛ*—brothers; *bāndhavān*—friends; *ativilaṅghya*—without caring for; *te*—Your; *anti*—dear shelter; *acyuta*—O infallible one; *āgatāḥ*—have come; *gati-vidaḥ*—who know everything of our activities; *tava*—of You; *udgīta*—by the singing flute; *mohitāḥ*—being attracted; *kitava*—O great cheater; *yoṣitaḥ*—beautiful women; *kaḥ*—who; *tyajet*—would give up; *niśi*—in the dead of night.

TRANSLATION

" 'O dear Kṛṣṇa, we gopīs have neglected the order of our husbands, sons, family, brothers and friends and have left their company to come to You. You know everything about our desires. We have come only because we are attracted by the supreme music of Your flute. But You are a great cheater, for who else would give up the company of young girls like us in the dead of night?'

PURPORT

This verse is from *Śrīmad-Bhāgavatam* (10.31.16).

TEXT 43

সর্বোত্তম ভজন এই সর্বভক্তি জিনি'।
অতএব কৃষ্ণ কহে,—'আমি তোমার ঋণী' ॥ ৪৩ ॥

sarvottama bhajana ei sarva-bhakti jini'
ataeva kṛṣṇa kahe, —'āmi tomāra ṛṇī'

SYNONYMS

sarva-uttama—above all; *bhajana*—devotional service; *ei*—this; *sarva-bhakti*—all types of *bhakti; jini'*—conquering; *ataeva*—therefore; *kṛṣṇa kahe*—Lord Kṛṣṇa says; *āmi*—I; *tomāra*—your; *ṛṇī*—debtor.

TRANSLATION

"The conjugal love of the gopīs is the most exalted devotional service, surpassing all other methods of bhakti. Therefore Lord Kṛṣṇa is obliged to say, 'My dear gopīs, I cannot repay you. Indeed, I am always indebted to you.'

TEXT 44

ন পারয়েঽহং নিরবদ্যসংযুজাং
স্বসাধুকৃত্যং বিবুধায়ুষাপি বঃ।
যা মাঽভজন্ দুর্জরগেহশৃঙ্খলাঃ
সংবৃশ্চ্য তদ্বঃ প্রতিযাতু সাধুনা ॥ ৪৪ ॥

na pāraye 'haṁ niravadya-saṁyujāṁ
sva-sādhu-kṛtyaṁ vibudhāyuṣāpi vaḥ
yā mābhajan durjaya-geha-śṛṅkhalāḥ
saṁvṛścya tad vaḥ pratiyātu sādhunā

SYNONYMS

na—not; *pāraye*—am able to make; *aham*—I; *niravadya-saṁyujām*—to those who are completely free from deceit; *sva-sādhu-kṛtyam*—proper compensation; *vibudha-āyuṣā*—with a lifetime as long as that of the demigods; *api*—although; *vaḥ*—to you; *yāḥ*—who; *mā*—Me; *abhajan*—have worshiped; *durjaya-geha-śṛṅkhalāḥ*—the chains of household life, which are difficult to overcome; *saṁvṛścya*—cutting; *tat*—that; *vaḥ*—of you; *pratiyātu*—let it be returned; *sādhunā*—by the good activity itself.

TRANSLATION

" 'O gopīs, I am not able to repay My debt for your spotless service, even within a lifetime of Brahmā. Your connection with Me is beyond reproach. You have worshiped Me, cutting off all domestic ties, which are difficult to break. Therefore please let your own glorious deeds be your compensation.'

PURPORT

This is a quotation from *Śrīmad-Bhāgavatam* (10.32.22).

TEXT 45

ঐশ্বর্য-জ্ঞান হৈতে কেবলা-ভাব—প্রধান ।
পৃথিবীতে ভক্ত নাহি উদ্ধব-সমান ॥ ৪৫ ॥

aiśvarya-jñāna haite kevalā-bhāva——pradhāna
pṛthivīte bhakta nāhi uddhava-samāna

SYNONYMS

aiśvarya-jñāna haite—than transcendental love in opulence; *kevalā-bhāva*—pure love; *pradhāna*—more prominent; *pṛthivīte*—on the surface of the world; *bhakta nāhi*—there is no devotee; *uddhava-samāna*—like Uddhava.

TRANSLATION

"Completely distinct from love of Kṛṣṇa in opulence, pure love of Kṛṣṇa is on the highest level. On the surface of the world there is no devotee greater than Uddhava.

TEXT 46

তেঁহ যাঁর পদধূলি করেন প্রার্থন ।
স্বরূপের সঙ্গে পাইলুঁ এ সব শিক্ষণ ॥ ৪৬ ॥

teṅha yāṅra pada-dhūli karena prārthana
svarūpera saṅge pāiluṅ e saba śikṣaṇa

SYNONYMS

teṅha—he; *yāṅra*—whose; *pada-dhūli*—dust of the lotus feet; *karena prārthana*—desires; *svarūpera saṅge*—from Svarūpa Dāmodara; *pāiluṅ*—I have gotten; *e saba*—all these; *śikṣaṇa*—instructions.

TRANSLATION

"Uddhava desires to take on his head the dust of the gopīs' lotus feet. I have learned about all these transcendental loving affairs of Lord Kṛṣṇa from Svarūpa Dāmodara.

TEXT 47

আসামহো চরণরেণুজুষামহং স্যাং
বৃন্দাবনে কিমপি গুল্মলতৌষধীনাম্ ।
যা দুস্ত্যজং স্বজনমার্যপথঞ্চ হিত্বা
ভেজুর্মুকুন্দপদবীং শ্রুতিভির্বিমৃগ্যাম্ ॥ ৪৭ ॥

āsām aho caraṇa-reṇu-juṣām ahaṁ syāṁ
vṛndāvane kim api gulma-latauṣadhīnām
yā dustyajaṁ svajanam ārya-pathaṁ ca hitvā
bhejur mukunda-padavīṁ śrutibhir vimṛgyām

SYNONYMS

āsām—of the *gopīs; aho*—oh; *caraṇa-reṇu*—the dust of the lotus feet; *juṣām*—devoted to; *aham syām*—let me become; *vṛndāvane*—in Vṛndāvana; *kim api*—anyone; *gulma-latā-auṣadhīnām*—among bushes, creepers and herbs; *yā*—they who; *dustyajam*—very difficult to give up; *sva-janam*—family members; *ārya-patham*—the path of chastity; *ca*—and; *hitvā*—giving up; *bhejuḥ*—worshiped; *mukunda-padavīm*—the lotus feet of Mukunda, Kṛṣṇa; *śrutibhiḥ*—by the *Vedas; vimṛgyām*—to be searched for.

TRANSLATION

" 'The gopīs of Vṛndāvana have given up the association of their husbands, sons and other family members, who are very difficult to give up, and they have forsaken the path of chastity to take shelter of the lotus feet of Mukunda, Kṛṣṇa, which one should search for by Vedic knowledge. Oh, let me be fortunate enough to be one of the bushes, creepers or herbs in Vṛndāvana because the gopīs trample them and bless them with the dust of their lotus feet.'

PURPORT

This verse from *Śrīmad-Bhāgavatam* (10.47.61) was spoken by Uddhava. When Uddhava was sent by Kṛṣṇa to see the condition of the *gopīs* in Vṛndāvana, he stayed there for a few months in their association and always talked with them about Kṛṣṇa. Although this greatly pleased the *gopīs* and other residents of Vrajabhūmi, Vṛndāvana, Uddhava saw that the *gopīs* were severely afflicted by their separation from Kṛṣṇa. Their hearts were so disturbed that their minds were sometimes deranged. Observing the unalloyed devotion and love of the *gopīs* for Kṛṣṇa, Uddhava desired to become a creeper, a blade of grass or an herb in Vṛndāvana so that sometimes the *gopīs* would trample him and he would receive the dust of their lotus feet on his head.

TEXT 48

হরিদাস-ঠাকুর—মহাভাগবত-প্রধান ।
প্রতি দিন লয় তেঁহ তিনলক্ষ নাম ॥ ৪৮ ॥

haridāsa-ṭhākura——mahā-bhāgavata-pradhāna
prati dina laya teṅha tina-lakṣa nāma

SYNONYMS

haridāsa-ṭhākura—Haridāsa Ṭhākura; *mahā-bhāgavata-pradhāna*—the topmost of all pure devotees; *prati dina*—every day; *laya*—chants; *teṅha*—he; *tina-lakṣa nāma*—300,000 holy names of the Lord.

TRANSLATION

"Haridāsa Ṭhākura, the teacher of the holy name, is among the most exalted of all devotees. Every day he chants 300,000 holy names of the Lord.

TEXT 49

নামের মহিমা আমি তাঁর ঠাঞি শিখিলুঁ ।
তাঁর প্রসাদে নামের মহিমা জানিলুঁ ॥ ৪৯ ॥

nāmera mahimā āmi tāṅra ṭhāñi śikhiluṅ
tāṅra prasāde nāmera mahimā jāniluṅ

SYNONYMS

nāmera mahimā—the glories of the holy name; *āmi*—I; *tāṅra ṭhāñi*—from him; *śikhiluṅ*—have learned; *tāṅra prasāde*—by his mercy; *nāmera*—of the holy name; *mahimā*—the glories; *jāniluṅ*—I could understand.

TRANSLATION

"I have learned about the glories of the Lord's holy name from Haridāsa Ṭhākura, and by his mercy I have understood these glories.

TEXTS 50-52

আচার্যরত্ন আচার্যনিধি পণ্ডিত-গদাধর ।
জগদানন্দ, দামোদর, শঙ্কর, বক্রেশ্বর ॥ ৫০ ॥
কাশীশ্বর, মুকুন্দ, বাসুদেব, মুরারি ।
আর যত ভক্তগণ গৌড়ে অবতরি' ॥ ৫১ ॥
কৃষ্ণ-নাম-প্রেম কৈলা জগতে প্রচার ।
ইঁহা সবার সঙ্গে কৃষ্ণভক্তি যে আমার"॥ ৫২ ॥

ācāryaratna ācāryanidhi paṇḍita-gadādhara
jagadānanda, dāmodara, śaṅkara, vakreśvara

kāśīśvara, mukunda, vāsudeva, murāri
āra yata bhakta-gaṇa gauḍe avatari'

kṛṣṇa-nāma-prema kailā jagate pracāra
iṅhā sabāra saṅge kṛṣṇa-bhakti ye āmāra"

SYNONYMS

ācāryaratna—Ācāryaratna; *ācāryanidhi*—Ācāryanidhi; *paṇḍita-gadādhara*—Gadādhara Paṇḍita; *jagadānanda*—Jagadānanda; *dāmodara*—Dāmodara; *śaṅkara*—Śaṅkara; *vakreśvara*—Vakreśvara; *kāśīśvara*—Kāśīśvara; *mukunda*—Mukunda; *vāsudeva*—Vāsudeva; *murāri*—Murāri; *āra*—and; *yata*—as many as; *bhakta-gaṇa*—devotees; *gauḍe*—in Bengal; *avatari'*—having descended; *kṛṣṇa-nāma*—the holy name of Lord Kṛṣṇa; *prema*—ecstatic love of Kṛṣṇa; *kailā*—did; *jagate*—all over the world; *pracāra*—preaching; *iṅhā sabāra*—of all of them; *saṅge*—by association; *kṛṣṇa-bhakti*—devotional service to Kṛṣṇa; *ye*—which; *āmāra*—My.

TRANSLATION

"Ācāryaratna, Ācāryanidhi, Gadādhara Paṇḍita, Jagadānanda, Dāmodara, Śaṅkara, Vakreśvara, Kāśīśvara, Mukunda, Vāsudeva, Murāri and many other devotees have descended in Bengal to preach to everyone the glories of the holy name of Kṛṣṇa and the value of love for Him. I have learned from them the meaning of devotional service to Kṛṣṇa."

TEXT 53

ভট্টের হৃদয়ে দৃঢ় অভিমান জানি' ।
ভঙ্গী করি' মহাপ্রভু কহে এত বাণী ॥ ৫৩ ॥

bhaṭṭera hṛdaye dṛḍha abhimāna jāni'
bhaṅgī kari' mahāprabhu kahe eta vāṇī

SYNONYMS

bhaṭṭera hṛdaye—in the heart of Vallabha Bhaṭṭa; *dṛḍha*—fixed; *abhimāna*—pride; *jāni'*—understanding; *bhaṅgī kari'*—making a hint; *mahāprabhu*—Śrī Caitanya Mahāprabhu; *kahe*—spoke; *eta vāṇī*—these words.

TRANSLATION

Knowing that Vallabha Bhaṭṭa's heart was full of pride, Śrī Caitanya Mahāprabhu spoke these words, hinting at how one can learn about devotional service.

PURPORT

Vallabha Bhaṭṭa was greatly proud of his knowledge in devotional service, and therefore he wanted to speak about Lord Śrī Caitanya Mahāprabhu without understanding the Lord's position. The Lord therefore hinted in many ways that if Vallabha Bhaṭṭa wanted to know what devotional service actually is, he would have to learn from all the devotees He mentioned, beginning with Advaita Ācārya, Lord Nityānanda, Sārvabhauma Bhaṭṭācārya and Rāmānanda Rāya. As Svarūpa Dāmodara has said, if one wants to learn the meaning of *Śrīmad-Bhāgavatam,* one must take lessons from a realized soul. One should not proudly think that one can understand the transcendental loving service of the Lord simply by reading books. One must become a servant of a Vaiṣṇava. As Narottama dāsa Ṭhākura has confirmed, *chāḍiyā vaiṣṇava-sevā nistāra pāyeche kebā:* one cannot be in a transcendental position unless one very faithfully serves a pure Vaiṣṇava. One must accept a Vaiṣṇava *guru* (*ādau gurv-āśrayam*), and then by questions and answers one should gradually learn what pure devotional service to Kṛṣṇa is. That is called the *paramparā* system.

TEXT 54

"আমি সে 'বৈষ্ণব',—ভক্তিসিদ্ধান্ত সব জানি।
আমি সে ভাগবত-অর্থ উত্তম বাখানি॥" ৫৪ ॥

"āmi se 'vaiṣṇava', ——bhakti-siddhānta saba jāni
āmi se bhāgavata-artha uttama vākhāni"

SYNONYMS

āmi—I; *se*—that; *vaiṣṇava*—Vaiṣṇava; *bhakti-siddhānta*—conclusions of devotional service; *saba*—all; *jāni*—I know; *āmi*—I; *se*—that; *bhāgavata-artha*—meaning of the *Bhāgavatam; uttama*—very well; *vākhāni*—can explain.

TRANSLATION

"I am a great Vaiṣṇava. Having learned all the conclusions of Vaiṣṇava philosophy, I can understand the meaning of Śrīmad-Bhāgavatam and explain it very well."

TEXT 55

ভট্টের মনেতে এই ছিল দীর্ঘ গর্ব।
প্রভুর বচন শুনি' সে হইল খর্ব॥ ৫৫ ॥

bhaṭṭera manete ei chila dīrgha garva
prabhura vacana śuni' se ha-ila kharva

SYNONYMS

bhaṭṭera manete—in the mind of Vallabha Bhaṭṭa; *ei*—this; *chila*—was existing; *dīrgha*—for a long time; *garva*—pride; *prabhura*—of Śrī Caitanya Mahāprabhu; *vacana*—the words; *śuni'*—by hearing; *se*—that; *ha-ila*—was; *kharva*—cut down.

TRANSLATION

Such pride had existed for a long time within Vallabha Bhaṭṭa's mind, but as he heard the preaching of Śrī Caitanya Mahāprabhu, his pride was cut down.

TEXT 56

প্রভুর মুখে বৈষ্ণবতা শুনিয়া সবার।
ভট্টের ইচ্ছা হৈল তাঁ-সবারে দেখিবার॥ ৫৬ ॥

prabhura mukhe vaiṣṇavatā śuniyā sabāra
bhaṭṭera icchā haila tāṅ-sabāre dekhibāra

SYNONYMS

prabhura mukhe—from the mouth of Śrī Caitanya Mahāprabhu; *vaiṣṇavatā*—the standard of Vaiṣṇavism; *śuniyā sabāra*—hearing of all the devotees; *bhaṭṭera*—of Vallabha Bhaṭṭa; *icchā*—desire; *haila*—was; *tāṅ-sabāre*—all of them; *dekhibāra*—to see.

TRANSLATION

When Vallabha Bhaṭṭa heard from the mouth of Śrī Caitanya Mahāprabhu about the pure Vaiṣṇavism of all these devotees, he immediately desired to see them.

TEXT 57

ভট্ট কহে,—"এ সব বৈষ্ণব রহে কোন্ স্থানে ?
কোন্ প্রকারে পাইমু ইহাঁ-সবার দর্শনে ? ৫৭ ॥

bhaṭṭa kahe, —"e saba vaiṣṇava rahe kon sthāne?
kon prakāre pāimu ihāṅ-sabāra darśane?

SYNONYMS

bhaṭṭa kahe—Vallabha Bhaṭṭa said; *e saba vaiṣṇava*—all these Vaiṣṇavas; *rahe*—live; *kon sthāne*—where; *kon prakāre*—how; *pāimu*—shall I attain; *ihāṅ-sabāra darśane*—seeing all these Vaiṣṇavas.

TRANSLATION

Vallabha Bhaṭṭa said, "Where do all these Vaiṣṇavas live, and how can I see them?"

TEXT 58

প্রভু কহে,—"কেহ গৌড়ে, কেহ দেশান্তরে ।
সব আসিয়াছে রথযাত্রা দেখিবারে ॥ ৫৮ ॥

prabhu kahe, —"keha gauḍe, keha deśāntare
saba āsiyāche ratha-yātrā dekhibāre

SYNONYMS

prabhu kahe—Śrī Caitanya Mahāprabhu replied; *keha gauḍe*—some in Bengal; *keha*—some; *deśa-antare*—in other states; *saba*—all; *āsiyāche*—have come; *ratha-yātrā dekhibāre*—to see the car festival of Lord Jagannātha.

TRANSLATION

Śrī Caitanya Mahāprabhu replied, "Although some of them live in Bengal and some in other states, they have all come here to see the Ratha-yātrā festival.

TEXT 59

ইহাঁই রহেন সবে, বাসা—নানা-স্থানে ।
ইহাঁই পাইবা তুমি সবার দর্শনে ॥" ৫৯ ॥

ihāṅi rahena sabe, vāsā —nānā-sthāne
ihāṅi pāibā tumi sabāra darśane"

SYNONYMS

ihāṅi—here; *rahena sabe*—all of them are living; *vāsā*—their residential places; *nānā-sthāne*—in various quarters; *ihāṅi*—here; *pāibā*—will get; *tumi*—you; *sabāra darśane*—everyone's audience.

TRANSLATION

"At present they are all living here. Their residences are in various quarters. Here you will get the audience of them all."

TEXT 60

তবে ভট্ট কহে বহু বিনয় বচন।
বহু দৈন্য করি' প্রভুরে কৈল নিমন্ত্রণ ॥ ৬০ ॥

tabe bhaṭṭa kahe bahu vinaya vacana
bahu dainya kari' prabhure kaila nimantraṇa

SYNONYMS

tabe—thereafter; *bhaṭṭa kahe*—Vallabha Bhaṭṭa said; *bahu*—very; *vinaya*—humble; *vacana*—words; *bahu dainya kari'*—in all humility; *prabhure*—Śrī Caitanya Mahāprabhu; *kaila nimantraṇa*—invited to dine.

TRANSLATION

Thereafter, with great submission and humility, Vallabha Bhaṭṭa invited Śrī Caitanya Mahāprabhu to dine at his home.

TEXT 61

আর দিন সব বৈষ্ণব প্রভু-স্থানে আইলা।
সবা-সনে মহাপ্রভু ভট্টে মিলাইলা ॥ ৬১ ॥

āra dina saba vaiṣṇava prabhu-sthāne āilā
sabā-sane mahāprabhu bhaṭṭe milāilā

SYNONYMS

āra dina—the next day; *saba vaiṣṇava*—all the Vaiṣṇavas; *prabhu-sthāne*—to the place of Śrī Caitanya Mahāprabhu; *āilā*—came; *sabā-sane*—with all of them; *mahāprabhu*—Śrī Caitanya Mahāprabhu; *bhaṭṭe milāilā*—introduced Vallabha Bhaṭṭa.

TRANSLATION

The next day, when all the Vaiṣṇavas came to the abode of Śrī Caitanya Mahāprabhu, the Lord introduced Vallabha Bhaṭṭa to them all.

TEXT 62

'বৈষ্ণবে'র তেজ দেখি' ভট্টের চমৎকার।
তাঁ-সবার আগে ভট্ট—খদ্যোত-আকার ॥ ৬২ ॥

'vaiṣṇave'ra teja dekhi' bhaṭṭera camatkāra
tāṅ-sabāra āge bhaṭṭa——khadyota-ākāra

SYNONYMS

vaiṣṇavera—of the Vaiṣṇavas; *teja*—the brilliance; *dekhi'*—seeing; *bhaṭṭera*—of Vallabha Bhaṭṭa; *camatkāra*—surprised; *tāṅ-sabāra*—of all of them; *āge*—in front; *bhaṭṭa*—Vallabha Bhaṭṭa; *khadyota-ākāra*—like a glowworm.

TRANSLATION

He was surprised to see the brilliance of their faces. Indeed, among them Vallabha Bhaṭṭa seemed just like a glowworm.

TEXT 63

তবে ভট্ট বহু মহাপ্রসাদ আনাইল।
গণ-সহ মহাপ্রভুরে ভোজন করাইল ॥ ৬৩ ॥

tabe bhaṭṭa bahu mahā-prasāda ānāila
gaṇa-saha mahāprabhure bhojana karāila

SYNONYMS

tabe—at that time; *bhaṭṭa*—Vallabha Bhaṭṭa; *bahu*—much; *mahā-prasāda*—Lord Jagannātha's remnants; *ānāila*—brought in; *gaṇa-saha mahāprabhure*—Śrī Caitanya Mahāprabhu with His associates; *bhojana karāila*—he fed.

TRANSLATION

Then Vallabha Bhaṭṭa brought in a great quantity of Lord Jagannātha's *mahā-prasāda* and sumptuously fed Lord Śrī Caitanya Mahāprabhu and His associates.

TEXT 64

পরমানন্দ পুরী-সঙ্গে সন্ন্যাসীর গণ ।
একদিকে বৈসে সব করিতে ভোজন ॥ ৬৪ ॥

paramānanda purī-saṅge sannyāsīra gaṇa
eka-dike vaise saba karite bhojana

SYNONYMS

paramānanda purī-saṅge—with Paramānanda Purī; *sannyāsīra gaṇa*—all the *sannyāsī* associates of Śrī Caitanya Mahāprabhu; *eka-dike*—on one side; *vaise*—sat down; *saba*—all; *karite bhojana*—to accept the *prasāda.*

TRANSLATION

All the sannyāsī associates of Śrī Caitanya Mahāprabhu headed by Paramānanda Purī, sat on one side and thus partook of the prasāda.

TEXT 65

অদ্বৈত, নিত্যানন্দ-রায়—পার্শ্বে দুইজন ।
মধ্যে মহাপ্রভু বসিলা, আগে-পাছে ভক্তগণ ॥ ৬৫ ॥

advaita, nityānanda-rāya——pārśve dui-jana
madhye mahāprabhu vasilā, āge-pāche bhakta-gaṇa

SYNONYMS

advaita—Advaita Ācārya; *nityānanda-rāya*—Lord Nityānanda; *pārśve*—on the sides; *dui-jana*—two personalities; *madhye*—in the middle; *mahāprabhu vasilā*—Śrī Caitanya Mahāprabhu sat down; *āge*—in front; *pāche*—behind; *bhakta-gaṇa*—all the devotees.

TRANSLATION

Śrī Caitanya Mahāprabhu sat in the midst of the devotees. Advaita Ācārya and Lord Nityānanda each sat on one side of the Lord. The other devotees sat in front of the Lord and behind Him.

TEXT 66

গৌড়ের ভক্ত যত কহিতে না পারি ।
অঙ্গনে বসিলা সব হঞা সারি সারি ॥ ৬৬ ॥

gauḍera bhakta yata kahite nā pāri
aṅgane vasilā saba hañā sāri sāri

SYNONYMS

gauḍera—of Bengal; *bhakta yata*—all the devotees; *kahite*—to mention; *nā pāri*—I am unable; *aṅgane*—in the courtyard; *vasilā*—sat down; *saba*—all; *hañā*—being; *sāri sāri*—in lines.

TRANSLATION

The devotees from Bengal, whom I am unable to count, all sat down in lines in the courtyard.

TEXT 67

প্রভুর ভক্তগণ দেখি' ভট্টের চমৎকার ।
প্রত্যেকে সবার পদে কৈল নমস্কার ॥ ৬৭ ॥

prabhura bhakta-gaṇa dekhi' bhaṭṭera camatkāra
pratyeke sabāra pade kaila namaskāra

SYNONYMS

prabhura—of Śrī Caitanya Mahāprabhu; *bhakta-gaṇa*—devotees; *dekhi'*—seeing; *bhaṭṭera*—of Vallabha Bhaṭṭa; *camatkāra*—surprise; *prati-eke*—unto each and every one; *sabāra*—of all; *pade*—at the lotus feet; *kaila namaskāra*—he offered obeisances.

TRANSLATION

When Vallabha Bhaṭṭa saw all the devotees of Śrī Caitanya Mahāprabhu, he was greatly surprised, but in devotion he offered his obeisances at the lotus feet of each and every one of them.

TEXT 68

স্বরূপ, জগদানন্দ, কাশীশ্বর, শঙ্কর ।
পরিবেশন করে, আর রাঘব, দামোদর ॥ ৬৮ ॥

svarūpa, jagadānanda, kāśīśvara, śaṅkara
pariveśana kare, āra rāghava, dāmodara

SYNONYMS

svarūpa—Svarūpa; *jagadānanda*—Jagadānanda; *kāśīśvara*—Kāśīśvara; *śaṅkara*—Śaṅkara; *pariveśana kare*—distribute; *āra*—and; *rāghava dāmodara*—Rāghava and Dāmodara.

TRANSLATION

Svarūpa Dāmodara, Jagadānanda, Kāśīśvara and Śaṅkara, along with Rāghava and Dāmodara Paṇḍita, took charge of distributing the prasāda.

TEXT 69

মহাপ্রসাদ বল্লভ-ভট্ট বহু আনাইল ।
প্রভু-সহ সন্ন্যাসিগণ ভোজনে বসিল ॥ ৬৯ ॥

mahā-prasāda vallabha-bhaṭṭa bahu ānāila
prabhu-saha sannyāsi-gaṇa bhojane vasila

SYNONYMS

mahā-prasāda—food offered to Śrī Jagannātha; *vallabha-bhaṭṭa*—Vallabha Bhaṭṭa; *bahu*—a large quantity; *ānāila*—brought; *prabhu-saha*—with Śrī Caitanya Mahāprabhu; *sannyāsi-gaṇa*—all the *sannyāsīs; bhojane vasila*—sat down to accept the *prasāda.*

TRANSLATION

Vallabha Bhaṭṭa had brought a large quantity of mahā-prasāda offered to Lord Jagannātha. Thus all the sannyāsīs sat down to eat with Śrī Caitanya Mahāprabhu.

TEXT 70

প্রসাদ পায় বৈষ্ণবগণ বলে, 'হরি' 'হরি' ।
হরি হরি ধ্বনি উঠে সব ব্রহ্মাণ্ড ভরি' ॥ ৭০ ॥

prasāda pāya vaiṣṇava-gaṇa bale, 'hari' 'hari'
hari hari dhvani uṭhe saba brahmāṇḍa bhari'

SYNONYMS

prasāda—the *prasāda; pāya*—accept; *vaiṣṇava-gaṇa*—all the Vaiṣṇavas; *bale*—chant; *hari hari*—Hari, Hari; *hari hari dhvani*—the vibration of Hari, Hari; *uṭhe*—rises; *saba brahmāṇḍa*—the entire universe; *bhari'*—filling.

TRANSLATION

Accepting the prasāda, all the Vaiṣṇavas chanted the holy names Hari, Hari. The rising vibration of the holy name of Hari filled the entire universe.

TEXT 71

**মালা, চন্দন, গুবাক, পান অনেক আনিল ।
সবা' পূজা করি' ভট্ট আনন্দিত হৈল ॥ ৭১ ॥**

mālā, candana, guvāka, pāna aneka ānila
sabā' pūjā kari' bhaṭṭa ānandita haila

SYNONYMS

mālā—garlands; *candana*—sandalwood pulp; *guvāka*—spices; *pāna*—betel; *aneka*—much; *ānila*—brought; *sabā' pūjā kari'*—worshiping all the Vaiṣṇavas; *bhaṭṭa*—Vallabha Bhaṭṭa; *ānandita haila*—became very happy.

TRANSLATION

When all the Vaiṣṇavas had finished eating, Vallabha Bhaṭṭa brought a large quantity of garlands, sandalwood pulp, spices and betel. He worshiped them very respectfully and became extremely happy.

TEXT 72

**রথযাত্রা-দিনে প্রভু কীর্তন আরম্ভিলা ।
পূর্ববৎ সাত সম্প্রদায় পৃথক্ করিলা ॥ ৭২ ॥**

ratha-yātrā-dine prabhu kīrtana ārambhilā
pūrvavat sāta sampradāya pṛthak karilā

SYNONYMS

ratha-yātrā-dine—on the day of the car festival; *prabhu*—Śrī Caitanya Mahāprabhu; *kīrtana ārambhilā*—began the congregational chanting; *pūrva-vat*—as previously; *sāta sampradāya*—in seven groups; *pṛthak karilā*—He divided.

TRANSLATION

On the day of the car festival, Śrī Caitanya Mahāprabhu began the congregational chanting. As He had done previously, He divided all the devotees into seven groups.

TEXTS 73-74

**অদ্বৈত, নিত্যানন্দ, হরিদাস, বক্রেশ্বর ।
শ্রীবাস, রাঘব, পণ্ডিত-গদাধর ॥ ৭৩ ॥**

সাত জন সাত-ঠাঞি করেন নর্তন ।
'হরিবোল' বলি' প্রভু করেন ভ্রমণ ॥ ৭৪ ॥

advaita, nityānanda, haridāsa, vakreśvara
śrīvāsa, rāghava, paṇḍita-gadādhara

sāta jana sāta-ṭhāñi karena nartana
'hari-bola' bali' prabhu karena bhramaṇa

SYNONYMS

advaita—Advaita Ācārya; *nityānanda*—Lord Nityānanda; *haridāsa*—Ṭhākura Haridāsa; *vakreśvara*—Vakreśvara; *śrīvāsa*—Śrīvāsa Ṭhākura; *rāghava*—Rāghava; *paṇḍita-gadādhara*—Gadādhara Paṇḍita; *sāta jana*—seven persons; *sāta-ṭhāñi*—in seven groups; *karena nartana*—dance; *hari-bola bali'*—uttering "Hari bol"; *prabhu*—Śrī Caitanya Mahāprabhu; *karena bhramaṇa*—wanders.

TRANSLATION

Seven devotees—Advaita, Nityānanda, Haridāsa Ṭhākura, Vakreśvara, Śrīvāsa Ṭhākura, Rāghava Paṇḍita and Gadādhara Paṇḍita—formed seven groups and began dancing. Śrī Caitanya Mahāprabhu, chanting "Hari bol," wandered from one group to another.

TEXT 75

চৌদ্দ মাদল বাজে উচ্চ সঙ্কীর্তন ।
এক এক নর্তকের প্রেমে ভাসিল ভুবন ॥ ৭৫ ॥

caudda mādala bāje ucca saṅkīrtana
eka eka nartakera preme bhāsila bhuvana

SYNONYMS

caudda mādala—fourteen *mṛdaṅgas; bāje*—were being played; *ucca saṅkīrtana*—loud congregational chanting; *eka eka*—of each group; *nartakera*—of the dancer; *preme*—in ecstatic love; *bhāsila bhuvana*—inundated the entire world.

TRANSLATION

Fourteen mṛdaṅgas resounded with the loud congregational chanting, and in each group was a dancer whose dance of ecstatic love inundated the entire world.

TEXT 76

দেখি' বল্লভ-ভট্টের হৈল চমৎকার।
আনন্দে বিহ্বল নাহি আপন-সাম্ভাল ॥ ৭৬ ॥

dekhi' vallabha-bhaṭṭera haila camatkāra
ānande vihvala nāhi āpana-sāmbhāla

SYNONYMS

dekhi'—seeing; *vallabha-bhaṭṭera*—of Vallabha Bhaṭṭa; *haila camatkāra*—was astonishment; *ānande vihvala*—overwhelmed by transcendental happiness; *nāhi*—there was not; *āpana-sāmbhāla*—keeping his normal position.

TRANSLATION

Seeing all this, Vallabha Bhaṭṭa was completely astonished. He was overwhelmed by transcendental bliss and lost himself.

TEXT 77

তবে মহাপ্রভু সবার নৃত্য রাখিলা।
পূর্ব্ববৎ আপনে নৃত্য করিতে লাগিলা ॥ ৭৭ ॥

tabe mahāprabhu sabāra nṛtya rākhilā
pūrvavat āpane nṛtya karite lāgilā

SYNONYMS

tabe—thereafter; *mahāprabhu*—Śrī Caitanya Mahāprabhu; *sabāra*—of all of them; *nṛtya rākhilā*—stopped the dancing; *pūrvavat*—as previously; *āpane*—personally; *nṛtya*—dancing; *karite lāgilā*—began to perform.

TRANSLATION

Then Śrī Caitanya Mahāprabhu stopped the dancing of the others, and as He had done previously, He personally began to dance.

TEXT 78

প্রভুর সৌন্দর্য দেখি আর প্রেমোদয়।
'এই ত' সাক্ষাৎ কৃষ্ণ' ভট্টের হইল নিশ্চয় ॥ ৭৮ ॥

prabhura saundarya dekhi āra premodaya
'ei ta' sākṣāt kṛṣṇa' bhaṭṭera ha-ila niścaya

SYNONYMS

prabhura—of Śrī Caitanya Mahāprabhu; *saundarya*—the beauty; *dekhi*—seeing; *āra*—also; *prema-udaya*—arousing of ecstatic love; *ei*—this; *ta'*—certainly; *sākṣāt*—directly; *kṛṣṇa*—Lord Kṛṣṇa; *bhaṭṭera*—of Vallabha Bhaṭṭa; *ha-ila*—was; *niścaya*—certainty.

TRANSLATION

Seeing the beauty of Śrī Caitanya Mahāprabhu and the awakening of His ecstatic love, Vallabha Bhaṭṭa concluded, "Here is Lord Kṛṣṇa, without a doubt."

TEXT 79

এত মত রথযাত্রা সকলে দেখিল।
প্রভুর চরিত্রে ভট্টের চমৎকার হৈল ॥ ৭৯ ॥

eta mata ratha-yātrā sakale dekhila
prabhura caritre bhaṭṭera camatkāra haila

SYNONYMS

eta mata—in this way; *ratha-yātrā*—the car festival; *sakale*—all; *dekhila*—saw; *prabhura caritre*—by the character of Śrī Caitanya Mahāprabhu; *bhaṭṭera*—of Vallabha Bhaṭṭa; *camatkāra haila*—there was astonishment.

TRANSLATION

Thus Vallabha Bhaṭṭa witnessed the car festival. He was simply astonished by the characteristics of Śrī Caitanya Mahāprabhu.

TEXT 80

যাত্রানন্তরে ভট্ট যাই মহাপ্রভু-স্থানে।
প্রভু-চরণে কিছু কৈল নিবেদনে ॥ ৮০ ॥

yātrānantare bhaṭṭa yāi mahāprabhu-sthāne
prabhu-caraṇe kichu kaila nivedane

SYNONYMS

yātrā-anantare—after the Ratha-yātrā; *bhaṭṭa*—Vallabha Bhaṭṭa; *yāi*—going; *mahāprabhu-sthāne*—to the place of Śrī Caitanya Mahāprabhu; *prabhu-caraṇe*—at the lotus feet of the Lord; *kichu*—some; *kaila*—made; *nivedane*—submission.

TRANSLATION

One day, after the festival was over, Vallabha Bhaṭṭa went to the abode of Śrī Caitanya Mahāprabhu and submitted a request at the lotus feet of the Lord.

TEXT 81

"ভাগবতের টীকা কিছু করিয়াছি লিখন।
আপনে মহাপ্রভু যদি করেন শ্রবণ॥" ৮১ ॥

"bhāgavatera ṭīkā kichu kariyāchi likhana
āpane mahāprabhu yadi karena śravaṇa"

SYNONYMS

bhāgavatera—on *Śrīmad-Bhāgavatam; ṭīkā*—commentary; *kichu*—some; *kariyāchi likhana*—I have written; *āpane*—You; *mahāprabhu*—Śrī Caitanya Mahāprabhu; *yadi*—if; *karena śravaṇa*—would hear.

TRANSLATION

"I have written some commentary on Śrīmad-Bhāgavatam," he said. "Would Your Lordship kindly hear it?"

TEXT 82

প্রভু কহে,—"ভাগবতার্থ বুঝিতে না পারি।
ভাগবতার্থ শুনিতে আমি নহি অধিকারী॥ ৮২ ॥

prabhu kahe, —"bhāgavatārtha bujhite nā pāri
bhāgavatārtha śunite āmi nahi adhikārī

SYNONYMS

prabhu kahe—Śrī Caitanya Mahāprabhu replied; *bhāgavata-artha*—the meaning of *Śrīmad-Bhāgavatam; bujhite nā pāri*—I cannot understand; *bhāgavata-artha*—the purport of *Śrīmad-Bhāgavatam; śunite*—to hear; *āmi nahi adhikārī*—I am not the proper person.

TRANSLATION

The Lord replied, "I do not understand the meaning of Śrīmad-Bhāgavatam. Indeed, I am not a suitable person to hear its meaning.

TEXT 83

বসি' কৃষ্ণনাম মাত্র করিয়ে গ্রহণে ।
সংখ্যা-নাম পূর্ণ মোর নহে রাত্রি-দিনে ॥ ৮৩ ॥

vasi' kṛṣṇa-nāma mātra kariye grahaṇe
saṅkhyā-nāma pūrṇa mora nahe rātri-dine

SYNONYMS

vasi'—sitting; *kṛṣṇa-nāma*—the holy name of Lord Kṛṣṇa; *mātra*—simply; *kariye grahaṇe*—I chant; *saṅkhyā-nāma*—a fixed number of rounds; *pūrṇa*—complete; *mora*—My; *nahe*—is not; *rātri-dine*—throughout the entire day and night.

TRANSLATION

"I simply sit and try to chant the holy name of Kṛṣṇa, and although I chant all day and night, I nevertheless cannot complete the chanting of my prescribed number of rounds."

TEXT 84

ভট্ট কহে,—"কৃষ্ণনামের অর্থ-ব্যাখ্যানে ।
বিস্তার কৈরাছি, তাহা করহ শ্রবণে ॥" ৮৪ ॥

bhaṭṭa kahe, "kṛṣṇa-nāmera artha-vyākhyāne
vistāra kairāchi, tāhā karaha śravaṇe"

SYNONYMS

bhaṭṭa kahe—Vallabha Bhaṭṭa said; *kṛṣṇa-nāmera*—of the holy name of Kṛṣṇa; *artha-vyākhyāne*—description of the meaning; *vistāra*—very elaborately; *kairāchi*—I have made; *tāhā*—that; *karaha śravaṇe*—kindly hear.

TRANSLATION

Vallabha Bhaṭṭa said, "I have tried to describe elaborately the meaning of Kṛṣṇa's holy name. Kindly hear the explanation."

TEXT 85

প্রভু কহে,—"কৃষ্ণনামের বহু অর্থ না মানি ।
'শ্যামসুন্দর' 'যশোদানন্দন',—এইমাত্র জানি ॥ ৮৫ ॥

prabhu kahe, ——"kṛṣṇa-nāmera bahu artha nā māni
"śyāma-sundara' 'yaśodā-nandana,' ——ei-mātra jāni

SYNONYMS

prabhu kahe—Lord Śrī Caitanya Mahāprabhu replied; *kṛṣṇa-nāmera*—of the holy name of Kṛṣṇa; *bahu artha*—many meanings; *nā māni*—I do not accept; *śyāma-sundara*—Śyāmasundara; *yaśodā-nandana*—Yaśodānandana; *ei-mātra*—only this; *jāni*—I know.

TRANSLATION

Lord Śrī Caitanya Mahāprabhu replied, "I do not accept many different meanings for the holy name of Kṛṣṇa. I know only that Lord Kṛṣṇa is Śyāmasundara and Yaśodānandana. That's all I know.

TEXT 86

তমালশ্যামলত্বিষি শ্রীযশোদাস্তনন্ধয়ে ।
কৃষ্ণনাম্নো রূঢ়িরিতি সর্বশাস্ত্র-বিনির্ণয়ঃ ॥ ৮৬ ॥

tamāla-śyāmala-tviṣi
śrī-yaśodā-stanandhaye
kṛṣṇa-nāmno rūḍhir iti
sarva-śāstra-vinirṇayaḥ

SYNONYMS

tamāla-śyāmala-tviṣi—whose complexion is dark blue, resembling a *tamāla* tree; *śrī-yaśodā-stanam-dhaye*—sucking the breast of mother Yaśodā; *kṛṣṇa-nāmnaḥ*—of the name Kṛṣṇa; *rūḍhiḥ*—the chief meaning; *iti*—thus; *sarva-śāstra*—of all revealed scriptures; *vinirṇayaḥ*—the conclusion.

TRANSLATION

" 'The only purport of the holy name of Kṛṣṇa is that He is dark blue like a tamāla tree and is the son of mother Yaśodā. This is the conclusion of all the revealed scriptures.'

PURPORT

This is a verse from the *Nāma-kaumuḍī.*

TEXT 87

এই অর্থ আমি মাত্র জানিয়ে নির্ধার ।
আর সর্ব-অর্থে মোর নাহি অধিকার ॥" ৮৭ ॥

ei artha āmi mātra jāniye nirdhāra
āra sarva-arthe mora nāhi adhikāra"

SYNONYMS

ei artha—this meaning; *āmi*—I; *mātra*—only; *jāniye*—know; *nirdhāra*—conclusion; *āra*—other; *sarva*—all; *arthe*—meanings; *mora*—My; *nāhi*—is not; *adhikāra*—capacity to understand.

TRANSLATION

"I conclusively know these two names, Śyāmasundara and Yaśodānandana. I do not understand any other meanings, nor have I the capacity to understand them."

TEXT 88

ফল্গুপ্রায় ভট্টের নামাদি সব-ব্যাখ্যা ।
সর্বজ্ঞ প্রভু জানি' তারে করেন উপেক্ষা ॥ ৮৮ ॥

phalgu-prāya bhaṭṭera nāmādi saba-vyākhyā
sarvajña prabhu jāni' tāre karena upekṣā

SYNONYMS

phalgu-prāya—generally useless; *bhaṭṭera*—of Vallabha Bhaṭṭa; *nāma-ādi*—the holy name and so on; *saba*—all; *vyākhyā*—explanations; *sarva-jña*—omniscient; *prabhu*—Śrī Caitanya Mahāprabhu; *jāni'*—knowing; *tāre*—him; *karena upekṣā*—neglects.

TRANSLATION

Lord Śrī Caitanya Mahāprabhu is omniscient. Therefore He could understand that Vallabha Bhaṭṭa's explanations of Kṛṣṇa's name and Śrīmad-Bhāgavatam were useless. Therefore He did not care about them.

TEXT 89

বিমনা হঞা ভট্ট গেলা নিজ-ঘর ।
প্রভু-বিষয়ে ভক্তি কিছু হইল অন্তর ॥ ৮৯ ॥

vimanā hañā bhaṭṭa gelā nija-ghara
prabhu-viṣaye bhakti kichu ha-ila antara

SYNONYMS

vimanā hañā—feeling morose; *bhaṭṭa*—Vallabha Bhaṭṭa; *gelā*—went; *nija-ghara*—to his home; *prabhu-viṣaye*—unto Śrī Caitanya Mahāprabhu; *bhakti*—devotion; *kichu*—somewhat; *ha-ila*—became; *antara*—different.

TRANSLATION

When Śrī Caitanya Mahāprabhu rigidly declined to hear his explanations, Vallabha Bhaṭṭa went home feeling morose. His faith and devotion to the Lord changed.

TEXT 90

তবে ভট্ট গেলা পণ্ডিত-গোসাঞির ঠাঞি ।
নানা মতে প্রীতি করি' করে আসা-যাই ॥ ৯০ ॥

tabe bhaṭṭa gelā paṇḍita-gosāñira ṭhāñi
nānā mate prīti kari' kare āsā-yāi

SYNONYMS

tabe—thereafter; *bhaṭṭa*—Vallabha Bhaṭṭa; *gelā*—went; *paṇḍita-gosāñira ṭhāñi*—to Gadādhara Paṇḍita Gosāñi; *nānā mate*—in various ways; *prīti kari'*—showing affection; *kare āsā-yāi*—comes and goes.

TRANSLATION

Thereafter, Vallabha Bhaṭṭa went to the home of Gadādhara Paṇḍita. He kept coming and going, showing affection in various ways, and thus maintained a relationship with him.

TEXT 91

প্রভুর উপেক্ষায় সব নীলাচলের জন ।
ভট্টের ব্যাখ্যান কিছু না করে শ্রবণ ॥ ৯১ ॥

prabhura upekṣāya saba nīlācalera jana
bhaṭṭera vyākhyāna kichu nā kare śravaṇa

SYNONYMS

prabhura—of Śrī Caitanya Mahāprabhu; *upekṣāya*—because of neglect; *saba*—all; *nīlācalera jana*—people in Jagannātha Purī; *bhaṭṭera vyākhyāna*—explanation of Vallabha Bhaṭṭa; *kichu*—any; *nā kare śravaṇa*—do not hear.

TRANSLATION

Because Śrī Caitanya Mahāprabhu did not take Vallabha Bhaṭṭa very seriously, none of the people in Jagannātha Purī would hear any of his explanations.

TEXT 92

লজ্জিত হৈল ভট্ট, হৈল অপমানে ।
দুঃখিত হঞা গেল পণ্ডিতের স্থানে ॥ ৯২ ॥

lajjita haila bhaṭṭa, haila apamāne
duḥkhita hañā gela paṇḍitera sthāne

SYNONYMS

lajjita—ashamed; *haila*—became; *bhaṭṭa*—Vallabha Bhaṭṭa; *haila apamāne*—felt insulted; *duḥkhita hañā*—being unhappy; *gela*—went; *paṇḍitera sthāne*—to Gadādhara Paṇḍita.

TRANSLATION

Ashamed, insulted and unhappy, Vallabha Bhaṭṭa went to Gadādhara Paṇḍita.

TEXT 93

দৈন্য করি' কহে,—"নিলুঁ তোমার শরণ ।
তুমি কৃপা করি' রাখ আমার জীবন ॥ ৯৩ ॥

dainya kari' kahe, —"niluṅ tomāra śaraṇa
tumi kṛpā kari' rākha āmāra jīvana

SYNONYMS

dainya kari'—with great humility; *kahe*—said; *niluṅ*—I have taken; *tomāra śaraṇa*—shelter of you; *tumi*—you; *kṛpā kari'*—being merciful; *rākha*—keep; *āmāra jīvana*—my life.

TRANSLATION

Approaching him with great humility, Vallabha Bhaṭṭa said, "I have taken shelter of you, my dear sir. Kindly be merciful to me and save my life.

TEXT 94

কৃষ্ণনাম-ব্যাখ্যা যদি করহ শ্রবণ ।
তবে মোর লজ্জা-পঙ্ক হয় প্রক্ষালন ॥" ৯৪ ॥

kṛṣṇa-nāma-vyākhyā yadi karaha śravaṇa
tabe mora lajjā-paṅka haya prakṣālana"

SYNONYMS

kṛṣṇa-nāma—of the name of Lord Kṛṣṇa; *vyākhyā*—explanation; *yadi*—if; *karaha śravaṇa*—you hear; *tabe*—then; *mora*—my; *lajjā-paṅka*—the mud of shame; *haya*—there is; *prakṣālana*—washing.

TRANSLATION

"Please hear my explanation of the meaning of Lord Kṛṣṇa's name. In that way the mud of the shame that has come upon me will be washed off."

TEXT 95

সঙ্কটে পড়িল পণ্ডিত, করয়ে সংশয় ।
কি করিবেন,—একো, করিতে না পারে নিশ্চয় ॥ ৯৫ ॥

saṅkaṭe paḍila paṇḍita, karaye saṁśaya
ki karibena, ——eko, karite nā pāre niścaya

SYNONYMS

saṅkaṭe—into a dilemma; *paḍila paṇḍita*—Paṇḍita Gosāñi fell; *karaye saṁśaya*—felt doubts; *ki karibena*—what he will do; *eko*—alone; *karite nā pāre niścaya*—cannot make a decision.

TRANSLATION

Thus Paṇḍita Gosāñi fell into a dilemma. He was in such doubt that he could not decide alone what to do.

PURPORT

Śrī Caitanya Mahāprabhu did not take Vallabha Bhaṭṭa very seriously. Therefore Paṇḍita Gosāñi, or Gadādhara Gosāñi, fell into perplexity. What would be his position if he heard Vallabha Bhaṭṭa's explanation of Śrī Kṛṣṇa's name? Certainly Śrī Caitanya Mahāprabhu would be displeased. Therefore Gadādhara Paṇḍita Gosāñi could not make a decision.

TEXT 96

যদ্যপি পণ্ডিত আর না কৈলা অঙ্গীকার ।
ভট্ট যাই' তবু পড়ে করি' বলাৎকার ॥ ৯৬ ॥

yadyapi paṇḍita āra nā kailā aṅgīkāra
bhaṭṭa yāi' tabu paḍe kari' balātkāra

SYNONYMS

yadyapi—although; *paṇḍita*—Gadādhara Paṇḍita; *āra*—also; *nā kailā aṅgīkāra*—did not accept; *bhaṭṭa*—Vallabha Bhaṭṭa; *yāi'*—going; *tabu*—still; *paḍe*—reads; *kari' balātkāra*—forcibly.

TRANSLATION

Although Gadādhara Paṇḍita Gosāñi did not want to hear it, Vallabha Bhaṭṭa began to read his explanation with great force.

TEXT 97

আভিজাত্যে পণ্ডিত করিতে নারে নিষেধন ।
"এ সঙ্কটে রাখ, কৃষ্ণ লইলাঙ শরণ ॥ ৯৭ ॥

ābhijātye paṇḍita karite nāre niṣedhana
"e saṅkaṭe rākha, kṛṣṇa la-ilāṅa śaraṇa

SYNONYMS

ābhijātye—because of his aristocracy; *paṇḍita*—Gadādhara Paṇḍita; *karite nāre niṣedhana*—could not forbid; *e saṅkaṭe*—in this danger; *rākha*—please protect; *kṛṣṇa*—O Lord Kṛṣṇa; *la-ilāṅa*—I have taken; *śaraṇa*—shelter.

TRANSLATION

Because Vallabha Bhaṭṭa was a learned brāhmaṇa, Gadādhara Paṇḍita could not forbid him. Thus he began to think of Lord Kṛṣṇa. "My dear Lord Kṛṣṇa," he requested, "please protect me in this danger. I have taken shelter of You.

TEXT 98

অন্তর্যামী প্রভু জানিবেন মোর মন ।
তাঁরে ভয় নাহি কিছু, 'বিষম' তাঁর গণ ॥"৯৮ ॥

antaryāmī prabhu jānibena mora mana
tāṅre bhaya nāhi kichu, 'viṣama' tāṅra gaṇa"

SYNONYMS

antaryāmī—existing in everyone's heart; *prabhu*—Śrī Caitanya Mahāprabhu; *jānibena*—will know; *mora mana*—my mind; *tāṅre*—of Him; *bhaya*—fear; *nāhi*—there is not; *kichu*—any; *viṣama*—very critical; *tāṅra gaṇa*—his associates.

TRANSLATION

"Śrī Caitanya Mahāprabhu is present in everyone's heart, and He will certainly know my mind. Therefore I do not fear Him. His associates, however, are extremely critical."

PURPORT

As the Supreme Personality of Godhead, Śrī Caitanya Mahāprabhu exists in everyone's heart. Therefore He would know the circumstances under which Paṇḍita Gosāñi agreed to hear Vallabha Bhaṭṭa's explanations, and certainly He would not be angry. However, the Vaiṣṇavas who were always with Śrī Caitanya Mahāprabhu might not understand Gadādhara Paṇḍita's inner consciousness, and they might accuse him of having compromised with Vallabha Bhaṭṭa, despite his having been neglected by Śrī Caitanya Mahāprabhu. Gadādhara Paṇḍita Gosāñi was seriously thinking in this way.

TEXT 99

যদ্যপি বিচারে পণ্ডিতের নাহি কিছু দোষ ।
তথাপি প্রভুর গণ তাঁরে করে প্রণয়-রোষ ॥ ৯৯ ॥

yadyapi vicāre paṇḍitera nāhi kichu doṣa
tathāpi prabhura gaṇa tāṅre kare praṇaya-roṣa

SYNONYMS

yadyapi—although; *vicāre*—conclusively; *paṇḍitera*—of Gadādhara Paṇḍita; *nāhi kichu doṣa*—there was no fault; *tathāpi*—still; *prabhura gaṇa*—associates of Śrī Caitanya Mahāprabhu; *tāṅre*—unto him; *kare praṇaya-roṣa*—showed affectionate anger.

TRANSLATION

Although Gadādhara Paṇḍita Gosāñi was not in the least at fault, some of Śrī Caitanya Mahāprabhu's devotees showed affectionate anger toward him.

TEXT 100

প্রত্যহ বল্লভ-ভট্ট আইসে প্রভু-স্থানে ।
'উদ্‌গ্রাহাদি' প্রায় করে আচার্যাদি-সনে ॥ ১০০ ॥

pratyaha vallabha-bhaṭṭa āise prabhu-sthāne
'udgrāhādi' prāya kare ācāryādi-sane

SYNONYMS

prati-aha—daily; *vallabha-bhaṭṭa*—Vallabha Bhaṭṭa; *āise*—comes; *prabhu-sthāne*—to the place of Lord Śrī Caitanya Mahāprabhu; *udgrāha-ādi prāya*—unnecessary argument; *kare*—does; *ācārya-ādi-sane*—with Advaita Ācārya and others.

TRANSLATION

Every day, Vallabha Bhaṭṭa would come to the place of Śrī Caitanya Mahāprabhu to engage in unnecessary arguments with Advaita Ācārya and other great personalities, such as Svarūpa Dāmodara.

TEXT 101

যেই কিছু করে ভট্ট 'সিদ্ধান্ত' স্থাপন ।
শুনিতেই আচার্য তাহা করেন খণ্ডন ॥ ১০১ ॥

yei kichu kare bhaṭṭa 'siddhānta' sthāpana
śunitei ācārya tāhā karena khaṇḍana

SYNONYMS

yei—whatever; *kichu*—any; *kare*—does; *bhaṭṭa*—Vallabha Bhaṭṭa; *siddhānta*—conclusion; *sthāpana*—establishing; *śunitei*—hearing; *ācārya*—Advaita Ācārya; *tāhā*—that; *karena khaṇḍana*—refuted.

TRANSLATION

Whatever conclusions Vallabha Bhaṭṭa eagerly presented were refuted by personalities like Advaita Ācārya.

TEXT 102

আচার্যাদি-আগে ভট্ট যবে যবে যায় ।
রাজহংস-মধ্যে যেন রহে বকপ্রায় ॥ ১০২ ॥

ācāryādi-āge bhaṭṭa yabe yabe yāya
rājahaṁsa-madhye yena rahe baka-prāya

SYNONYMS

ācārya-ādi-āge—in front of Advaita Ācārya and others; *bhaṭṭa*—Vallabha Bhaṭṭa; *yabe yabe*—whenever; *yāya*—goes; *rāja-haṁsa-madhye*—in a society of white swans; *yena*—as; *rahe*—remained; *baka-prāya*—like a duck.

TRANSLATION

Whenever Vallabha Bhaṭṭa entered the society of devotees, headed by Advaita Ācārya, he was like a duck in a society of white swans.

TEXT 103

একদিন ভট্ট পুছিল আচার্যেরে।
"জীব-'প্রকৃতি' 'পতি' করি' মানয়ে কৃষ্ণেরে ॥ ১০৩॥

eka-dina bhaṭṭa puchila ācāryere
"jīva-'prakṛti' 'pati' kari' mānaye kṛṣṇere

SYNONYMS

eka-dina—one day; *bhaṭṭa*—Vallabha Bhaṭṭa; *puchila ācāryere*—inquired from Advaita Ācārya; *jīva*—the living entity; *prakṛti*—female; *pati*—husband; *kari'*—as; *mānaye kṛṣṇere*—accepts Kṛṣṇa.

TRANSLATION

One day Vallabha Bhaṭṭa said to Advaita Ācārya, "Every living entity is female [prakṛti] and considers Kṛṣṇa her husband [pati].

TEXT 104

পতিব্রতা হঞা পতির নাম নাহি লয়।
তোমরা কৃষ্ণনাম-লহ,– কোন্ ধর্ম হয় ?"১০৪ ॥

pati-vratā hañā patira nāma nāhi laya
tomarā kṛṣṇa-nāma-laha, —kon dharma haya?"

SYNONYMS

pati-vratā—devoted to the husband; *hañā*—being; *patira*—of the husband; *nāma*—name; *nāhi laya*—does not utter; *tomarā*—all of you; *kṛṣṇa-nāma-laha*—chant the name of Kṛṣṇa; *kon*—what; *dharma*—religious principle; *haya*—is it.

TRANSLATION

"It is the duty of a chaste wife, devoted to her husband, not to utter her husband's name, but all of you chant the name of Kṛṣṇa. How can this be called a religious principle?"

TEXT 105

আচার্য কহে,—"আগে তোমার 'ধর্ম' মূর্তিমান্।
ইঁহারে পুছহ, ইঁহ করিবেন ইহার সমাধান ॥ ১০৫॥

ācārya kahe, —"āge tomāra 'dharma' mūrtimān
iṅhāre puchaha, iṅha karibena ihāra samādhāna

SYNONYMS

ācārya kahe—Advaita Ācārya said; *āge*—in front; *tomāra*—of you; *dharma*—religious principles; *mūrtimān*—personified; *iṅhāre puchaha*—ask Him; *iṅha*—He; *karibena*—will make; *ihāra*—of this; *samādhāna*—solution.

TRANSLATION

Advaita Ācārya responded, "In front of you is Lord Śrī Caitanya Mahāprabhu, the personification of religious principles. You should ask Him, for He will give you the proper answer."

TEXT 106

শুনি' প্রভু কহেন,—"তুমি না জান ধর্মমর্ম ।
স্বামি-আজ্ঞা পালে,—এই পতিব্রতা-ধর্ম ॥ ১০৬ ॥

śuni' prabhu kahena, —"tumi nā jāna dharma-marma
svāmi-ājñā pāle, —ei pati-vratā-dharma

SYNONYMS

śuni'—hearing; *prabhu kahena*—Śrī Caitanya Mahāprabhu said; *tumi*—you; *nā jāna*—do not know; *dharma-marma*—real religious principles; *svāmi*—of the husband; *ājñā*—order; *pāle*—obeys; *ei*—this; *pati-vratā-dharma*—the religious principle of a chaste woman.

TRANSLATION

Hearing this, Lord Śrī Caitanya Mahāprabhu said, "My dear Vallabha Bhaṭṭa, you do not know religious principles. Actually, the first duty of a chaste woman is to carry out the order of her husband.

TEXT 107

পতির আজ্ঞা,—নিরন্তর তাঁর নাম লইতে ।
পতির আজ্ঞা পতিব্রতা না পারে লঙ্ঘিতে ॥ ১০৭ ॥

patira ājñā, —nirantara tāṅra nāma la-ite
patira ājñā pati-vratā nā pāre laṅghite

SYNONYMS

patira ājñā—the husband's order; *nirantara*—always; *tāṅra*—His; *nāma*—name; *la-ite*—to chant; *patira ājñā*—the order of the husband; *pati-vratā*—a chaste, devoted wife; *nā pāre laṅghite*—cannot deny.

TRANSLATION

"The order of Kṛṣṇa is to chant His name incessantly. Therefore one who is chaste and adherent to the husband Kṛṣṇa must chant the Lord's name, for she cannot deny the husband's order.

TEXT 108

অতএব নাম লয়, নামের 'ফল' পায়।
নামের ফলে কৃষ্ণপদে 'প্রেম' উপজায় ॥"১০৮ ॥

ataeva nāma laya, nāmera 'phala' pāya
nāmera phale kṛṣṇa-pade 'prema' upajāya"

SYNONYMS

ataeva—therefore; *nāma laya*—chants the holy name; *nāmera*—of the name; *phala*—result; *pāya*—gets; *nāmera phale*—as a result of chanting the holy name; *kṛṣṇa-pade*—at the lotus feet of Kṛṣṇa; *prema*—ecstatic love; *upajāya*—develops.

TRANSLATION

"Following this religious principle, a pure devotee of Lord Kṛṣṇa always chants the holy name. As a result of this, he gets the fruit of ecstatic love for Kṛṣṇa."

TEXT 109

শুনিয়া বল্লভ-ভট্ট হৈল নির্বচন।
ঘরে যাই' মনে দুঃখে করেন চিন্তন ॥ ১০৯ ॥

śuniyā vallabha-bhaṭṭa haila nirvacana
ghare yāi' mane duḥkhe karena cintana

SYNONYMS

śuniyā—hearing; *vallabha-bhaṭṭa*—Vallabha Bhaṭṭa; *haila*—became; *nirvacana*—speechless; *ghare yāi'*—returning home; *mane*—in the mind; *duḥkhe*—unhappy; *karena cintana*—began to consider.

TRANSLATION

Hearing this, Vallabha Bhaṭṭa was speechless. He returned home greatly unhappy and began to consider thus.

TEXTS 110-111

"নিত্য আমার এই সভায় হয় কক্ষা-পাত।
একদিন উপরে যদি হয় মোর বাত্ ॥ ১১০ ॥
তবে সুখ হয়, আর সব লজ্জা যায়।
স্ব-বচন স্থাপিতে আমি কি করি উপায়? ১১১ ॥

"nitya āmāra ei sabhāya haya kakṣā-pāta
eka-dina upare yadi haya mora vāt

tabe sukha haya, āra saba lajjā yāya
sva-vacana sthāpite āmi ki kari upāya?

SYNONYMS

nitya—daily; *āmāra*—my; *ei*—this; *sabhāya*—in the assembly; *haya*—there is; *kakṣā-pāta*—defeat; *eka-dina*—one day; *upare*—on top; *yadi*—if; *haya*—are; *mora*—my; *vāt*—words; *tabe*—then; *sukha*—happiness; *haya*—is; *āra*—and; *saba*—all; *lajjā*—shame; *yāya*—goes; *sva-vacana*—my statement; *sthāpite*—to establish; *āmi*—I; *ki*—what; *kari*—shall adopt; *upāya*—means.

TRANSLATION

"Every day I am defeated in this assembly. If by chance I am one day victorious, that will be a great source of happiness for me, and all my shame will go away. But what means shall I adopt to establish my statements?"

TEXT 112

আর দিন আসি' বসিলা প্রভুরে নমস্করি'।
সভাতে কহেন কিছু মনে গর্ব করি' ॥ ১১২ ॥

āra dina āsi' vasilā prabhure namaskari'
sabhāte kahena kichu mane garva kari'

SYNONYMS

āra dina—the next day; *āsi'*—coming; *vasilā*—sat down; *prabhure namaskari'*—offering obeisances to Lord Śrī Caitanya Mahāprabhu; *sabhāte*—in the assembly; *kahena*—he said; *kichu*—something; *mane*—within the mind; *garva kari'*—being proud.

TRANSLATION

The next day when he came to the assembly of Śrī Caitanya Mahāprabhu, he sat down after offering obeisances to the Lord and said something with great pride.

TEXT 113

"ভাগবতে স্বামীর ব্যাখ্যান কৈরাছি খণ্ডন ।
লইতে না পারি তাঁর ব্যাখ্যান-বচন ॥ ১১৩ ॥

"bhāgavate svāmīra vyākhyāna kairāchi khaṇḍana
la-ite nā pāri tāṅra vyākhyāna-vacana

SYNONYMS

bhāgavate—in my commentary on *Śrīmad-Bhāgavatam; svāmīra*—of Śrīdhara Svāmī; *vyākhyāna*—explanation; *kairāchi khaṇḍana*—I have refuted; *la-ite nā pāri*—I cannot accept; *tāṅra*—his; *vyākhyāna-vacana*—words of explanation.

TRANSLATION

"In my commentary on Śrīmad-Bhāgavatam," he said, "I have refuted the explanations of Śrīdhara Svāmī. I cannot accept his explanations.

TEXT 114

সেই ব্যাখ্যা করেন যাহাঁ যেই পড়ে আনি' ।
একবাক্যতা নাহি, তাতে 'স্বামী' নাহি মানি ॥"১১৪॥

sei vyākhyā karena yāhāṅ yei paḍe āni'
eka-vākyatā nāhi, tāte 'svāmī' nāhi māni"

SYNONYMS

sei—he; *vyākhyā karena*—explains; *yāhāṅ*—wherever; *yei*—whatever; *paḍe*—reads; *āni'*—accepting; *eka-vākyatā*—consistency; *nāhi*—there is not; *tāte*—therefore; *svāmī*—Śrīdhara Svāmī; *nāhi māni*—I cannot accept.

TRANSLATION

"Whatever Śrīdhara Svāmī reads he explains according to the circumstances. Therefore he is inconsistent in his explanations and cannot be accepted as an authority."

TEXT 115

প্রভু হাসি' কহে,—"স্বামী না মানে যেই জন ।
বেশ্যার ভিতরে তারে করিয়ে গণন ॥" ১১৫ ॥

prabhu hāsi' kahe, —"svāmī nā māne yei jana
veśyāra bhitare tāre kariye gaṇana"

SYNONYMS

prabhu—Śrī Caitanya Mahāprabhu; *hāsi'*—smiling; *kahe*—said; *svāmī*—husband; *nā māne*—does not accept; *yei jana*—anyone who; *veśyāra bhitare*—among the prostitutes; *tāre*—him; *kariye gaṇana*—I count.

TRANSLATION

Śrī Caitanya Mahāprabhu smilingly replied, "One who does not accept the svāmī [husband] as an authority I consider a prostitute."

TEXT 116

এত কহি' মহাপ্রভু মৌন ধরিলা ।
শুনিয়া সবার মনে সন্তোষ হইলা ॥ ১১৬ ॥

eta kahi' mahāprabhu mauna dharilā
śuniyā sabāra mane santoṣa ha-ilā

SYNONYMS

eta kahi'—saying this; *mahāprabhu*—Śrī Caitanya Mahāprabhu; *mauna dharilā*—became very grave; *śuniyā*—hearing; *sabāra*—of all the devotees; *mane*—in the mind; *santoṣa ha-ilā*—there was great satisfaction.

TRANSLATION

After saying this, Śrī Caitanya Mahāprabhu was very grave. All the devotees present derived great satisfaction from hearing this statement.

TEXT 117

জগতের হিত লাগি' গৌর-অবতার ।
অন্তরের অভিমান জানেন তাহার ॥ ১১৭ ॥

jagatera hita lāgi' gaura-avatāra
antarera abhimāna jānena tāhāra

SYNONYMS

jagatera—of the entire world; *hita lāgi'*—for the benefit; *gaura-avatāra*—the incarnation of Śrī Caitanya Mahāprabhu; *antarera abhimāna*—internal pride; *jānena*—understands; *tāhāra*—his.

TRANSLATION

Śrī Caitanya Mahāprabhu descended as an incarnation for the benefit of the entire world. Thus He knew the mind of Vallabha Bhaṭṭa very well.

TEXT 118

নানা অবজ্ঞানে ভট্টে শোধেন ভগবান্ ।
কৃষ্ণ যৈছে খণ্ডিলেন ইন্দ্রের অভিমান ॥ ১১৮ ॥

nānā avajñāne bhaṭṭe śodhena bhagavān
kṛṣṇa yaiche khaṇḍilena indrera abhimāna

SYNONYMS

nānā—various; *avajñāne*—by disrespect; *bhaṭṭe*—Vallabha Bhaṭṭa; *śodhena*—purifies; *bhagavān*—the Supreme Personality of Godhead; *kṛṣṇa*—Lord Kṛṣṇa; *yaiche*—as; *khaṇḍilena*—cuts down; *indrera abhimāna*—the pride of Indra.

TRANSLATION

By various hints and refutations, Lord Caitanya, the Supreme Personality of Godhead, corrected Vallabha Bhaṭṭa exactly as Kṛṣṇa had cut down the false pride of Indra.

PURPORT

Indra, the King of heaven, was very proud of his position. Therefore when the residents of Vṛndāvana decided not to perform the Indra-yajña but to perform the Govardhana-yajña in accordance with the instructions of Kṛṣṇa, Indra, because of his false pride, wanted to chastise the residents of Vṛndāvana. Thinking himself extremely powerful, Indra poured incessant rain upon Vṛndāvana, but Lord Kṛṣṇa immediately cut down his pride by lifting the Govardhana Hill as an umbrella to save the residents of Vṛndāvana. In this way Kṛṣṇa proved Indra's power most insignificant in the presence of His own omnipotence.

TEXT 119

অজ্ঞ জীব নিজ-'হিতে' 'অহিত' করি' মানে ।
গর্ব চূর্ণ হৈলে, পাছে উঘাড়ে নয়নে ॥ ১১৯ ॥

ajña jīva nija-'hite' 'ahita' kari' māne
garva cūrṇa haile, pāche ughāḍe nayane

SYNONYMS

ajña jīva—the ignorant living entity; *nija-hite*—his personal benefit; *ahita kari' māne*—considers a loss; *garva cūrṇa haile*—when pride is cut down; *pāche*—afterward; *ughāḍe nayane*—the eyes open.

TRANSLATION

An ignorant living being does not recognize his actual profit. Because of ignorance and material pride, he sometimes considers profit a loss, but when his pride is cut down he can actually see his true benefit.

TEXT 120

ঘরে আসি' রাত্র্যে ভট্ট চিন্তিতে লাগিল ।
"পূর্বে প্রয়াগে মোরে মহা-কৃপা কৈল ॥ ১২০ ॥

ghare āsi' rātrye bhaṭṭa cintite lāgila
"pūrve prayāge more mahā-kṛpā kaila

SYNONYMS

ghare āsi'—coming home; *rātrye*—at night; *bhaṭṭa*—Vallabha Bhaṭṭa; *cintite lāgila*—began to think; *pūrve*—previously; *prayāge*—at Prayāga; *more*—unto me; *mahā-kṛpā kaila*—showed great mercy.

TRANSLATION

Returning home that night, Vallabha Bhaṭṭa thought, "Previously, at Prayāga, Lord Caitanya was very kind to me.

TEXT 121

স্বগণ-সহিতে মোর মানিলা নিমন্ত্রণ ।
এবে কেনে প্রভুর মোতে ফিরি' গেল মন ? ১২১ ॥

svagaṇa-sahite mora mānilā nimantraṇa
ebe kene prabhura mote phiri' gela mana?

SYNONYMS

sva-gaṇa-sahite—accompanied by His personal associates; *mora*—my; *mānilā*—accepted; *nimantraṇa*—invitation; *ebe*—now; *kene*—why; *prabhura*—

of Śrī Caitanya Mahāprabhu; *mote*—unto me; *phiri' gela*—has changed; *mana*—mind.

TRANSLATION

"He accepted my invitation with His other devotees, and He was kind to me. Why has He now changed so much here at Jagannātha Purī?

TEXT 122

'আমি জিতি',—এই গর্ব-শূন্য হউক ইঁহার চিত।
ঈশ্বর-স্বভাব,—করেন সবাকার হিত ॥ ১২২ ॥

'āmi jiti', —ei garva-śūnya ha-uka iṅhāra cita
īśvara-svabhāva, —karena sabākāra hita

SYNONYMS

āmi jiti—let me become victorious; *ei*—this; *garva*—pride; *śūnya*—devoid of; *ha-uka*—let be; *iṅhāra cita*—this person's mind; *īśvara-svabhāva*—the characteristic of the Supreme Personality of Godhead; *karena*—He does; *sabākāra*—of everyone; *hita*—benefit.

TRANSLATION

"Being very proud of my learning, I am thinking, 'Let me become victorious.' Śrī Caitanya Mahāprabhu, however, is trying to purify me by nullifying this false pride, for a characteristic of the Supreme Personality of Godhead is that He acts for everyone's welfare.

TEXT 123

আপনা জানাইতে আমি করি অভিমান।
সে গর্ব খণ্ডাইতে মোর করেন অপমান ॥ ১২৩ ॥

āpanā jānāite āmi kari abhimāna
se garva khaṇḍāite mora karena apamāna

SYNONYMS

āpanā jānāite—advertising myself; *āmi*—I; *kari abhimāna*—am falsely proud; *se garva*—that pride; *khaṇḍāite*—to cut down; *mora karena apamāna*—He insults me.

TRANSLATION

"I am falsely proud, advertising myself as a learned scholar. Therefore Śrī Caitanya Mahāprabhu insults me just to favor me by cutting down this false pride.

TEXT 124

আমার 'হিত' করেন,—ইহো আমি মানি 'দুঃখ'।
কৃষ্ণের উপরে কৈল যেন ইন্দ্র মহামূর্খ॥" ১২৪ ॥

āmāra 'hita' karena,——iho āmi māni 'duḥkha'
kṛṣṇera upare kaila yena indra mahā-mūrkha"

SYNONYMS

āmāra—my; *hita*—benefit; *karena*—He is doing; *iho*—this; *āmi*—I; *māni*—consider; *duḥkha*—unhappiness; *kṛṣṇera upare*—upon Kṛṣṇa; *kaila*—did; *yena*—as; *indra*—Indra; *mahā-mūrkha*—the great fool.

TRANSLATION

"He is actually acting for my benefit, although I interpret His actions as insults. This is exactly like the incident in which Lord Kṛṣṇa cut down Indra, the great, puffed-up fool, to correct him."

TEXT 125

এত চিন্তি' প্রাতে আসি' প্রভুর চরণে।
দৈন্য করি' স্তুতি করি' লইল শরণে ॥ ১২৫ ॥

eta cinti' prāte āsi' prabhura caraṇe
dainya kari' stuti kari' la-ila śaraṇe

SYNONYMS

eta cinti'—considering this; *prāte*—in the morning; *āsi'*—coming; *prabhura caraṇe*—to the lotus feet of Śrī Caitanya Mahāprabhu; *dainya kari'*—with great humility; *stuti kari'*—offering many prayers; *la-ila śaraṇe*—took shelter.

TRANSLATION

Thinking in this way, Vallabha Bhaṭṭa approached Śrī Caitanya Mahāprabhu the next morning, and in great humility, offering many prayers, he sought shelter and surrendered at the lotus feet of the Lord.

TEXT 126

"আমি অজ্ঞ জীব,—অজ্ঞোচিত কর্ম কৈলুঁ।
তোমার আগে মূর্খ আমি পাণ্ডিত্য প্রকাশিলুঁ॥১২৬॥

"āmi ajña jīva, —ajñocita karma kailuṅ
tomāra āge mūrkha āmi pāṇḍitya prakāśiluṅ

SYNONYMS

āmi—I; *ajña jīva*—a foolish living being; *ajña-ucita*—fit for a fool; *karma*—activity; *kailuṅ*—I have done; *tomāra āge*—before You; *mūrkha*—a fool; *āmi*—I; *pāṇḍitya prakāśiluṅ*—have tried to demonstrate learning.

TRANSLATION

Vallabha Bhaṭṭa admitted, "I am a great fool, and indeed I have acted like a fool by trying to demonstrate to You my learning.

TEXT 127

তুমি—ঈশ্বর, নিজোচিত কৃপা যে করিলা।
অপমান করি' সর্ব গর্ব খণ্ডাইলা॥ ১২৭ ॥

tumi—īśvara, nijocita kṛpā ye karilā
apamāna kari' sarva garva khaṇḍāilā

SYNONYMS

tumi—You; *īśvara*—the Supreme Personality of Godhead; *nija-ucita*—exactly befitting Your position; *kṛpā*—mercy; *ye*—that; *karilā*—You showed; *apamāna kari'*—by insulting; *sarva*—all; *garva*—pride; *khaṇḍāilā*—You have cut down.

TRANSLATION

"My dear Lord, You are the Supreme Personality of Godhead. You have showed mercy to me in a way just befitting Your position by insulting me to cut down all my false pride.

TEXT 128

আমি—অজ্ঞ, 'হিত'-স্থানে মানি 'অপমানে'।
ইন্দ্র যেন কৃষ্ণের নিন্দা করিল অজ্ঞানে॥ ১২৮ ॥

āmi—ajña, 'hita'-sthāne māni 'apamāne'
indra yena kṛṣṇera nindā karila ajñāne

SYNONYMS

āmi—I; *ajña*—ignorant fool; *hita-sthāne*—what is for my benefit; *māni*—I consider; *apamāne*—as an insult; *indra*—King Indra; *yena*—as; *kṛṣṇera*—of Lord Kṛṣṇa; *nindā*—offense; *karila*—did; *ajñāne*—out of ignorance.

TRANSLATION

"I am an ignorant fool, for I interpret as an insult what is meant for my benefit, just like King Indra, who out of ignorance tried to surpass Kṛṣṇa, the Supreme Lord.

TEXT 129

তোমার কৃপা-অঞ্জনে এবে গর্ব-আন্ধ্য গেল ।
তুমি এত কৃপা কৈলা,—এবে 'জ্ঞান' হৈল ॥১২৯॥

tomāra kṛpā-añjane ebe garva-āndhya gela
tumi eta kṛpā kailā, ——ebe 'jñāna' haila

SYNONYMS

tomāra kṛpā-añjane—by the eye-ointment of Your mercy; *ebe*—now; *garva-āndhya*—the blindness of false pride; *gela*—has gone; *tumi*—You; *eta*—such; *kṛpā*—mercy; *kailā*—have shown; *ebe*—now; *jñāna*—knowledge; *haila*—has become.

TRANSLATION

"My dear Lord, You have cured the blindness of my false pride by smearing my eyes with the ointment of Your mercy. You have bestowed so much mercy upon me that my ignorance is now gone.

TEXT 130

অপরাধ কৈনু, ক্ষম, লইনু শরণ ।
কৃপা করি' মোর মাথে ধরহ চরণ ॥" ১৩০ ॥

aparādha kainu, kṣama, la-inu śaraṇa
kṛpā kari' mora māthe dharaha caraṇa"

SYNONYMS

aparādha kainu—I have committed offenses; *kṣama*—please excuse; *la-inu śaraṇa*—I have taken shelter; *kṛpā kari'*—being merciful; *mora māthe*—on my head; *dharaha caraṇa*—please keep Your lotus feet.

TRANSLATION

"My dear Lord, I have committed offenses. Please excuse me. I seek shelter of You. Please be merciful unto me by placing Your lotus feet on my head."

TEXT 131

প্রভু কহে,—"তুমি 'পণ্ডিত' 'মহাভাগবত' ।
দুইগুণ যাহাঁ, তাহাঁ নাহি গর্ব-পর্বত ॥ ১৩১ ॥

prabhu kahe——"tumi 'paṇḍita' 'mahā-bhāgavata'
dui-guṇa yāhāṅ, tāhāṅ nāhi garva-parvata

SYNONYMS

prabhu kahe—Śrī Caitanya Mahāprabhu said; *tumi*—you; *paṇḍita*—very learned scholar; *mahā-bhāgavata*—great devotee; *dui-guṇa*—two qualities; *yāhāṅ*—wherever; *tāhāṅ*—there; *nāhi*—there cannot be; *garva-parvata*—the mountain of pride.

TRANSLATION

Lord Śrī Caitanya Mahāprabhu said, "You are both a greatly learned scholar and a great devotee. Wherever there are two such attributes, there cannot be a mountain of false pride.

TEXT 132

শ্রীধরস্বামী নিন্দি' নিজ-টীকা কর !
শ্রীধরস্বামী নাহি মান',—এত 'গর্ব' ধর ! ১৩২ ॥

śrīdhara-svāmī nindi' nija-ṭīkā kara!
śrīdhara-svāmī nāhi māna', ——eta 'garva' dhara!

SYNONYMS

śrīdhara-svāmī—a great commentator on *Śrīmad-Bhāgavatam; nindi'*—blaspheming; *nija-ṭīkā*—your own commentary; *kara*—you make; *śrīdhara-svāmī*—Śrīdhara Svāmī; *nāhi māna'*—you do not accept; *eta*—this; *garva*—pride; *dhara*—you bear.

TRANSLATION

"You have dared criticize Śrīdhara Svāmī, and you have begun your own commentary on Śrīmad-Bhāgavatam, not accepting his authority. That is your false pride.

TEXT 133

শ্রীধরস্বামি-প্রসাদে 'ভাগবত' জানি।
জগদ্গুরু শ্রীধরস্বামী 'গুরু' করি' মানি ॥ ১৩৩ ॥

śrīdhara-svāmī-prasāde 'bhāgavata' jāni
jagad-guru śrīdhara-svāmī 'guru' kari' māni

SYNONYMS

śrīdhara-svāmī—of Śrīdhara Svāmī; *prasāde*—by the mercy; *bhāgavata jāni*—we can understand *Śrīmad-Bhāgavatam; jagat-guru*—the spiritual master of the entire world; *śrīdhara-svāmī*—Śrīdhara Svāmī; *guru kari'*—as a spiritual master; *māni*—I accept.

TRANSLATION

"Śrīdhara Svāmī is the spiritual master of the entire world because by his mercy we can understand Śrīmad-Bhāgavatam. I therefore accept him as a spiritual master.

TEXT 134

শ্রীধর-উপরে গর্বে যে কিছু লিখিবে।
'অর্থব্যস্ত' লিখন সেই, লোকে না মানিবে ॥ ১৩৪ ॥

śrīdhara-upare garve ye kichu likhibe
'artha-vyasta' likhana sei, loke nā mānibe

SYNONYMS

śrīdhara-upare—above Śrīdhara Svāmī; *garve*—in false pride; *ye kichu likhibe*—whatever you write; *artha-vyasta*—the opposite meaning; *likhana sei*—such writing; *loke nā mānibe*—no one will care about it.

TRANSLATION

"Whatever you might write due to false pride, trying to surpass Śrīdhara Svāmī, would carry a contrary purport. Therefore no one would pay attention to it.

PURPORT

Śrīmad-Bhāgavatam has many *ṭikās,* or commentaries, following the *paramparā* system, but Śrīdhāra Svāmī's is first. The commentaries of all the other *ācāryas* follow his. The *paramparā* system does not allow one to deviate from the commentaries of the previous *ācāryas*. By depending upon the previous *ācāryas,* one can write beautiful commentaries. However, one cannot defy the previous *ācāryas*. The false pride that makes one think that he can write better than the previous *ācāryas* will make one's comments faulty. At the present moment it has become fashionable for everyone to write in his own way, but such writing is never accepted by serious devotees. Because of false pride, every scholar and philosopher wants to exhibit his learning by interpreting the *śāstras,* especially *Bhagavad-gītā* and *Śrīmad-Bhāgavatam,* in his own way. This system of commenting in one's own way is fully condemned by Śrī Caitanya Mahāprabhu. Therefore He says, *'artha-vyasta' likhana sei*. Commentaries written according to one's own philosophical way are never accepted; no one will appreciate such commentaries on the revealed scriptures.

TEXT 135

শ্রীধরের অনুগত যে করে লিখন ।
সব লোক মান্য করি' করিবে গ্রহণ ॥ ১৩৫ ॥

śrīdharera anugata ye kare likhana
saba loka mānya kari' karibe grahaṇa

SYNONYMS

śrīdharera—of Śrīdhara Svāmī; *anugata*—following in the footsteps; *ye*—anyone who; *kare likhana*—writes; *saba loka*—everyone; *mānya kari'*—with great honor; *karibe grahaṇa*—will accept.

TRANSLATION

"One who comments on Śrīmad-Bhāgavatam following in the footsteps of Śrīdhara Svāmī will be honored and accepted by everyone.

TEXT 136

শ্রীধরানুগত কর ভাগবত-ব্যাখ্যান ।
অভিমান ছাড়ি' ভজ কৃষ্ণ ভগবান্ ॥ ১৩৬ ॥

śrīdharānugata kara bhāgavata-vyākhyāna
abhimāna chāḍi' bhaja kṛṣṇa bhagavān

SYNONYMS

śrīdhara-anugata—following in the footsteps of Śrīdhara Svāmī; *kara*—put forth; *bhāgavata-vyākhyāna*—an explanation of *Śrīmad-Bhāgavatam; abhimāna chāḍi'*—giving up false pride or false conceptions; *bhaja*—worship; *kṛṣṇa bhagavān*—the Supreme Personality of Godhead Kṛṣṇa.

TRANSLATION

"Put forth your explanation of Śrīmad-Bhāgavatam following in the footsteps of Śrīdhara Svāmī. Giving up your false pride, worship the Supreme Personality of Godhead, Kṛṣṇa.

TEXT 137

অপরাধ ছাড়ি' কর কৃষ্ণসঙ্কীর্তন ।
অচিরাৎ পাবে তবে কৃষ্ণের চরণ ॥"১৩৭ ॥

aparādha chāḍi' kara kṛṣṇa-saṅkīrtana
acirāt pābe tabe kṛṣṇera caraṇa"

SYNONYMS

aparādha chāḍi'—giving up offenses; *kara kṛṣṇa-saṅkīrtana*—chant the holy name of the Lord; *acirāt*—very soon; *pābe*—you will get; *tabe*—thereupon; *kṛṣṇera caraṇa*—shelter at the lotus feet of Lord Kṛṣṇa.

TRANSLATION

"Abandoning your offenses, chant the Hare Kṛṣṇa mahā-mantra, the holy names of the Lord. Then very soon you will achieve shelter at the lotus feet of Kṛṣṇa."

TEXT 138

ভট্ট কহে,—"যদি মোরে হইলা প্রসন্ন ।
একদিন পুনঃ মোর মান' নিমন্ত্রণ ॥" ১৩৮ ॥

bhaṭṭa kahe, —"yadi more ha-ilā prasanna
eka-dina punaḥ mora māna' nimantraṇa"

SYNONYMS

bhaṭṭa kahe—Vallabha Bhaṭṭa said; *yadi*—if; *more*—with me; *ha-ilā prasanna*—You are pleased; *eka-dina*—one day; *punaḥ*—again; *mora*—my; *māna'*—accept; *nimantraṇa*—invitation.

TRANSLATION

Vallabha Bhaṭṭa Ācārya requested Śrī Caitanya Mahāprabhu, "If You are actually pleased with me, please accept my invitation once again."

TEXT 139

প্রভু অবতীর্ণ হৈলা জগৎ তারিতে ।
মানিলেন নিমন্ত্রণ, তারে সুখ দিতে ॥ ১৩৯ ॥

prabhu avatīrṇa hailā jagat tārite
mānilena nimantraṇa, tāre sukha dite

SYNONYMS

prabhu—Śrī Caitanya Mahāprabhu; *avatīrṇa hailā*—made His advent; *jagat*—the universe; *tārite*—to deliver; *mānilena*—He accepted; *nimantraṇa*—the invitation; *tāre*—to him; *sukha*—happiness; *dite*—to give.

TRANSLATION

Śrī Caitanya Mahāprabhu, who had descended to deliver the entire universe, accepted the invitation of Vallabha Bhaṭṭa just to give him happiness.

TEXT 140

জগতের 'হিত' হউক,—এই প্রভুর মন ।
দণ্ড করি' করে তার হৃদয় শোধন ॥ ১৪০ ॥

jagatera 'hita' ha-uka——ei prabhura mana
daṇḍa kari' kare tāra hṛdaya śodhana

SYNONYMS

jagatera—of the entire world; *hita*—welfare; *ha-uka*—let there be; *ei*—this; *prabhura mana*—the mind of Śrī Caitanya Mahāprabhu; *daṇḍa kari'*—punishing; *kare*—does; *tāra*—his; *hṛdaya*—heart; *śodhana*—purifying.

TRANSLATION

Śrī Caitanya Mahāprabhu is always eager to see everyone in the material world happy. Therefore sometimes He chastises someone just to purify his heart.

TEXT 141

স্বগণ-সহিত প্রভুর নিমন্ত্রণ কৈলা ।
মহাপ্রভু তারে তবে প্রসন্ন হইলা ॥ ১৪১ ॥

svagaṇa-sahita prabhura nimantraṇa kailā
mahāprabhu tāre tabe prasanna ha-ilā

SYNONYMS

sva-gaṇa-sahita—with His associates; *prabhura*—of Śrī Caitanya Mahāprabhu; *nimantraṇa*—invitation; *kailā*—made; *mahāprabhu*—Śrī Caitanya Mahāprabhu; *tāre*—upon him; *tabe*—then; *prasanna ha-ilā*—became very pleased.

TRANSLATION

When Vallabha Bhaṭṭa invited Śrī Caitanya Mahāprabhu and His associates, the Lord was very pleased with him.

TEXT 142

জগদানন্দ-পণ্ডিতের শুদ্ধ গাঢ় ভাব ।
সত্যভামা-প্রায় প্রেম 'বাম্য-স্বভাব' ॥ ১৪২ ॥

jagadānanda-paṇḍitera śuddha gāḍha bhāva
satyabhāmā-prāya prema 'vāmya-svabhāva'

SYNONYMS

jagadānanda-paṇḍitera—of Jagadānanda Paṇḍita; *śuddha*—pure; *gāḍha*—deep; *bhāva*—ecstatic love; *satyabhāmā-prāya*—like Satyabhāmā; *prema*—his love for the Lord; *vāmya-svabhāva*—quarrelsome nature.

TRANSLATION

Jagadānanda Paṇḍita's pure ecstatic love for Śrī Caitanya Mahāprabhu was very deep. It can be compared to the love of Satyabhāmā, who always quarreled with Lord Kṛṣṇa.

TEXT 143

বার-বার প্রণয় কলহ করে প্রভু-সনে ।
অন্যোহন্যে খট্‌মটি চলে দুইজনে ॥ ১৪৩ ॥

bāra-bāra praṇaya kalaha kare prabhu-sane
anyonye khaṭmaṭi cale dui-jane

SYNONYMS

bāra-bāra—again and again; *praṇaya*—loving; *kalaha*—quarrel; *kare*—makes; *prabhu-sane*—with Śrī Caitanya Mahāprabhu; *anyonye*—mutual; *khaṭmaṭi*—picking a quarrel; *cale*—goes on; *dui-jane*—between the two.

TRANSLATION

Jagadānanda Paṇḍita was accustomed to provoking loving quarrels with the Lord. There was always some disagreement between them.

TEXT 144

গদাধর-পণ্ডিতের শুদ্ধ গাঢ় ভাব ।
রুক্মিণী-দেবীর যৈছে 'দক্ষিণ-স্বভাব' ॥ ১৪৪ ॥

gadādhara-paṇḍitera śuddha gāḍha bhāva
rukmiṇī-devīra yaiche 'dakṣiṇa-svabhāva'

SYNONYMS

gadādhara-paṇḍitera—of Gadādhara Paṇḍita; *śuddha*—pure; *gāḍha*—deep; *bhāva*—ecstatic love; *rukmiṇī-devīra*—of Rukmiṇīdevī; *yaiche*—as; *dakṣiṇa-svabhāva*—submissive nature.

TRANSLATION

Gadādhara Paṇḍita's pure ecstatic love for Śrī Caitanya Mahāprabhu was also very deep. It was like that of Rukmiṇīdevī, who was always especially submissive to Kṛṣṇa.

TEXT 145

তাঁর প্রণয়-রোষ দেখিতে প্রভুর ইচ্ছা হয় ।
ঐশ্বর্য-জ্ঞানে তাঁর রোষ নাহি উপজয় ॥ ১৪৫ ॥

tāṅra praṇaya-roṣa dekhite prabhura icchā haya
aiśvarya-jñāne tāṅra roṣa nāhi upajaya

SYNONYMS

tāṅra—his; *praṇaya-roṣa*—affectionate anger; *dekhite*—to see; *prabhura*—of Śrī Caitanya Mahāprabhu; *icchā haya*—there is a desire; *aiśvarya-jñāne*—due to knowledge of opulences; *tāṅra*—his; *roṣa*—anger; *nāhi*—not; *upajaya*—is awakened.

TRANSLATION

Lord Śrī Caitanya Mahāprabhu sometimes desired to see Gadādhara Paṇḍita's affectionate anger, but because of knowledge of the Lord's opulences, his anger was never invoked.

PURPORT

Joking with Rukmiṇīdevī in Dvārakā, Kṛṣṇa once advised her to accept another husband because He thought Himself unfit for her. Rukmiṇīdevī, however, unable to understand His joking words, took them very seriously and immediately fell to the ground in fear of separation from Him. In the pastimes of Lord Śrī Caitanya Mahāprabhu, Jagadānanda Paṇḍita was always in disagreement with the Lord like Satyabhāmā, whereas Gadādhara Paṇḍita was always awed by the Lord's opulence and was therefore submissive to the Lord under all circumstances.

TEXT 146

এই লক্ষ্য পাঞা প্রভু কৈলা রোষাভাস।
শুনি' পণ্ডিতের চিত্তে উপজিল ত্রাস ॥ ১৪৬ ॥

ei lakṣya pāñā prabhu kailā roṣābhāsa
śuni' paṇḍitera citte upajila trāsa

SYNONYMS

ei—this; *lakṣya*—aim; *pāñā*—taking; *prabhu*—Śrī Caitanya Mahāprabhu; *kailā roṣa-ābhāsa*—made a semblance of anger; *śuni'*—hearing; *paṇḍitera*—of Gadādhara Paṇḍita; *citte*—in the heart; *upajila*—arose; *trāsa*—fear.

TRANSLATION

For this purpose Śrī Caitanya Mahāprabhu sometimes showed His apparent anger. Hearing of this anger inspired great fear in the heart of Gadādhara Paṇḍita.

TEXT 147

পূর্বে যেন কৃষ্ণ যদি পরিহাস কৈল।
শুনি' রুক্মিণীর মনে ত্রাস উপজিল ॥ ১৪৭ ॥

pūrve yena kṛṣṇa yadi parihāsa kaila
śuni' rukmiṇīra mane trāsa upajila

SYNONYMS

pūrve—previously; *yena*—as; *kṛṣṇa*—Lord Kṛṣṇa; *yadi*—when; *parihāsa kaila*—play a joke; *śuni'*—hearing; *rukmiṇīra mane*—in the mind of Rukmiṇīdevī; *trāsa*—fear; *upajila*—arose.

TRANSLATION

Previously, in kṛṣṇa-līlā, when Lord Kṛṣṇa wanted to joke with Rukmiṇīdevī, she took His words seriously, and fear awoke within her mind.

TEXT 148

বল্লভ-ভট্টের হয় বাৎসল্য-উপাসন।
বালগোপাল-মন্ত্রে তেঁহো করেন সেবন ॥ ১৪৮ ॥

vallabha-bhaṭṭera haya vātsalya-upāsana
bāla-gopāla-mantre teṅho karena sevana

SYNONYMS

vallabha-bhaṭṭera—of Vallabha Bhaṭṭa; *haya*—there is; *vātsalya-upāsana*—worship as a parent; *bāla-gopāla-mantre*—with the *mantra* of Bāla-gopāla, child Kṛṣṇa; *teṅho*—he; *karena*—practices; *sevana*—worship.

TRANSLATION

Vallabha Bhaṭṭa was accustomed to worshiping the Lord as child Kṛṣṇa. Therefore he had been initiated into the Bāla-gopāla mantra and was thus worshiping the Lord.

TEXT 149

পণ্ডিতের সনে তার মন ফিরি' গেল।
কিশোরগোপাল-উপাসনায় মন দিল ॥ ১৪৯ ॥

paṇḍitera sane tāra mana phiri' gela
kiśora-gopāla-upāsanāya mana dila

SYNONYMS

paṇḍitera sane—in the association of Gadādhara Paṇḍita; *tāra*—his; *mana*—mind; *phiri' gela*—became converted; *kiśora-gopāla*—of Kṛṣṇa as a young boy; *upāsanāya*—to the worship; *mana dila*—he gave his mind.

TRANSLATION

In the association of Gadādhara Paṇḍita, his mind was converted, and he dedicated his mind to worshiping Kiśora-gopāla, Kṛṣṇa as a young boy.

TEXT 150

পণ্ডিতের ঠাঞি চাহে মন্ত্রাদি শিখিতে।
পণ্ডিত কহে,—"এই কর্ম নহে আমা হৈতে ॥ ১৫০ ॥

paṇḍitera ṭhāñi cāhe mantrādi śikhite
paṇḍita kahe, —"ei karma nahe āmā haite

SYNONYMS

paṇḍitera ṭhāñi—from Gadādhara Paṇḍita; *cāhe*—wanted; *mantra-ādi śikhite*—to be initiated; *paṇḍita kahe*—Gadādhara Paṇḍita said; *ei karma*—this work; *nahe āmā haite*—is not possible for me.

TRANSLATION

Vallabha Bhaṭṭa wanted to be initiated by Gadādhara Paṇḍita, but Gadādhara Paṇḍita refused, saying, "The work of acting as a spiritual master is not possible for me.

TEXT 151

আমি—পরতন্ত্র, আমার প্রভু—গৌরচন্দ্র।
তাঁর আজ্ঞা বিনা আমি না হই 'স্বতন্ত্র' ॥ ১৫১ ॥

āmi—paratantra, āmāra prabhu—gauracandra
tāṅra ājñā vinā āmi nā ha-i 'svatantra'

SYNONYMS

āmi—I; *paratantra*—dependent; *āmāra prabhu*—my Lord; *gauracandra*—Lord Śrī Caitanya Mahāprabhu; *tāṅra*—His; *ājñā*—order; *vinā*—without; *āmi*—I; *nā*—not; *ha-i*—am; *svatantra*—independent.

TRANSLATION

"I am completely dependent. My Lord is Gauracandra, Śrī Caitanya Mahāprabhu. I cannot do anything independently, without His order.

TEXT 152

তুমি যে আমার ঠাঞি কর আগমন।
তাহাতেই প্রভু মোরে দেন ওলাহন ॥" ১৫২ ॥

tumi ye āmāra ṭhāñi kara āgamana
tāhātei prabhu more dena olāhana"

SYNONYMS

tumi—you; *ye*—that; *āmāra ṭhāñi*—to me; *kara āgamana*—come; *tāhātei*—due to that; *prabhu*—Śrī Caitanya Mahāprabhu; *more*—unto me; *dena*—gives; *olāhana*—punishment by words.

TRANSLATION

"My dear Vallabha Bhaṭṭa, your coming to me is not appreciated by Śrī Caitanya Mahāprabhu. Therefore He sometimes speaks to chastise me."

TEXTS 153-154

এইমত ভট্টের কথেক দিন গেল ।
শেষে যদি প্রভু তারে সুপ্রসন্ন হৈল ॥ ১৫৩ ॥
নিমন্ত্রণের দিনে পণ্ডিতে বোলাইলা ।
স্বরূপ, জগদানন্দ, গোবিন্দে পাঠাইলা ॥ ১৫৪ ॥

ei-mata bhaṭṭera katheka dina gela
śeṣe yadi prabhu tāre suprasanna haila

nimantraṇera dine paṇḍite bolāilā
svarūpa, jagadānanda, govinde pāṭhāilā

SYNONYMS

ei-mata—in this way; *bhaṭṭera*—of Vallabha Bhaṭṭa; *katheka dina*—some days; *gela*—passed; *śeṣe*—at last; *yadi*—when; *prabhu*—Śrī Caitanya Mahāprabhu; *tāre*—upon him; *su-prasanna haila*—became very pleased; *nimantraṇera dine*—on the day of invitation; *paṇḍite bolāilā*—He called for Gadādhara Paṇḍita; *svarūpa*—Svarūpa Dāmodara; *jagadānanda*—Jagadānanda Paṇḍita; *govinde*—Govinda; *pāṭhāilā*—He sent.

TRANSLATION

Some days passed, and when Śrī Caitanya Mahāprabhu, finally pleased with Vallabha Bhaṭṭa, accepted his invitation, the Lord sent Svarūpa Dāmodara, Jagadānanda Paṇḍita and Govinda to call for Gadādhara Paṇḍita.

TEXT 155

পথে পণ্ডিতেরে স্বরূপ কহেন বচন।
"পরীক্ষিতে প্রভু তোমারে কৈলা উপেক্ষণ॥ ১৫৫॥

pathe paṇḍitere svarūpa kahena vacana
"parīkṣite prabhu tomāre kailā upekṣaṇa

SYNONYMS

pathe—on the way; *paṇḍitere*—unto Gadādhara Paṇḍita; *svarūpa*—Svarūpa Dāmodara; *kahena vacana*—said some words; *parīkṣite*—to test; *prabhu*—Lord Śrī Caitanya Mahāprabhu; *tomāre*—you; *kailā upekṣaṇa*—neglected.

TRANSLATION

On the way, Svarūpa Dāmodara said to Gadādhara Paṇḍita, "Śrī Caitanya Mahāprabhu wanted to test you. Therefore He neglected you.

TEXT 156

তুমি কেনে আসি' তাঁরে না দিলা ওলাহন?
ভীতপ্রায় হঞা কাঁহে করিলা সহন?" ১৫৬॥

tumi kene āsi' tāṅre nā dilā olāhana?
bhīta-prāya hañā kāṅhe karilā sahana?"

SYNONYMS

tumi—you; *kene*—why; *āsi'*—coming; *tāṅre*—unto Him; *nā dilā*—did not give; *olāhana*—chastisement; *bhīta-prāya*—as if fearful; *hañā*—being; *kāṅhe*—why; *karilā sahana*—did you tolerate.

TRANSLATION

"Why did you not retaliate by reproaching Him? Why did you fearfully tolerate His criticism?"

TEXT 157

পণ্ডিত কহেন,—প্রভু স্বতন্ত্র সর্বজ্ঞ-শিরোমণি।
তাঁর সনে 'হঠ' করি,—ভাল নাহি মানি॥ ১৫৭॥

paṇḍita kahena,——prabhu svatantra sarvajña-śiromaṇi
tāṅra sane 'haṭha' kari,——bhāla nāhi māni

SYNONYMS

paṇḍita kahena—Gadādhara Paṇḍita said; *prabhu*—Lord Śrī Caitanya Mahāprabhu; *svatantra*—independent; *sarvajña-śiromaṇi*—the best of the omniscient; *tāṅra sane*—with Him; *haṭha kari*—if I talk on an equal level; *bhāla*—good; *nāhi māni*—I do not think it is.

TRANSLATION

Gadādhara Paṇḍita said, "Lord Śrī Caitanya Mahāprabhu is completely independent. He is the topmost omniscient personality. It would not look well for me to talk to Him as if His equal.

TEXT 158

যেই কহে, সেই সহি নিজ-শিরে ধরি'।
আপনে করিবেন কৃপা গুণ-দোষ বিচারি' ॥" ১৫৮ ॥

yei kahe, sei sahi nija-śire dhari'
āpane karibena kṛpā guṇa-doṣa vicāri' "

SYNONYMS

yei kahe—whatever He says; *sei sahi*—I tolerate that; *nija-śire*—on my head; *dhari'*—bearing; *āpane*—automatically; *karibena kṛpā*—He will be merciful; *guṇa-doṣa*—attributes and faults; *vicāri'*—after considering.

TRANSLATION

"I can tolerate whatever He says, bearing it upon my head. He will automatically be merciful to me after considering my faults and attributes."

TEXT 159

এত বলি' পণ্ডিত প্রভুর স্থানে আইলা।
রোদন করিয়া প্রভুর চরণে পড়িলা ॥ ১৫৯ ॥

eta bali' paṇḍita prabhura sthāne āilā
rodana kariyā prabhura caraṇe paḍilā

SYNONYMS

eta bali'—saying this; *paṇḍita*—Gadādhara Paṇḍita; *prabhura sthāne*—to Śrī Caitanya Mahāprabhu; *āilā*—came; *rodana kariyā*—crying; *prabhura*—of Śrī Caitanya Mahāprabhu; *caraṇe*—at the lotus feet; *paḍilā*—fell down.

TRANSLATION

After saying this, Gadādhara Paṇḍita went to Śrī Caitanya Mahāprabhu and fell down crying at the lotus feet of the Lord.

TEXT 160

ঈষৎ হাসিয়া প্রভু কৈলা আলিঙ্গন।
সবারে শুনাঞা কহেন মধুর বচন ॥ ১৬০ ॥

īṣat hāsiyā prabhu kailā āliṅgana
sabāre śunāñā kahena madhura vacana

SYNONYMS

īṣat hāsiyā—smiling slightly; *prabhu*—Śrī Caitanya Mahāprabhu; *kailā āliṅgana*—embraced; *sabāre*—all others; *śunāñā*—causing to hear; *kahena*—began to say; *madhura vacana*—sweet words.

TRANSLATION

Smiling slightly, the Lord embraced him and spoke sweet words so that others would also hear.

TEXT 161

"আমি চালাইলুঁ তোমা, তুমি না চলিলা।
ক্রোধে কিছু না কহিলা, সকল সহিলা ॥ ১৬১ ॥

"āmi cālāiluṅ tomā, tumi nā calilā
krodhe kichu nā kahilā, sakala sahilā

SYNONYMS

āmi—I; *cālāiluṅ*—tried to agitate; *tomā*—you; *tumi*—you; *nā calilā*—did not become agitated; *krodhe*—in anger; *kichu*—anything; *nā kahilā*—you did not say; *sakala*—everything; *sahilā*—you tolerated.

TRANSLATION

"I wanted to agitate you," the Lord said, "but you did not become agitated. Indeed, you could not say anything angry. Instead, you tolerated everything.

TEXT 162

আমার ভঙ্গীতে তোমার মন না চলিলা।
সুদৃঢ় সরলভাবে আমারে কিনিলা ॥"১৬২ ॥

āmāra bhaṅgīte tomāra mana nā calilā
sudṛḍha sarala-bhāve āmāre kinilā"

SYNONYMS

āmāra bhaṅgīte—by My trick; *tomāra mana*—your mind; *nā calilā*—did not become disturbed; *sudṛḍha*—firm; *sarala-bhāve*—by simplicity; *āmāre*—Me; *kinilā*—you have purchased.

TRANSLATION

"Your mind was not disturbed by My tricks. Rather, you stayed fixed in your simplicity. In this way you have purchased Me."

TEXT 163

পণ্ডিতের ভাব-মুদ্রা কহন না যায়।
'গদাধর-প্রাণনাথ' নাম হৈল যায়॥ ১৬৩॥

paṇḍitera bhāva-mudrā kahana nā yāya
'gadādhara-prāṇa-nātha' nāma haila yāya

SYNONYMS

paṇḍitera—of Gadādhara Paṇḍita; *bhāva-mudrā*—characteristics and ecstatic love; *kahana nā yāya*—cannot be described; *gadādhara-prāṇa-nātha*—the Lord of the life of Gadādhara; *nāma*—name; *haila*—became; *yāya*—goes.

TRANSLATION

No one can describe the characteristics and ecstatic love of Gadādhara Paṇḍita. Therefore another name for Śrī Caitanya Mahāprabhu is Gadādhara-prāṇanātha, "the life and soul of Gadādhara Paṇḍita."

TEXT 164

পণ্ডিতে প্রভুর প্রসাদ কহন না যায়।
'গদাইর গৌরাঙ্গ' বলি' যাঁরে লোকে গায়॥ ১৬৪॥

paṇḍite prabhura prasāda kahana nā yāya
'gadāira gaurāṅga' bali' yāṅre loke gāya

SYNONYMS

paṇḍite—upon Gadādhara Paṇḍita; *prabhura*—of Śrī Caitanya Mahāprabhu; *prasāda*—mercy; *kahana nā yāya*—no one can explain; *gadāira gaurāṅga*—the

Gaurāṅga of Gadādhara Paṇḍita; *bali'*—as; *yāṅre*—whom; *loke gāya*—people say.

TRANSLATION

No one can say how merciful the Lord is to Gadādhara Paṇḍita, but people know the Lord as Gadāira Gaura, "the Lord Gaurāṅga of Gadādhara Paṇḍita."

TEXT 165

চৈতন্যপ্রভুর লীলা কে বুঝিতে পারে ?
একলীলায় বহে গঙ্গার শত শত ধারে ॥ ১৬৫ ॥

caitanya-prabhura līlā ke bujhite pāre?
eka-līlāya vahe gaṅgāra śata śata dhāre

SYNONYMS

caitanya-prabhura līlā—the pastimes of Lord Śrī Caitanya Mahāprabhu; *ke*—who; *bujhite pāre*—can understand; *eka-līlāya*—in one activity; *vahe*—flow; *gaṅgāra*—of the Ganges; *śata śata dhāre*—hundreds and hundreds of branches.

TRANSLATION

No one can understand the pastimes of Śrī Caitanya Mahāprabhu. They are like the Ganges, for hundreds and thousands of branches flow from even one of His activities.

TEXT 166

পণ্ডিতের সৌজন্য, ব্রহ্মণ্যতা-গুণ ।
দৃঢ় প্রেমমুদ্রা লোকে করিলা খ্যাপন ॥ ১৬৬ ॥

paṇḍitera saujanya, brahmaṇyatā-guṇa
dṛḍha prema-mudrā loke karilā khyāpana

SYNONYMS

paṇḍitera saujanya—the gentle behavior of Gadādhara Paṇḍita; *brahmaṇyatā-guṇa*—the attributes of a perfect *brāhmaṇa; dṛḍha*—firm; *prema-mudrā*—characteristic of love; *loke*—people; *karilā khyāpana*—proclaimed.

TRANSLATION

Gadādhara Paṇḍita is celebrated all over the world for his gentle behavior, his brahminical attributes and his steady love for Śrī Caitanya Mahāprabhu.

TEXT 167

অভিমান-পঙ্ক ধুঞা ভট্টেরে শোধিলা ।
সেইদ্বারা আর সব লোকে শিখাইলা ॥ ১৬৭ ॥

abhimāna-paṅka dhuñā bhaṭṭere śodhilā
sei-dvārā āra saba loke śikhāilā

SYNONYMS

abhimāna-paṅka—the mud of false pride; *dhuñā*—washing; *bhaṭṭere śodhilā*—purified Vallabha Bhaṭṭa; *sei-dvārā*—by that; *āra saba*—all other; *loke*—persons; *śikhāilā*—instructed.

TRANSLATION

The Lord purified Vallabha Bhaṭṭa by cleansing him of the mud of false pride. By such activities the Lord also instructed others.

TEXT 168

অন্তরে 'অনুগ্রহ', বাহ্যে 'উপেক্ষার প্রায়' ।
বাহ্যার্থ যেই লয়, সেই নাশ যায় ॥ ১৬৮ ॥

antare 'anugraha,' bāhye 'upekṣāra prāya'
bāhyārtha yei laya, sei nāśa yāya

SYNONYMS

antare—within the heart; *anugraha*—mercy; *bāhye*—externally; *upekṣāra prāya*—like neglect; *bāhya-artha*—the external meaning; *yei*—anyone who; *laya*—takes; *sei*—he; *nāśa yāya*—becomes vanquished.

TRANSLATION

Śrī Caitanya Mahāprabhu was actually always merciful within His heart, but He was sometimes externally negligent of His devotees. We should not be preoccupied with His external feature, however, for if we do so we shall be vanquished.

TEXT 169

নিগূঢ় চৈতন্যলীলা বুঝিতে কা'র শক্তি ?
সেই বুঝে, গৌরচন্দ্রে যাঁর দৃঢ় ভক্তি ॥ ১৬৯ ॥

nigūḍha caitanya-līlā bujhite kā'ra śakti?
sei bujhe, gauracandre yāṅra dṛḍha bhakti

SYNONYMS

nigūḍha—very deep; *caitanya-līlā*—the pastimes of Lord Caitanya; *bujhite*—to understand; *kā'ra*—of whom; *śakti*—the power; *sei bujhe*—he understands; *gauracandre*—unto Lord Śrī Caitanya Mahāprabhu; *yāṅra*—whose; *dṛḍha bhakti*—fixed devotion.

TRANSLATION

The pastimes of Śrī Caitanya Mahāprabhu are very deep. Who can understand them? Only one who has firm, deep devotion to His lotus feet.

TEXT 170

দিনান্তরে পণ্ডিত কৈল প্রভুর নিমন্ত্রণ ।
প্রভু তাহাঁ ভিক্ষা কৈল লঞা নিজগণ ॥ ১৭০ ।

dināntare paṇḍita kaila prabhura nimantraṇa
prabhu tāhāṅ bhikṣā kaila lañā nija-gaṇa

SYNONYMS

dina-antare—another day; *paṇḍita*—Gadādhara Paṇḍita; *kaila prabhura nimantraṇa*—invited Śrī Caitanya Mahāprabhu; *prabhu*—Śrī Caitanya Mahāprabhu; *tāhāṅ*—there; *bhikṣā kaila*—took *prasāda; lañā nija-gaṇa*—with His personal associates.

TRANSLATION

Another day, Gadādhara Paṇḍita invited Śrī Caitanya Mahāprabhu to dinner. The Lord took prasāda at his home with His personal associates.

PURPORT

Śrīla Bhaktisiddhānta Sarasvatī Ṭhākura comments that Lord Śrī Caitanya Mahāprabhu acted as a very merciful well-wisher toward Vallabha Bhaṭṭa by externally neglecting him in many ways to purify him of his false pride in being a learned scholar. The Lord neglected Gadādhara Paṇḍita for a few days because of his associating with Vallabha Bhaṭṭa. Actually He was not at all displeased with Gadādhara Paṇḍita. Indeed, because Gadādhara Paṇḍita is the personal potency of Lord Caitanya Mahāprabhu, there is no chance of the Lord's being dissatisfied with him. However, a person who is too attracted to externals cannot understand the deep meaning of these dealings of Śrī Caitanya Mahāprabhu. If one therefore becomes disrespectful to Gadādhara Paṇḍita, he will surely be vanquished.

TEXT 171

তাহাঁই বল্লভ-ভট্ট প্রভুর আজ্ঞা লৈল ।
পণ্ডিত-ঠাঞি পূর্বপ্রার্থিত সব সিদ্ধি হৈল ॥ ১৭১ ॥

tāhāṅi vallabha-bhaṭṭa prabhura ājñā laila
paṇḍita-ṭhāñi pūrva-prārthita saba siddhi haila

SYNONYMS

tāhāṅi—there; *vallabha-bhaṭṭa*—Vallabha Bhaṭṭa; *prabhura ājñā*—the permission of Śrī Caitanya Mahāprabhu; *laila*—took; *paṇḍita-ṭhāñi*—from Gadādhara Paṇḍita; *pūrva-prārthita*—as previously petitioned; *saba siddhi haila*—everything was perfectly executed.

TRANSLATION

There Vallabha Bhaṭṭa took permission from Lord Caitanya Mahāprabhu, and his desire to be initiated by Gadādhara Paṇḍita was thus fulfilled.

TEXT 172

এই ত' কহিলুঁ বল্লভ-ভট্টের মিলন ।
যাহার শ্রবণে পায় গৌরপ্রেমধন ॥ ১৭২ ॥

ei ta' kahiluṅ vallabha-bhaṭṭera milana
yāhāra śravaṇe pāya gaura-prema-dhana

SYNONYMS

ei ta' kahiluṅ—thus I have explained; *vallabha-bhaṭṭera milana*—the meeting of Vallabha Bhaṭṭa; *yāhāra śravaṇe*—by hearing which; *pāya*—one can get; *gaura-prema-dhana*—the treasure of love for Śrī Caitanya Mahāprabhu.

TRANSLATION

I have thus explained the Lord's meeting with Vallabha Bhaṭṭa. By hearing of this incident, one can achieve the treasure of love for Śrī Caitanya Mahāprabhu.

TEXT 173

শ্রীরূপ-রঘুনাথ-পদে যার আশ।
চৈতন্যচরিতামৃত কহে কৃষ্ণদাস ॥ ১৭৩ ॥

śrī-rūpa-raghunātha-pade yāra āśa
caitanya-caritāmṛta kahe kṛṣṇadāsa

SYNONYMS

śrī-rūpa—Śrīla Rūpa Gosvāmī; *raghunātha*—Śrīla Raghunātha dāsa Gosvāmī; *pade*—at the lotus feet; *yāra*—whose; *āśa*—expectation; *caitanya-caritāmṛta*—the book named *Caitanya-caritāmṛta; kahe*—describes; *kṛṣṇadāsa*—Śrīla Kṛṣṇadāsa Kavirāja Gosvāmī.

TRANSLATION

Praying at the lotus feet of Śrī Rūpa and Śrī Raghunātha, always desiring their mercy, I, Kṛṣṇadāsa, narrate Śrī Caitanya-caritāmṛta, following in their footsteps.

Thus end the Bhaktivedanta purports to the Śrī Caitanya-caritāmṛta, Antya-līlā, *Seventh Chapter, describing the meeting of Vallabha Bhaṭṭa with Śrī Caitanya Mahāprabhu.*

CHAPTER 8

Rāmacandra Purī Criticizes the Lord

The following summary of the Eighth Chapter is given by Śrīla Bhaktivinoda Ṭhākura in his *Amṛta-pravāha-bhāṣya.* This chapter describes the history of the Lord's dealings with Rāmacandra Purī. Although Rāmacandra Purī was one of the disciples of Mādhavendra Purī, he was influenced by dry Māyāvādīs, and therefore he criticized Mādhavendra Purī. Therefore Mādhavendra Purī accused him of being an offender and rejected him. Because Rāmacandra Purī had been rejected by his spiritual master, he became concerned only with finding faults in others and advising them according to dry Māyāvāda philosophy. For this reason he was not very respectful to the Vaiṣṇavas, and later he became so fallen that he began criticizing Śrī Caitanya Mahāprabhu for His eating. Hearing his criticisms, Śrī Caitanya Mahāprabhu reduced His eating, but after Rāmacandra Purī left Jagannātha Purī, the Lord resumed His usual behavior.

TEXT 1

তং বন্দে কৃষ্ণচৈতন্যং রামচন্দ্রপুরীভয়াৎ ।
লৌকিকাহারতঃ স্বং যো ভিক্ষান্নং সমকোচয়ৎ ॥১॥

taṁ vande kṛṣṇa-caitanyaṁ
rāmacandra-purī-bhayāt
laukikāhārataḥ svaṁ yo
bhikṣānnaṁ samakocayat

SYNONYMS

tam—to Him; *vande*—I offer my respectful obeisances; *kṛṣṇa-caitanyam*—Lord Śrī Caitanya Mahāprabhu; *rāmacandra-purī-bhayāt*—due to fear of Rāmacandra Purī; *laukika*—ordinary; *āhārataḥ*—from eating; *svam*—His own; *yaḥ*—who; *bhikṣā-annam*—quantity of food; *samakocayat*—reduced.

TRANSLATION

Let me offer my respectful obeisances to Śrī Caitanya Mahāprabhu, who reduced His eating due to fear of the criticism of Rāmacandra Purī.

TEXT 2

জয় জয় শ্রীচৈতন্য করুণাসিন্ধু-অবতার।
ব্রহ্মা-শিবাদিক ভজে চরণ যাঁহার ॥ ২ ॥

jaya jaya śrī-caitanya karuṇā-sindhu-avatāra
brahmā-śivādika bhaje caraṇa yāṅhāra

SYNONYMS

jaya jaya—all glories; *śrī-caitanya*—to Śrī Caitanya Mahāprabhu; *karuṇā-sindhu-avatāra*—the incarnation of the ocean of mercy; *brahmā-śiva-ādika*—demigods, beginning from Lord Brahmā and Śiva; *bhaje*—worship; *caraṇa*—lotus feet; *yāṅhāra*—whose.

TRANSLATION

All glories to Śrī Caitanya Mahāprabhu, the incarnation of the ocean of mercy. His lotus feet are worshiped by demigods like Lord Brahmā and Lord Śiva.

TEXT 3

জয় জয় অবধূতচন্দ্র নিত্যানন্দ।
জগৎ বাঁধিল যেঁহ দিয়া প্রেমফাঁদ ॥ ৩ ॥

jaya jaya avadhūta-candra nityānanda
jagat bāṅdhila yeṅha diyā prema-phāṅda

SYNONYMS

jaya jaya—all glories; *avadhūta-candra*—to the moon of mendicants; *nityānanda*—Lord Nityānanda; *jagat*—the world; *bāṅdhila*—bound; *yeṅha*—who; *diyā*—by; *prema-phāṅda*—the noose of ecstatic love of Kṛṣṇa.

TRANSLATION

All glories to Nityānanda Prabhu, the greatest of mendicants, who bound the entire world with a knot of ecstatic love for God.

TEXT 4

জয় জয় অদ্বৈত ঈশ্বর অবতার।
কৃষ্ণ অবতারি' কৈল জগৎ-নিস্তার ॥ ৪ ॥

jaya jaya advaita īśvara avatāra
kṛṣṇa avatāri' kaila jagat-nistāra

SYNONYMS

jaya jaya —all glories; *advaita*—to Advaita Ācārya; *īśvara*—of the Supreme Personality of Godhead; *avatāra*—incarnation; *kṛṣṇa avatāri'*—inducing Kṛṣṇa to descend; *kaila*—did; *jagat-nistāra*—deliverance of the entire world.

TRANSLATION

All glories to Advaita Prabhu, the incarnation of the Supreme Personality of Godhead. He induced Kṛṣṇa to descend and thus delivered the entire world.

TEXT 5

জয় জয় শ্রীবাসাদি যত ভক্তগণ ।
শ্রীকৃষ্ণচৈতন্য প্রভু—যাঁর প্রাণধন ॥ ৫ ॥

jaya jaya śrīvāsādi yata bhakta-gaṇa
śrī-kṛṣṇa-caitanya prabhu——yāṅra prāṇa-dhana

SYNONYMS

jaya jaya—all glories; *śrīvāsa-ādi*—headed by Śrīvāsa Ṭhākura; *yata bhakta-gaṇa*—to all the devotees; *śrī-kṛṣṇa-caitanya prabhu*—Śrī Caitanya Mahāprabhu; *yāṅra*—whose; *prāṇa-dhana*—life and soul.

TRANSLATION

All glories to all the devotees, headed by Śrīvāsa Ṭhākura. Śrī Kṛṣṇa Caitanya Mahāprabhu is their life and soul.

TEXT 6

এইমত গৌরচন্দ্র নিজভক্ত-সঙ্গে ।
নীলাচলে ক্রীড়া করে কৃষ্ণপ্রেমতরঙ্গে ॥ ৬ ॥

ei-mata gauracandra nija-bhakta-saṅge
nīlācale krīḍā kare kṛṣṇa-prema-taraṅge

SYNONYMS

ei-mata—in this way; *gauracandra*—Lord Śrī Caitanya Mahāprabhu; *nija-bhakta-saṅge*—with His own devotees; *nīlācale*—at Jagannātha Purī; *krīḍā kare*—executes different pastimes; *kṛṣṇa-prema-taraṅge*—in the waves of love of Kṛṣṇa.

TRANSLATION

Thus Śrī Caitanya Mahāprabhu, at Jagannātha Purī, performed His various pastimes with His own devotees in the waves of love for Kṛṣṇa.

TEXT 7

হেনকালে রামচন্দ্রপুরী-গোসাঞি আইলা।
পরমানন্দ-পুরীরে আর প্রভুরে মিলিলা॥ ৭॥

hena-kāle rāmacandra-purī-gosāñi āilā
paramānanda-purīre āra prabhure mililā

SYNONYMS

hena-kāle—at this time; *rāmacandra-purī-gosāñi*—a *sannyāsī* named Rāmacandra Purī; *āilā*—came; *paramānanda-purīre*—Paramānanda Purī; *āra*—and; *prabhure*—Śrī Caitanya Mahāprabhu; *mililā*—met.

TRANSLATION

Then a sannyāsī named Rāmacandra Purī Gosāñi came to see Paramānanda Purī and Śrī Caitanya Mahāprabhu.

TEXT 8

পরমানন্দ-পুরী কৈল চরণ বন্দন।
পুরী-গোসাঞি কৈল তাঁরে দৃঢ় আলিঙ্গন॥ ৮॥

paramānanda-purī kaila caraṇa vandana
purī-gosāñi kaila tāṅre dṛḍha āliṅgana

SYNONYMS

paramānanda-purī—Paramānanda Purī; *kaila*—did; *caraṇa*—unto the feet; *vandana*—offering obeisances; *purī-gosāñi*—Rāmacandra Purī; *kaila*—did; *tāṅre*—unto him; *dṛḍha*—strong; *āliṅgana*—embracing.

TRANSLATION

Paramānanda Purī offered respects at the feet of Rāmacandra Purī, and Rāmacandra Purī strongly embraced him.

PURPORT

Because Rāmacandra Purī was a disciple of Mādhavendra Purī, both Paramānanda Purī and Śrī Caitanya Mahāprabhu offered him respectful obeisances. Śrīla

Bhaktisiddhānta Sarasvatī Ṭhākura comments that although Rāmacandra Purī was naturally very envious and although he was against the principles of Vaiṣṇavism—or, in other words, against the principles of the Supreme Personality of Godhead and His devotees—common people nevertheless addressed him as Gosvāmī or Gosāñi because he was superficially in the renounced order and dressed like a *sannyāsī*. In the modern age the title *gosvāmī* is used by a caste of *gṛhasthas*, but formerly it was not. Rūpa Gosvāmī and Sanātana Gosvāmī, for example, were called *gosvāmī* because they were in the renounced order. Similarly, because Paramānanda Purī was a *sannyāsī*, he was called Purī Gosvāmī. By careful scrutiny, therefore, one will find that *gosvāmī* is not the title for a certain caste; rather, it is properly the title for a person in the renounced order.

TEXT 9

মহাপ্রভু কৈলা তাঁরে দণ্ডবৎ নতি ।
আলিঙ্গন করি' তেঁহো কৈল কৃষ্ণস্মৃতি ॥ ৯ ॥

mahāprabhu kailā tāṅre daṇḍavat nati
āliṅgana kari' teṅho kaila kṛṣṇa-smṛti

SYNONYMS

mahāprabhu—Śrī Caitanya Mahāprabhu; *kailā*—did; *tāṅre*—unto him; *daṇḍavat nati*—offering obeisances; *āliṅgana kari'*—embracing; *teṅho*—Rāmacandra Purī; *kaila*—did; *kṛṣṇa-smṛti*—remembrance of Kṛṣṇa.

TRANSLATION

Śrī Caitanya Mahāprabhu also offered obeisances unto Rāmacandra Purī, who then embraced Him and thus remembered Kṛṣṇa.

PURPORT

Śrī Caitanya Mahāprabhu offered obeisances to Rāmacandra Purī in consideration of his being a disciple of Śrīla Mādhavendra Purī, the spiritual master of His own spiritual master, Īśvara Purī. When a Vaiṣṇava *sannyāsī* meets another Vaiṣṇava *sannyāsī*, they both remember Kṛṣṇa. Even Māyāvādī *sannyāsīs* generally remember Nārāyaṇa, who is also Kṛṣṇa, by saying *oṁ namo bhagavate nārāyaṇa* or *namo nārāyaṇa*. Thus it is the duty of a *sannyāsī* to remember Kṛṣṇa. According to *smṛti-śāstra*, a *sannyāsī* does not offer obeisances or blessings to anyone. It is said, *sannyāsī nirāśīr nirnamaskriyaḥ*: a *sannyāsī* should not offer anyone blessings or obeisances.

TEXT 10

তিনজনে ইষ্টগোষ্ঠী কৈলা কতক্ষণ ।
জগদানন্দ-পণ্ডিত তাঁরে কৈলা নিমন্ত্রণ ॥ ১০ ॥

tina-jane iṣṭha-goṣṭhī kailā kata-kṣaṇa
jagadānanda-paṇḍita tāṅre kailā nimantraṇa

SYNONYMS

tina-jane—three persons; *iṣṭha-goṣṭhī*—discussion on Kṛṣṇa; *kailā*—performed; *kata-kṣaṇa*—for some time; *jagadānanda-paṇḍita*—Jagadānanda Paṇḍita; *tāṅre*—Rāmacandra Purī; *kailā nimantraṇa*—invited.

TRANSLATION

The three of them talked about Kṛṣṇa for some time, and then Jagadānanda came and extended an invitation to Rāmacandra Purī.

TEXT 11

জগন্নাথের প্রসাদ আনিলা ভিক্ষার লাগিয়া ।
যথেষ্ট ভিক্ষা করিলা তেঁহো নিন্দার লাগিয়া ॥ ১১ ॥

jagannāthera prasāda ānilā bhikṣāra lāgiyā
yatheṣṭa bhikṣā karilā teṅho nindāra lāgiyā

SYNONYMS

jagannāthera prasāda—remnants of the food of Lord Jagannātha; *ānilā*—brought; *bhikṣāra lāgiyā*—for feeding; *yatheṣṭa bhikṣā karilā*—ate sumptuously; *teṅho*—he; *nindāra lāgiyā*—to find some fault.

TRANSLATION

A large quantity of the remnants of food from Lord Jagannātha was brought in for distribution. Rāmacandra Purī ate sumptuously, and then he wanted to find faults in Jagadānanda Paṇḍita.

TEXT 12

ভিক্ষা করি' কহে পুরী,—"শুন, জগদানন্দ ।
অবশেষ প্রসাদ তুমি করহ ভক্ষণ ॥" ১২ ॥

bhikṣā kari' kahe purī,—"śuna, jagadānanda
avaśeṣa prasāda tumi karaha bhakṣaṇa"

SYNONYMS

bhikṣā kari'—after finishing the lunch; *kahe purī*—Rāmacandra Purī began to speak; *śuna, jagadānanda*—my dear Jagadānanda, just hear; *avaśeṣa prasāda*—the remaining *prasāda; tumi*—you; *karaha bhakṣaṇa*—eat.

TRANSLATION

After finishing the meal, Rāmacandra Purī requested, "My dear Jagadānanda, please listen. You eat the food that is left."

TEXT 13

আগ্রহ করিয়া তাঁরে বসি' খাওয়াইল ।
আপনে আগ্রহ করি' পরিবেশন কৈল ॥ ১৩ ॥

āgraha kariyā tāṅre vasi' khāoyāila
āpane āgraha kari' pariveśana kaila

SYNONYMS

āgraha kariyā—with great eagerness; *tāṅre vasi'*—seating him; *khāoyāila*—he fed; *āpane*—personally; *āgraha kari'*—with great eagerness; *pariveśana kaila*—administered the *prasāda.*

TRANSLATION

With great eagerness Rāmacandra Purī seated Jagadānanda Paṇḍita and personally served him prasāda.

TEXT 14

আগ্রহ করিয়া পুনঃ পুনঃ খাওয়াইল ।
আচমন কৈলে নিন্দা করিতে লাগিল ॥ ১৪ ॥

āgraha kariyā punaḥ punaḥ khāoyāila
ācamana kaile nindā karite lāgila

SYNONYMS

āgraha kariyā—with eagerness; *punaḥ punaḥ*—again and again; *khāoyāila*—fed; *ācamana kaile*—when he had washed his hands and mouth; *nindā karite lāgila*—began to criticize.

TRANSLATION

Encouraging him again and again, Rāmacandra Purī fed him sumptuously, but when Jagadānanda had washed his hands and mouth, Rāmacandra Purī began criticizing him.

TEXT 15

"শুনি, চৈতন্যগণ করে বহুত ভক্ষণ।
'সত্য' সেই বাক্য,—সাক্ষাৎ দেখিলুঁ এখন ॥ ১৫ ॥

"śuni, caitanya-gaṇa kare bahuta bhakṣaṇa
'satya' sei vākya,——sākṣāt dekhiluṅ ekhana

SYNONYMS

śuni—I have heard; *caitanya-gaṇa*—the followers of Śrī Caitanya Mahāprabhu; *kare bahuta bhakṣaṇa*—eat more than necessary; *satya*—true; *sei vākya*—that statement; *sākṣāt*—directly; *dekhiluṅ*—I have seen; *ekhana*—now.

TRANSLATION

"I have heard," he said, "that the followers of Caitanya Mahāprabhu eat more than necessary. Now I have directly seen that this is true.

TEXT 16

সন্ন্যাসীরে এত খাওয়াঞা করে ধর্ম নাশ।
বৈরাগী হঞা এত খায়, বৈরাগ্যের নাহি 'ভাস'॥"১৬॥

sannyāsīre eta khāoyāñā kare dharma nāśa
vairāgī hañā eta khāya, vairāgyera nāhi 'bhāsa' "

SYNONYMS

sannyāsīre—unto a *sannyāsī; eta*—so much; *khāoyāñā*—feeding; *kare dharma nāśa*—destroys the regulative principles; *vairāgī hañā*—being in the renounced order; *eta*—so much; *khāya*—eats; *vairāgyera nāhi bhāsa*—there is no trace of renunciation.

TRANSLATION

"Feeding a sannyāsī too much breaks his regulative principles, for when a sannyāsī eats too much, his renunciation is destroyed."

TEXT 17

এই ত' স্বভাব তাঁর আগ্রহ করিয়া।
পিছে নিন্দা করে, আগে বহুত খাওয়াঞা ॥ ১৭ ॥

ei ta' svabhāva tāṅra āgraha kariyā
piche nindā kare, āge bahuta khāoyāñā

SYNONYMS

ei—this; *ta'*—certainly; *sva-bhāva*—characteristic; *tāṅra*—his; *āgraha kariyā*—with great eagerness; *piche*—afterward; *nindā kare*—criticizes; *āge*—at first; *bahuta*—much; *khāoyāñā*—feeding.

TRANSLATION

The characteristic of Rāmacandra Purī was that first he would induce someone to eat more than necessary and then he would criticize him.

TEXT 18

পূর্বে যবে মাধবেন্দ্র করেন অন্তর্ধান ।
রামচন্দ্রপুরী তবে আইলা তাঁর স্থান ॥ ১৮ ॥

pūrve yabe mādhavendra karena antardhāna
rāmacandra-purī tabe āilā tāṅra sthāna

SYNONYMS

pūrve—formerly; *yabe*—when; *mādhavendra*—Mādhavendra Purī; *karena antardhāna*—was about to die; *rāmacandra-purī*—Rāmacandra Purī; *tabe*—at that time; *āilā*—came; *tāṅra sthāna*—to his place.

TRANSLATION

Formerly, when Mādhavendra Purī was at the last stage of his life, Rāmacandra Purī came to where he was staying.

TEXT 19

পুরী-গোসাঞি করে কৃষ্ণনাম-সঙ্কীর্তন ।
'মথুরা না পাইনু' বলি' করেন ক্রন্দন ॥ ১৯ ॥

purī-gosāñi kare kṛṣṇa-nāma-saṅkīrtana
'mathurā nā pāinu' bali' karena krandana

SYNONYMS

purī-gosāñi—Mādhavendra Purī; *kare*—was performing; *kṛṣṇa-nāma-saṅkīrtana*—the chanting of the holy name of Lord Kṛṣṇa; *mathurā nā pāinu*—I did not get shelter at Mathurā; *bali'*—saying; *karena krandana*—was crying.

TRANSLATION

Mādhavendra Purī was chanting the holy name of Kṛṣṇa, and sometimes he would cry, "O my Lord, I did not get shelter at Mathurā."

TEXT 20

রামচন্দ্রপুরী তবে উপদেশে তাঁরে।
শিষ্য হঞা গুরুকে কহে, ভয় নাহি করে ॥ ২০ ॥

rāmacandra-purī tabe upadeśe tāṅre
śiṣya hañā guruke kahe, bhaya nāhi kare

SYNONYMS

rāmacandra-purī—Rāmacandra Purī; *tabe*—then; *upadeśe tāṅre*—instructed him; *śiṣya hañā*—being a disciple; *guruke kahe*—said to his spiritual master; *bhaya nāhi kare*—without fear.

TRANSLATION

Then Rāmacandra Purī was so foolish that he fearlessly dared to instruct his spiritual master.

TEXT 21

"তুমি—পূর্ণ-ব্রহ্মানন্দ, করহ স্মরণ।
ব্রহ্মবিৎ হঞা কেনে করহ রোদন?" ২১ ॥

"tumi——pūrṇa-brahmānanda, karaha smaraṇa
brahmavit hañā kene karaha rodana?"

SYNONYMS

tumi—you; *pūrṇa-brahma-ānanda*—full in transcendental bliss; *karaha smaraṇa*—you should remember; *brahma-vit hañā*—being fully aware of Brahman; *kene*—why; *karaha rodana*—are you crying.

TRANSLATION

"If you are in full transcendental bliss," he said, "you should now remember only Brahman. Why are you crying?"

PURPORT

As stated in *Bhagavad-gītā, brahma-bhūtaḥ prasannātmā:* a Brahman realized person is always happy. *Na śocati na kāṅkṣati:* he neither laments nor aspires for anything. Not knowing why Mādhavendra Purī was crying, Rāmacandra Purī tried to become his advisor. Thus he committed a great offense, for a disciple should never try to instruct his spiritual master.

TEXT 22

**শুনি' মাধবেন্দ্র-মনে ক্রোধ উপজিল ।
'দূর, দূর, পাপিষ্ঠ' বলি' ভৎর্সনা করিল ॥ ২২ ॥**

śuni' mādhavendra-mane krodha upajila
'dūra, dūra, pāpiṣṭha' bali' bhartsanā karila

SYNONYMS

śuni'—hearing; *mādhavendra*—of Mādhavendra Purī; *mane*—in the mind; *krodha*—anger; *upajila*—arose; *dūra dūra*—get out; *pāpiṣṭha*—you sinful rascal; *bali'*—saying; *bhartsanā karila*—he chastised.

TRANSLATION

Hearing this instruction, Mādhavendra Purī, greatly angry, rebuked him by saying, "Get out, you sinful rascal!

PURPORT

Rāmacandra Purī could not understand that his spiritual master, Mādhavendra Purī, was feeling transcendental separation. His lamentation was not material. Rather, it proceeded from the highest stage of ecstatic love of Kṛṣṇa. When he was crying in separation, "I could not achieve Kṛṣṇa! I could not reach Mathurā!" this was not ordinary material lamentation. Rāmacandra Purī was not sufficiently expert to understand the feelings of Mādhavendra Purī, but nevertheless he thought himself very advanced. Therefore, regarding Mādhavendra Purī's expressions as ordinary material lamentation, he advised him to remember Brahman because he was latently an impersonalist. Mādhavendra Purī understood Rāmacandra Purī's position as a great fool and therefore immediately rebuked him. Such a reprimand from the spiritual master is certainly for the betterment of the disciple.

TEXT 23

**'কৃষ্ণ না পাইনু, না পাইনু 'মথুরা' ।
আপন-দুঃখে মরোঁ — এই দিতে আইল জ্বালা ॥২৩॥**

'kṛṣṇa nā pāinu, nā pāinu 'mathurā'
āpana-duḥkhe maroṅ——ei dite āila jvālā

SYNONYMS

kṛṣṇa—Lord Kṛṣṇa; *nā pāinu*—I did not get; *nā pāinu*—did not get; *mathurā*—Mathurā; *āpana-duḥkhe*—in my own unhappiness; *maroṅ*—I am dying; *ei*—this person; *dite āila jvālā*—has come to give more pain.

TRANSLATION

"O my Lord Kṛṣṇa, I could not reach You, nor could I reach Your abode, Mathurā. I am dying in my unhappiness, and now this rascal has come to give me more pain.

TEXT 24

মোরে মুখ না দেখাবি তুই, যাও যথি-তথি ।
তোরে দেখি' মৈলে মোর হবে অসদ্গতি ॥ ২৪ ॥

more mukha nā dekhābi tui, yāo yathi-tathi
tore dekhi' maile mora habe asad-gati

SYNONYMS

more—to me; *mukha*—face; *nā dekhābi*—do not show; *tui*—you; *yāo*—go; *yathi-tathi*—anywhere else; *tore*—you; *dekhi'*—seeing; *maile*—if I die; *mora habe asat-gati*—I shall not get my destination.

TRANSLATION

"Don't show your face to me! Go anywhere else you like. If I die seeing your face, I shall not achieve the destination of my life.

TEXT 25

কৃষ্ণ না পাইনু মুঞি মরোঁ আপনার দুঃখে ।
মোরে 'ব্রহ্ম' উপদেশে এই ছার মূর্খে ॥" ২৫ ॥

kṛṣṇa nā pāinu muñi maroṅ āpanāra duḥkhe
more 'brahma' upadeśe ei chāra mūrkhe"

SYNONYMS

kṛṣṇa—Kṛṣṇa; *nā pāinu*—could not get; *muñi*—I; *maroṅ*—I die; *āpanāra duḥkhe*—in my own unhappiness; *more*—to me; *brahma*—Brahman; *upadeśe*—instructs; *ei*—this; *chāra*—condemned; *mūrkhe*—fool.

TRANSLATION

"I am dying without achieving the shelter of Kṛṣṇa, and therefore I am greatly unhappy. Now this condemned foolish rascal has come to instruct me about Brahman."

TEXT 26

এই যে শ্রীমাধবেন্দ্র শ্রীপাদ উপেক্ষা করিল ।
সেই অপরাধে ইঁহার 'বাসনা' জন্মিল ॥ ২৬ ॥

ei ye śrī-mādhavendra śrī-pāda upekṣā karila
sei aparādhe iṅhāra 'vāsanā' janmila

SYNONYMS

ei—this; *ye*—that; *śrī-mādhavendra śrī-pāda*—His Lordship Mādhavendra Purī; *upekṣā karila*—neglected or denounced; *sei aparādhe*—because of the offense; *iṅhāra*—of Rāmacandra Purī; *vāsanā*—material desire; *janmila*—arose.

TRANSLATION

Rāmacandra Purī was thus denounced by Mādhavendra Purī. Due to his offense, gradually material desire appeared within him.

PURPORT

The word *vāsanā* ("material desires") refers to dry speculative knowledge. Such speculative knowledge is only material. As confirmed in *Śrīmad-Bhāgavatam* (10.14.4), a person without devotional service who simply wants to know things (*kevala-bodha-labdhaye*) gains only dry speculative knowledge but no spiritual profit. This is also confirmed in the *Bhakti-sandarbha* (111), wherein it is said:

jīvan-muktā api punar
yānti saṁsāra-vāsanām
yady acintya-mahā-śaktau
bhagavaty aparādhinaḥ

"Even though one is liberated in this life, if one offends the Supreme Personality of Godhead he falls down in the midst of material desires, of which dry speculation about spiritual realization is one."

In his *Laghu-toṣaṇī* commentary on *Śrīmad-Bhāgavatam* (10.2.32), Jīva Gosvāmī says;

jīvan-muktā api punar
bandhanaṁ yānti karmabhiḥ
yady acintya-mahā-śaktau
bhagavaty aparādhinaḥ

"Even if one is liberated in this life, he becomes addicted to material desires because of offenses to the Supreme Personality of Godhead."

A similar quotation from one of the *Purāṇas* also appears in the *Viṣṇu-bhakti-candrodaya:*

jivān-muktāḥ prapadyante
kvacit saṁsāra-vāsanām
yogino na vilipyante
karmabhir bhagavat-parāḥ

"Even liberated souls sometimes fall down to material desires, but those who fully engaged in devotional service to the Supreme Personality of Godhead are not affected by such desires."

These are references from authoritative revealed scriptures. If one becomes an offender to his spiritual master or the Supreme Personality of Godhead, he falls down to the material platform to merely speculate.

TEXT 27

শুষ্ক-ব্রহ্মজ্ঞানী, নাহি কৃষ্ণের 'সম্বন্ধ' ।
সর্ব লোক নিন্দা করে, নিন্দাতে নির্বন্ধ ॥ ২৭ ॥

śuṣka-brahma-jñānī, nāhi kṛṣṇera 'sambandha'
sarva loka nindā kare, nindāte nirbandha

SYNONYMS

śuṣka—dry; *brahma-jñānī*—impersonalist philosopher; *nāhi*—there is not; *kṛṣṇera*—with Lord Kṛṣṇa; *sambandha*—relationship; *sarva*—all; *loka*—persons; *nindā kare*—criticizes; *nindāte nirbandha*—fixed in blaspheming.

TRANSLATION

One who is attached to dry speculative knowledge has no relationship with Kṛṣṇa. His occupation is criticizing Vaiṣṇavas. Thus he is situated in criticism.

PURPORT

Śrīla Bhaktisiddhānta Sarasvatī Ṭhākura has explained in his *Anubhāṣya* that the word *nirbandha* indicates that Rāmacandra Purī had a steady desire to criticize others. Impersonalist Māyāvādīs who have no relationship with Kṛṣṇa, who cannot take to devotional service and who simply engage in material arguments to understand Brahman regard devotional service to Kṛṣṇa as *karma-kāṇḍa,* or fruitive activities. According to them, devotional service to Kṛṣṇa is but another means for attaining *dharma, artha, kāma* and *mokṣa.* Therefore they criticize the devotees for engaging in material activities. They think that devotional service is *māyā* and that Kṛṣṇa or Viṣṇu is also *māyā.* Therefore they are called Māyāvādīs. Such a mentality awakens in a person who is an offender to Kṛṣṇa and His devotees.

TEXT 28

ঈশ্বরপুরী গোসাঞি করে শ্রীপাদ-সেবন।
স্বহস্তে করেন মলমূত্রাদি মার্জন ॥ ২৮ ॥

īśvara-purī gosāñi kare śrī-pāda-sevana
svahaste karena mala-mūtrādi mārjana

SYNONYMS

īśvara-purī—Īśvara Purī; *gosāñi*—Gosvāmī; *kare*—performs; *śrī-pāda-sevana*—service to Mādhavendra Purī; *sva-haste*—with his own hand; *karena*—performs; *mala-mūtra-ādi*—stool, urine, and so on; *mārjana*—cleaning.

TRANSLATION

Īśvara Purī, the spiritual master of Śrī Caitanya Mahāprabhu, performed service to Mādhavendra Purī, cleaning up his stool and urine with his own hand.

TEXT 29

নিরন্তর কৃষ্ণনাম করায় স্মরণ।
কৃষ্ণনাম, কৃষ্ণলীলা শুনায় অনুক্ষণ ॥ ২৯ ॥

nirantara kṛṣṇa-nāma karāya smaraṇa
kṛṣṇa-nāma, kṛṣṇa-līlā śunāya anukṣaṇa

SYNONYMS

nirantara—always; *kṛṣṇa-nāma*—the name of Lord Kṛṣṇa; *karāya smaraṇa*—was reminding; *kṛṣṇa-nāma*—the holy name of Kṛṣṇa; *kṛṣṇa-līlā*—pastimes of Kṛṣṇa; *śunāya anukṣaṇa*—was always causing to hear.

TRANSLATION

Īśvara Purī was always chanting the holy name and pastimes of Lord Kṛṣṇa for Mādhavendra Purī to hear. In this way he helped Mādhavendra Purī remember the holy name and pastimes of Lord Kṛṣṇa at the time of death.

TEXT 30

তুষ্ট হঞা পুরী তাঁরে কৈলা আলিঙ্গন।
বর দিলা—'কৃষ্ণে তোমার হউক প্রেমধন' ॥ ৩০ ॥

tuṣṭa hañā purī tāṅre kailā āliṅgana
vara dilā——'kṛṣṇe tomāra ha-uka prema-dhana'

SYNONYMS

tuṣṭa hañā—being pleased; *purī*—Mādhavendra Purī; *tāṅre*—him; *kailā āliṅgana*—embraced; *vara dilā*—gave the benediction; *kṛṣṇe*—unto Kṛṣṇa; *tomāra*—your; *ha-uka*—let there be; *prema-dhana*—the wealth of love.

TRANSLATION

Pleased with Īśvara Purī, Mādhavendra Purī embraced him and gave him the benediction that he would be a great devotee and lover of Kṛṣṇa.

TEXT 31

সেই হৈতে ঈশ্বরপুরী –'প্রেমের সাগর' ।
রামচন্দ্রপুরী হৈল সর্বনিন্দাকর ॥ ৩১ ॥

sei haite īśvara-purī——'premera sāgara'
rāmacandra-purī haila sarva-nindākara

SYNONYMS

sei haite—from that; *īśvara-purī*—Īśvara Purī; *premera sāgara*—the ocean of ecstatic love; *rāmacandra-purī*—Rāmacandra Purī; *haila*—became; *sarva-nindākara*—critic of all others.

TRANSLATION

Thus Īśvara Purī became like an ocean of ecstatic love for Kṛṣṇa, whereas Rāmacandra Purī became a dry speculator and a critic of everyone else.

TEXT 32

মহদনুগ্রহ-নিগ্রহের 'সাক্ষী' দুইজনে ।
এই দুইদ্বারে শিখাইলা জগজনে ॥ ৩২ ॥

mahad-anugraha-nigrahera 'sākṣī' dui-jane
ei dui-dvāre śikhāilā jaga-jane

SYNONYMS

mahat—of an exalted personality; *anugraha*—of the blessing; *nigrahera*—of chastisement; *sākṣī*—giving evidence; *dui-jane*—two persons; *ei dui-dvāre*—by these two; *śikhāilā*—instructed; *jaga-jane*—the people of the world.

TRANSLATION

Īśvara Purī received the blessing of Mādhavendra Purī, whereas Rāmacandra Purī received a rebuke from him. Therefore these two persons, Īśvara Purī and Rāmacandra Purī, are examples of the objects of a great personality's benediction and punishment. Mādhavendra Purī instructed the entire world by presenting these two examples.

TEXT 33

জগদ্গুরু মাধবেন্দ্র করি' প্রেম দান ।
এই শ্লোক পড়ি' তেঁহো কৈল অন্তর্ধান ॥ ৩৩

jagad-guru mādhavendra kari' prema dāna
ei śloka paḍi' teṅho kaila antardhāna

SYNONYMS

jagat-guru—the spiritual master of the entire world; *mādhavendra*—Mādhavendra Purī; *kari' prema dāna*—giving ecstatic love of Kṛṣṇa as charity; *ei śloka paḍi'*—reciting this verse; *teṅho*—he; *kaila antardhāna*—passed away from this material world.

TRANSLATION

His Divine Grace Mādhavendra Purī, the spiritual master of the entire world, thus distributed ecstatic love for Kṛṣṇa. While passing away from the material world, he chanted the following verse.

TEXT 34

অয়ি দীনদয়ার্দ্রনাথ হে
মথুরানাথ কদাবলোক্যসে ।
হৃদয়ং ত্বদলোককাতরং
দয়িত ভ্রাম্যতি কিং করোম্যহম্ ॥ ৩৪ ॥

ayi dīna-dayārdra nātha he
mathurā-nātha kadāvalokyase
hṛdayaṁ tvad-aloka-kātaraṁ
dayita bhrāmyati kiṁ karomy aham

SYNONYMS

ayi—O my Lord; *dīna*—on the poor; *dayā-ārdra*—compassionate; *nātha*—O master; *he*—O; *mathurā-nātha*—the master of Mathurā; *kadā*—when;

avalokyase—I shall see you; *hṛdayam*—my heart; *tvat*—of You; *aloka*—without seeing; *kātaram*—very much aggrieved; *dayita*—O most beloved; *bhrāmyati*—becomes overwhelmed; *kim*—what; *karomi*—shall do; *aham*—I.

TRANSLATION

"O my Lord! O most merciful master! O master of Mathurā! When shall I see You again? Because of my not seeing You, my agitated heart has become unsteady. O most beloved one, what shall I do now?"

TEXT 35

এই শ্লোকে কৃষ্ণপ্রেম করে উপদেশ ।
কৃষ্ণের বিরহে ভক্তের ভাববিশেষ ॥ ৩৫ ॥

ei śloke kṛṣṇa-prema kare upadeśa
kṛṣṇera virahe bhaktera bhāva-viśeṣa

SYNONYMS

ei śloke—in this verse; *kṛṣṇa-prema*—love of Kṛṣṇa; *kare upadeśa*—instructs; *kṛṣṇera virahe*—by feeling separation from Kṛṣṇa; *bhaktera*—of the devotee; *bhāva-viśeṣa*—transcendental situation.

TRANSLATION

In this verse Mādhavendra Purī instructs how to achieve ecstatic love for Kṛṣṇa. By feeling separation from Kṛṣṇa, one becomes spiritually situated.

TEXT 36

পৃথিবীতে রোপণ করি' গেলা প্রেমাঙ্কুর ।
সেই প্রেমাঙ্কুরের বৃক্ষ –চৈতন্যঠাকুর ॥ ৩৬ ॥

pṛthivīte ropaṇa kari' gelā premāṅkura
sei premāṅkurera vṛkṣa——caitanya-ṭhākura

SYNONYMS

pṛthivīte—within this material world; *ropaṇa kari'*—sowing; *gelā*—went; *prema-aṅkura*—the seed of ecstatic love for Kṛṣṇa; *sei prema-aṅkurera*—of that seed of ecstatic love for Kṛṣṇa; *vṛkṣa*—the tree; *caitanya-ṭhākura*—Lord Śrī Caitanya Mahāprabhu.

TRANSLATION

Mādhavendra Purī sowed the seed of ecstatic love for Kṛṣṇa within this material world and then departed. That seed later became a great tree in the form of Śrī Caitanya Mahāprabhu.

TEXT 37

প্রস্তাবে কহিলুঁ পুরী-গোসাঞির নির্যাণ ।
যেই ইহা শুনে, সেই বড় ভাগ্যবান্ ॥ ৩৭ ॥

prastāve kahiluṅ purī-gosāñira niryāṇa
yei ihā śune, sei baḍa bhāgyavān

SYNONYMS

prastāve—incidentally; *kahiluṅ*—I have described; *purī-gosāñira*—of Mādhavendra Purī; *niryāṇa*—the passing away; *yei*—one who; *ihā*—this; *śune*—hears; *sei*—he; *baḍa bhāgyavān*—very fortunate.

TRANSLATION

I have incidentally described the passing away of Mādhavendra Purī. Anyone who hears this must be considered very fortunate.

TEXT 38

রামচন্দ্রপুরী ঐছে রহিলা নীলাচলে ।
বিরক্ত স্বভাব, কভু রহে কোন স্থলে ॥ ৩৮ ॥

rāmacandra-purī aiche rahilā nīlācale
virakta svabhāva, kabhu rahe kona sthale

SYNONYMS

rāmacandra-purī—Rāmacandra Purī; *aiche*—in this way; *rahilā nīlācale*—remained at Jagannātha Purī; *virakta*—renounced; *sva-bhāva*—as is the custom; *kabhu*—sometimes; *rahe*—he remained; *kona sthale*—at a particular place.

TRANSLATION

Thus Rāmacandra Purī stayed at Jagannātha Purī. As customary for those in the renounced order, he would sometimes stay someplace and then go away.

TEXT 39

অনিমন্ত্রণ ভিক্ষা করে, নাহিক নির্ণয় ।
অন্যের ভিক্ষার স্থিতির লয়েন নিশ্চয় ॥ ৩৯ ॥

animantraṇa bhikṣā kare, nāhika nirṇaya
anyera bhikṣāra sthitira layena niścaya

SYNONYMS

animantraṇa—without being invited; *bhikṣā kare*—accepts food; *nāhika nirṇaya*—there is no certainty; *anyera*—of others; *bhikṣāra*—of acceptance of *prasāda; sthitira*—of the situation; *layena niścaya*—takes account.

TRANSLATION

There was no certainty of where Rāmacandra Purī would take his meal, for he would do so even uninvited. Nevertheless, he was very particular to keep account of how others were taking their meals.

TEXT 40

প্রভুর নিমন্ত্রণে লাগে কৌড়ি চারি পণ ।
কভু কাশীশ্বর, গোবিন্দ খান তিন জন ॥ ৪০ ॥

prabhura nimantraṇe lāge kauḍi cāri paṇa
kabhu kāśīśvara, govinda khāna tina jana

SYNONYMS

prabhura—of Śrī Caitanya Mahāprabhu; *nimantraṇe*—for invitation; *lāge*—is required; *kauḍi cāri paṇa*—four times eighty small conchshells; *kabhu kāśīśvara*—sometimes Kāśīśvara; *govinda*—the personal servant of Caitanya Mahāprabhu; *khāna*—eat; *tina jana*—three persons.

TRANSLATION

To invite Śrī Caitanya Mahāprabhu would cost 320 kauḍis [small conchshells]. This would provide lunch for three people, including Śrī Caitanya Mahāprabhu and sometimes Kāśīśvara and Govinda.

TEXT 41

প্রত্যহ প্রভুর ভিক্ষা ইতি-উতি হয় ।
কেহ যদি মূল্য আনে, চারিপণ-নির্ণয় ॥ ৪১ ॥

pratyaha prabhura bhikṣā iti-uti haya
keha yadi mūlya āne, cāri-paṇa-nirṇaya

SYNONYMS

prati-aha—daily; *prabhura*—of Śrī Caitanya Mahāprabhu; *bhikṣā*—alms; *iti-uti*—here and there; *haya*—is; *keha*—someone; *yadi*—if; *mūlya āne*—pays; *cāri-paṇa*—four times eighty small conchshells; *nirṇaya*—as a fixed amount.

TRANSLATION

Every day the Lord would take His meal at a different place, and if someone was prepared to pay for a meal, the price was fixed at only four paṇas.

TEXT 42

প্রভুর স্থিতি, রীতি, ভিক্ষা, শয়ন, প্রয়াণ ।
রামচন্দ্রপুরী করে সর্বানুসন্ধান ॥ ৪২ ॥

prabhura sthiti, rīti, bhikṣā, śayana, prayāṇa
rāmacandra-purī kare sarvānusandhāna

SYNONYMS

prabhura—of Śrī Caitanya Mahāprabhu; *sthiti*—situation; *rīti*—regulative principles; *bhikṣā*—accepting lunch; *śayana*—sleeping; *prayāṇa*—movement; *rāmacandra-purī*—Rāmacandra Purī; *kare sarva-anusandhāna*—takes all information of.

TRANSLATION

Rāmacandra Purī concerned himself with gathering all sorts of information about how Śrī Caitanya Mahāprabhu was situated, including His regulative principles, His lunch, His sleep and His movements.

TEXT 43

প্রভুর যতেক গুণ স্পর্শিতে নারিল ।
ছিদ্র চাহি' বুলে, কাহাঁ ছিদ্র না পাইল ॥ ৪৩ ॥

prabhura yateka guṇa sparśite nārila
chidra cāhi' bule, kāṅhā chidra nā pāila

SYNONYMS

prabhura—of Śrī Caitanya Mahāprabhu; *yateka guṇa*—all the transcendental attributes; *sparśite nārila*—could not touch or understand; *chidra cāhi'*—looking for faults; *bule*—he goes about; *kāṅhā*—anywhere; *chidra*—fault; *nā pāila*—he could not find.

TRANSLATION

Because Rāmacandra Purī was interested only in finding faults, he could not understand the transcendental qualities of Śrī Caitanya Mahāprabhu. His only concern was finding faults, but still he could not find any.

TEXT 44

'সন্ন্যাসী হঞা করে মিষ্টান্ন ভক্ষণ ।
এই ভোগে হয় কৈছে ইন্দ্রিয়-বারণ' ? ৪৪ ॥

'sannyāsī hañā kare miṣṭānna bhakṣaṇa
ei bhoge haya kaiche indriya-vāraṇa'?

SYNONYMS

sannyāsī hañā—being a *sannyāsī; kare miṣṭānna bhakṣaṇa*—eats sweetmeats; *ei bhoge*—by this eating; *haya*—there is; *kaiche*—how; *indriya-vāraṇa*—controlling the senses.

TRANSLATION

At last he found a fault. "How can a person in the renounced order eat so many sweetmeats?" he said. "If one eats sweets, controlling the senses is very difficult."

TEXT 45

এই নিন্দা করি' কহে সর্বলোক-স্থানে ।
প্রভুরে দেখিতেহ অবশ্য আইসে প্রতিদিনে ॥ ৪৫ ॥

ei nindā kari' kahe sarva-loka-sthāne
prabhure dekhiteha avaśya āise prati-dine

SYNONYMS

ei nindā—this criticism; *kari'*—making; *kahe*—speaks; *sarva-loka-sthāne*—to everyone; *prabhure*—Śrī Caitanya Mahāprabhu; *dekhiteha*—to see, still; *avaśya*—certainly; *āise*—comes; *prati-dine*—daily.

TRANSLATION

In this way Rāmacandra Purī blasphemed Śrī Caitanya Mahāprabhu before everyone, but nevertheless he would regularly come to see the Lord every day.

TEXT 46

প্রভু গুরুবুদ্ধ্যে করেন সম্ভ্রম, সম্মান।
তেঁহো ছিদ্র চাহি' বুলে,—এই তার কাম ॥ ৪৬ ॥

prabhu guru-buddhye karena sambhrama, sammāna
teṅho chidra cāhi' bule, ——ei tāra kāma

SYNONYMS

prabhu—Śrī Caitanya Mahāprabhu; *guru-buddhye*—accepting him as a Godbrother of His spiritual master; *karena sambhrama sammāna*—offers full respect and obeisances; *teṅho*—Rāmacandra Purī; *chidra cāhi'*—trying to find fault; *bule*—goes about; *ei*—this; *tāra*—his; *kāma*—business.

TRANSLATION

When they met, the Lord would offer him respectful obeisances, considering him a Godbrother of His spiritual master. Rāmacandra Purī's business, however, was to search for faults in the Lord.

TEXT 47

যত নিন্দা করে তাহা প্রভু সব জানে।
তথাপি আদর করে বড়ই সম্ভ্রমে ॥ ৪৭ ॥

yata nindā kare tāhā prabhu saba jāne
tathāpi ādara kare baḍa-i sambhrame

SYNONYMS

yata—whatever; *nindā*—blasphemy; *kare*—does; *tāhā*—that; *prabhu*—Śrī Caitanya Mahāprabhu; *saba*—all; *jāne*—knows; *tathāpi*—still; *ādara kare*—offers respect; *baḍa-i sambhrame*—with great attention.

TRANSLATION

Śrī Caitanya Mahāprabhu knew that Rāmacandra Purī was criticizing Him before everyone, but whenever Rāmacandra Purī came to see Him, the Lord offered him respects with great attention.

TEXT 48

একদিন প্রাতঃকালে আইলা প্রভুর ঘর।
পিপীলিকা দেখি' কিছু কহেন উত্তর ॥ ৪৮ ॥

eka-dina prātaḥ-kāle āilā prabhura ghara
pipīlikā dekhi' kichu kahena uttara

SYNONYMS

eka-dina—one day; *prātaḥ-kāle*—in the morning; *āilā*—came; *prabhura ghara*—to the place of Śrī Caitanya Mahāprabhu; *pipīlikā dekhi'*—seeing many ants; *kichu kahena uttara*—began to say something critical.

TRANSLATION

One day Rāmacandra Purī came in the morning to the abode of Śrī Caitanya Mahāprabhu. Seeing many ants, he said something to criticize the Lord.

TEXT 49

"রাত্রাবত্র ঐক্ষবমাসীঃ, তেন পিপীলিকাঃ সঞ্চরন্তি।
অহো! বিরক্তানাং সন্ন্যাসিনামিয়মিন্দ্রিয়লালসেতি
ব্রুবন্নুত্থায় গতঃ॥" ৪৯ ॥

"rātrāv atra aikṣavam āsīt, tena
pipīlikāḥ sañcaranti aho! viraktānāṁ
sannyāsinām iyam indriya-lālaseti
bruvann utthāya gataḥ."

SYNONYMS

rātrau—at night; *atra*—here; *aikṣavam*—sugar candy; *āsīt*—was; *tena*—by that; *pipīlikāḥ*—ants; *sañcaranti*—wander about; *aho*—alas; *viraktānām*—renounced; *sannyāsinām*—of *sannyāsīs; iyam*—this; *indriya*—to the senses; *lālasa*—attachment; *iti*—thus; *bruvan*—speaking; *utthāya*—getting up; *gataḥ*—left.

TRANSLATION

"Last night there was sugar candy here," he said. "Therefore ants are wandering about. Alas, this renounced sannyāsī is attached to such sense gratification!" After speaking in this way, he got up and left.

TEXT 50

প্রভু পরম্পরায় নিন্দা কৈরাছেন শ্রবণ।
এবে সাক্ষাৎ শুনিলেন 'কল্পিত' নিন্দন॥ ৫০ ॥

prabhu paramparāya nindā kairāchena śravaṇa
ebe sākṣāt śunilena 'kalpita' nindana

SYNONYMS

prabhu—Śrī Caitanya Mahāprabhu; *paramparāya*—by hearsay; *nindā*—blasphemy; *kairāchena śravaṇa*—had heard; *ebe*—now; *sākṣāt*—directly; *śunilena*—He heard; *kalpita*—imaginary; *nindana*—blasphemy.

TRANSLATION

Śrī Caitanya Mahāprabhu had heard rumors about Rāmacandra Purī's blasphemy. Now He directly heard his fanciful accusations.

PURPORT

Rāmacandra Purī could find no faults in the character of Śrī Caitanya Mahāprabhu, for He is situated in a transcendental position as the Supreme Personality of Godhead. Ants are generally found everywhere, but when Rāmacandra Purī saw ants crawling in the abode of the Lord, he took for granted that they must have been there because Caitanya Mahāprabhu had been eating sweetmeats. He thus discovered imaginary faults in the Lord and then left.

TEXT 51

সহজেই পিপীলিকা সর্বত্র বেড়ায়।
তাহাতে তর্ক উঠাঞা দোষ লাগায়॥ ৫১॥

sahajei pipīlikā sarvatra beḍāya
tāhāte tarka uṭhāñā doṣa lāgāya

SYNONYMS

sahajei—generally; *pipīlikā*—ants; *sarvatra*—everywhere; *beḍāya*—loiter; *tāhāte*—by that; *tarka uṭhāñā*—raising a controversy; *doṣa lāgāya*—find faults.

TRANSLATION

Ants generally crawl about here, there and everywhere, but Rāmacandra Purī, looking for imaginary faults, criticized Śrī Caitanya Mahāprabhu by alleging that there had been sweetmeats in His room.

TEXT 52

শুনি' তাহা প্রভুর সঙ্কোচ-ভয় মনে।
গোবিন্দে বোলাঞা কিছু কহেন বচনে॥ ৫২॥

śuni' tāhā prabhura saṅkoca-bhaya mane
govinde bolāñā kichu kahena vacane

SYNONYMS

śuni'—hearing; *tāhā*—that; *prabhura*—of Śrī Caitanya; *saṅkoca*—doubt; *bhaya*—fear; *mane*—in the mind; *govinde bolāñā*—calling for Govinda; *kichu*—some; *kahena*—spoke; *vacane*—words.

TRANSLATION

After hearing this criticism, Śrī Caitanya Mahāprabhu was doubtful and apprehensive. Therefore He called Govinda and instructed him as follows.

TEXT 53

"আজি হৈতে ভিক্ষা আমার এই ত' নিয়ম ।
পিণ্ডাভোগের এক চৌঠি, পাঁচগণ্ডার ব্যঞ্জন ॥ ৫৩ ॥

"āji haite bhikṣā āmāra ei ta' niyama
piṇḍā-bhogera eka cauṭhi, pāṅca-gaṇḍāra vyañjana

SYNONYMS

āji haite—from today; *bhikṣā āmāra*—My accepting *prasāda; ei*—this; *ta'*—certainly; *niyama*—the rule; *piṇḍā-bhogera*—of Lord Jagannātha's *prasāda; eka cauṭhi*—one-fourth of a pot; *pāṅca-gaṇḍāra vyañjana*—vegetables costing five *gaṇḍās* (one *gaṇḍā* equals four *kauḍis*).

TRANSLATION

"From today on it will be a rule that I shall accept only one-fourth of a pot of Lord Jagannātha's prasāda and five gaṇḍās worth of vegetables.

TEXT 54

ইহা বই অধিক আর কিছু না আনিবা ।
অধিক আনিলে আমা এথা না দেখিবা ॥" ৫৪ ॥

ihā ba-i adhika āra kichu nā ānibā
adhika ānile āmā ethā nā dekhibā"

SYNONYMS

ihā ba-i—except for this; *adhika*—more; *āra*—extra; *kichu*—anything; *nā ānibā*—do not bring; *adhika ānile*—if more is brought; *āmā*—Me; *ethā*—here; *nā dekhibā*—you will not see.

TRANSLATION

"If you bring any more than this, you will not see Me here anymore."

TEXT 55

সকল বৈষ্ণবে গোবিন্দ কহে এই বাত্‌।
শুনি' সবার মাথে যৈছে হৈল বজ্রাঘাত ॥ ৫৫ ॥

sakala vaiṣṇave govinda kahe ei vāt
śuni' sabāra māthe yaiche haila vajrāghāta

SYNONYMS

sakala vaiṣṇave—to all the Vaiṣṇavas; *govinda*—Govinda; *kahe*—informs; *ei vāt*—this message; *śuni'*—hearing; *sabāra māthe*—on everyone's head; *yaiche*—as if; *haila*—there was; *vajra-āghāta*—striking of lightning.

TRANSLATION

Govinda relayed this message to all the devotees. When they heard it, they felt as if their heads had been struck by thunderbolts.

TEXT 56

রামচন্দ্রপুরীকে সবায় দেয় তিরস্কার।
'এই পাপিষ্ঠ আসি' প্রাণ লইল সবার' ॥ ৫৬ ॥

rāmacandra-purīke sabāya deya tiraskāra
'ei pāpiṣṭha āsi' prāṇa la-ila sabāra'

SYNONYMS

rāmacandra-purīke—unto Rāmacandra Purī; *sabāya*—all the devotees; *deya tiraskāra*—offer chastisement; *ei pāpiṣṭha*—this sinful man; *āsi'*—coming; *prāṇa*—life; *la-ila*—has taken; *sabāra*—of everyone.

TRANSLATION

All the devotees condemned Rāmacandra Purī, saying, "This sinful man has come here and taken our lives."

TEXTS 57-58

সেইদিন একবিপ্র কৈল নিমন্ত্রণ।
এক-চৌঠি ভাত, পাঁচ-গণ্ডার ব্যঞ্জন ॥ ৫৭ ॥
এইমাত্র গোবিন্দ কৈল অঙ্গীকার।
মাথায় ঘা মারে বিপ্র, করে হাহাকার ॥ ৫৮ ॥

sei-dina eka-vipra kaila nimantraṇa
eka-cauṭhi bhāta, pāṅca-gaṇḍāra vyañjana

ei-mātra govinda kaila aṅgīkāra
māthāya ghā māre vipra, kare hāhākāra

SYNONYMS

sei-dina—that day; *eka-vipra*—one *brāhmaṇa; kaila nimantraṇa*—invited; *eka-cauṭhi bhāta*—one-fourth of a pot of rice; *pāṅca-gaṇḍāra vyañjana*—vegetables worth only five *gaṇḍās; ei-mātra*—only this; *govinda*—the servant of Lord Caitanya Mahāprabhu; *kaila aṅgīkāra*—accepted; *māthāya*—his head; *ghā māre*—struck; *vipra*—the *brāhmaṇa; kare hāhā-kāra*—began to say, "alas, alas."

TRANSLATION

That day, a brāhmaṇa extended an invitation to Śrī Caitanya Mahāprabhu. When Govinda accepted only five gaṇḍās worth of vegetables and a fourth of a pot of rice, the brāhmaṇa, in great despair, struck his head with his hand and cried, "Alas! Alas!"

TEXT 59

সেই ভাত-ব্যঞ্জন প্রভু অর্ধেক খাইল ।
যে কিছু রহিল, তাহা গোবিন্দ পাইল ॥ ৫৯ ॥

sei bhāta-vyañjana prabhu ardheka khāila
ye kichu rahila, tāhā govinda pāila

SYNONYMS

sei—that; *bhāta*—rice; *vyañjana*—vegetable; *prabhu*—Śrī Caitanya Mahāprabhu; *ardheka khāila*—ate half; *ye kichu rahila*—whatever remained; *tāhā*—that; *govinda*—Govinda; *pāila*—got.

TRANSLATION

Śrī Caitanya Mahāprabhu ate only half of the rice and vegetables, and whatever remained was taken by Govinda.

TEXT 60

অর্ধাশন করেন প্রভু, গোবিন্দ অর্ধাশন ।
সব ভক্তগণ তবে ছাড়িল ভোজন ॥ ৬০ ॥

ardhāśana karena prabhu, govinda ardhāśana
saba bhakta-gaṇa tabe chāḍila bhojana

SYNONYMS

ardha-aśana karena—eats half; *prabhu*—Śrī Caitanya Mahāprabhu; *govinda*—Govinda; *ardha-aśana*—eats half; *saba bhakta-gaṇa*—all the devotees; *tabe*—at that time; *chāḍila bhojana*—gave up eating.

TRANSLATION

Thus both Śrī Caitanya Mahāprabhu and Govinda ate only half the food they needed. Because of this, all the other devotees gave up eating.

TEXT 61

গোবিন্দ-কাশীশ্বরে প্রভু কৈলা আজ্ঞাপন ।
'দুঁহে অন্যত্র মাগি' কর উদর ভরণ' ॥ ৬১ ॥

govinda-kāśīśvare prabhu kailā ājñāpana
'duṅhe anyatra māgi' kara udara bharaṇa'

SYNONYMS

govinda-kāśīśvare—unto Govinda and Kāśīśvara; *prabhu*—Śrī Caitanya Mahāprabhu; *kailā*—made; *ājñāpana*—order; *duṅhe*—both of you; *anyatra*—elsewhere; *māgi'*—begging; *kara udara bharaṇa*—fill your bellies.

TRANSLATION

Śrī Caitanya Mahāprabhu ordered Govinda and Kāśīśvara, "You may both take alms elsewhere to fill your bellies."

TEXT 62

এইরূপ মহাদুঃখে দিন কত গেল ।
শুনি' রামচন্দ্রপুরী প্রভু-পাশ আইল ॥ ৬২ ॥

ei-rūpa mahā-duḥkhe dina kata gela
śuni' rāmacandra-purī prabhu-pāśa āila

SYNONYMS

ei-rūpa—in this way; *mahā-duḥkhe*—in great unhappiness; *dina kata*—some days; *gela*—passed; *śuni'*—hearing; *rāmacandra-purī*—Rāmacandra Purī; *prabhu-pāśa āila*—came to Śrī Caitanya Mahāprabhu.

TRANSLATION

In this way, some days passed in great unhappiness. Hearing of all this, Rāmacandra Purī went to Śrī Caitanya Mahāprabhu.

TEXT 63

প্রণাম করি' প্রভু কৈলা চরণ বন্দন ।
প্রভুরে কহয়ে কিছু হাসিয়া বচন ॥ ৬৩ ॥

praṇāma kari' prabhu kailā caraṇa vandana
prabhure kahaye kichu hāsiyā vacana

SYNONYMS

praṇāma kari'—offering obeisances; *prabhu*—Śrī Caitanya Mahāprabhu; *kailā caraṇa vandana*—offered respect at his feet; *prabhure*—to Caitanya Mahāprabhu; *kahaye*—he says; *kichu*—some; *hāsiyā*—smiling; *vacana*—words.

TRANSLATION

Śrī Caitanya Mahāprabhu offered His obeisances to Rāmacandra Purī, worshiping his feet. Then Rāmacandra Purī smiled and spoke to the Lord.

TEXT 64

"সন্ন্যাসীর ধর্ম নহে 'ইন্দ্রিয়-তর্পণ' ।
যৈছে তৈছে করে মাত্র উদর ভরণ ॥ ৬৪ ॥

"sannyāsīra dharma nahe 'indriya-tarpaṇa'
yaiche taiche kare mātra udara bharaṇa

SYNONYMS

sannyāsīra—of a *sannyāsī; dharma*—religious principle; *nahe*—is not; *indriya-tarpaṇa*—to gratify the senses; *yaiche taiche*—some way or other; *kare*—does; *mātra*—only; *udara bharaṇa*—filling the belly.

TRANSLATION

Rāmacandra Purī advised, "It is not the business of a sannyāsī to gratify his senses. He should fill his belly some way or other.

TEXT 65

তোমারে ক্ষীণ দেখি, শুনি,—কর অর্ধাশন ।
এই 'শুষ্ক-বৈরাগ্য' নহে সন্ন্যাসীর 'ধর্ম' ॥ ৬৫ ॥

tomāre kṣīṇa dekhi, śuni, ——kara ardhāśana
ei 'śuṣka-vairāgya' nahe sannyāsīra 'dharma'

SYNONYMS

tomāre—You; *kṣīṇa*—skinny; *dekhi*—I see; *śuni*—I have heard; *kara ardha-aśana*—You are eating half; *ei*—this; *śuṣka-vairāgya*—dry renunciation; *nahe*—is not; *sannyāsīra dharma*—the religion of a *sannyāsī.*

TRANSLATION

"I have heard that You have cut Your eating in half. Indeed, I see that You are skinny. Such dry renunciation is also not the religion of a sannyāsī.

TEXT 66

যথাযোগ্য উদর ভরে, না করে 'বিষয়' ভোগ ।
সন্ন্যাসীর তবে সিদ্ধ হয় জ্ঞানযোগ ॥ ৬৬ ॥

yathā-yogya udara bhare, nā kare 'viṣaya' bhoga
sannyāsīra tabe siddha haya jñāna-yoga

SYNONYMS

yathā-yogya—as much as necessary; *udara bhare*—fills the belly; *nā kare*—does not do; *viṣaya bhoga*—material enjoyment; *sannyāsīra*—of a *sannyāsī; tabe*—then; *siddha*—perfect; *haya*—is; *jñāna-yoga*—spiritual advancement in knowledge.

TRANSLATION

"A sannyāsī eats as much as necessary to maintain his body, but he does not enjoy satisfying his senses materially. Thus a sannyāsī becomes perfect in his spiritual advancement in knowledge.

TEXTS 67-68

নাত্যশ্নতোঽপি যোগোঽস্তি ন চৈকান্তমনশ্নতঃ ।
ন চাতিস্বপ্নশীলস্য জাগ্রতো নৈব চার্জুন ॥ ৬৭ ॥
যুক্তাহারবিহারস্য যুক্তচেষ্টস্য কর্মসু ।
যুক্তস্বপ্নাববোধস্য যোগো ভবতি দুঃখহা ॥" ৬৮ ॥

nātyaśnato 'pi yogo 'sti
na caikāntam anaśnataḥ

na cātisvapna-śīlasya
jāgrato naiva cārjuna

yuktāhāra-vihārasya
yukta-ceṣṭasya karmasu
yukta-svapnāvabodhasya
yogo bhavati duḥkhahā"

SYNONYMS

na—not; *ati-aśnataḥ*—of one who eats too much; *api*—certainly; *yogaḥ*—linking with the Supreme; *asti*—there is; *na*—not; *ca*—also; *ekāntam*—solely; *anaśnataḥ*—of one who abstains from eating; *na*—not; *ca*—also; *ati-svapna-śīlasya*—of one who dreams too much in sleep; *jāgrataḥ*—of one who keeps awake; *na*—not; *eva*—certainly; *ca*—also; *arjuna*—O Arjuna; *yukta*—as much as necessary; *āhāra*—eating; *vihārasya*—of one whose sense enjoyment; *yukta*—proper; *ceṣṭasya*—of one whose endeavor; *karmasu*—in executing duties; *yukta*—as much as necessary; *svapna*—dreaming while asleep; *avabodhasya*—of one whose keeping awake; *yogaḥ*—practice of *yoga; bhavati*—is; *duḥkha-hā*—diminishing sufferings.

TRANSLATION

" 'My dear Arjuna, one cannot perform mystic yoga if he eats more than necessary or needlessly fasts, sleeps and dreams too much or does not sleep enough. One should eat and enjoy his senses as much as necessary, one should properly endeavor to execute his duties, and one should regulate his sleep and wakefulness. Thus one can become freed from material pains by executing mystic yoga.' "

PURPORT

This is a quotation from *Bhagavad-gītā* (6.16-17).

TEXT 69

প্রভু কহে,—"অজ্ঞ বালক মুই 'শিষ্য' তোমার ।
মোরে শিক্ষা দেহ',—এই ভাগ্য আমার ॥" ৬৯ ॥

prabhu kahe, —"ajña bālaka mui 'śiṣya' tomāra
more śikṣā deha', —ei bhāgya āmāra"

SYNONYMS

prabhu kahe—Śrī Caitanya Mahāprabhu said; *ajña*—ignorant; *bālaka*—boy; *mui*—I; *śiṣya tomāra*—your disciple; *more*—Me; *śikṣā deha'*—you are instructing; *ei*—this; *bhāgya āmāra*—My great fortune.

TRANSLATION

Śrī Caitanya Mahāprabhu then humbly submitted, "I am just like an ignorant boy and am like your disciple. It is My great fortune that you are instructing Me."

TEXT 70

এত শুনি' রামচন্দ্রপুরী উঠি' গেলা।
ভক্তগণ অর্ধাশন করে,—পুরী গোসাঞি শুনিলা ॥

eta śuni' rāmacandra-purī uṭhi' gelā
bhakta-gaṇa ardhāśana kare, ——purī gosāñi śunilā

SYNONYMS

eta śuni'—hearing this; *rāmacandra-purī*—Rāmacandra Purī; *uṭhi' gelā*—got up and left; *bhakta-gaṇa*—the devotees; *ardha-aśana kare*—were taking half the quantity of food; *purī gosāñi*—Rāmacandra Purī; *śunilā*—heard.

TRANSLATION

Hearing this, Rāmacandra Purī got up and left. He also heard from various sources that all the devotees of Śrī Caitanya Mahāprabhu were eating half as much as usual.

TEXT 71

আর দিন ভক্তগণ-সহ পরমানন্দপুরী।
প্রভু-পাশে নিবেদিলা দৈন্য-বিনয় করি' ॥ ৭১ ॥

āra dina bhakta-gaṇa-saha paramānanda-purī
prabhu-pāśe nivedilā dainya-vinaya kari'

SYNONYMS

āra dina—the next day; *bhakta-gaṇa-saha*—with the other devotees; *paramānanda-purī*—Paramānanda Purī; *prabhu-pāśe*—before Śrī Caitanya Mahāprabhu; *nivedilā*—submitted; *dainya-vinaya kari'*—in great humility and submission.

TRANSLATION

The next day, Paramānanda Purī and other devotees approached Śrī Caitanya Mahāprabhu with great humility and submission.

TEXT 72

"রামচন্দ্রপুরী হয় নিন্দুক-স্বভাব।
তার বোলে অন্ন ছাড়ি' কিবা হবে লাভ? ৭২॥

"rāmacandra-purī haya ninduka-svabhāva
tāra bole anna chāḍi' kibā habe lābha?

SYNONYMS

rāmacandra-purī—Rāmacandra Purī; *haya*—is; *ninduka-svabhāva*—a critic by nature; *tāra bole*—by his words; *anna chāḍi'*—giving up eating properly; *kibā*—what; *habe*—will be; *lābha*—profit.

TRANSLATION

Paramānanda Purī said, "My Godbrother Rāmacandra Purī is by nature a bad critic. If You give up eating because of his words, what will be the profit?

TEXT 73

পুরীর স্বভাব,—যথেষ্ট আহার করাঞা।
যে না খায়, তারে খাওয়ায় যতন করিয়া॥ ৭৩॥

purīra svabhāva, ——yatheṣṭa āhāra karāñā
ye nā khāya, tāre khāoyāya yatana kariyā

SYNONYMS

purīra svabhāva—Rāmacandra Purī's character; *yathā-iṣṭa*—as much as desired; *āhāra karāñā*—getting someone to eat; *ye*—what; *nā khāya*—one does not eat; *tāre khāoyāya*—causes him to eat; *yatana kariyā*—with great attention.

TRANSLATION

"It is the nature of Rāmacandra Purī that first he lets one eat as much as desired, and if one does not eat more than necessary, with great attention he makes him eat more.

TEXT 74

খাওয়াঞা পুনঃ তারে করয়ে নিন্দন।
'এত অন্ন খাও,—তোমার কত আছে ধন? ৭৪॥

khāoyāñā punaḥ tāre karaye nindana
'eta anna khāo, ——tomāra kata āche dhana?

SYNONYMS

khāoyāñā—after feeding; *punaḥ*—again; *tāre*—him; *karaye nindana*—criticizes; *eta*—so much; *anna*—food; *khāo*—you eat; *tomāra*—your; *kata*—how much; *āche*—is there; *dhana*—wealth.

TRANSLATION

"In this way he induces one to eat more than necessary, and then he directly criticizes him, saying, 'You eat so much. How much money do you have in your treasury?

TEXT 75

সন্ন্যাসীকে এত খাওয়াঞা কর ধর্ম নাশ !
অতএব জানিনু,—তোমার কিছু নাহি ভাস' ॥ ৭৫ ॥

sannyāsīke eta khāoyāñā kara dharma nāśa!
ataeva jāninu, ——tomāra kichu nāhi bhāsa'

SYNONYMS

sannyāsīke—*sannyāsīs;* *eta*—so much; *khāoyāñā*—inducing to eat; *kara dharma nāśa*—you spoil their religious principles; *ataeva*—therefore; *jāninu*—I can understand; *tomāra*—your; *kichu nāhi bhāsa*—there is no advancement.

TRANSLATION

" 'Also, by inducing sannyāsīs to eat so much, you spoil their religious principles. Therefore I can understand that you have no advancement.'

TEXT 76

কে কৈছে ব্যবহারে, কেবা কৈছে খায় ।
এই অনুসন্ধান তেঁহো করয় সদায় ॥ ৭৬ ॥

ke kaiche vyavahāre, kebā kaiche khāya
ei anusandhāna teṅho karaya sadāya

SYNONYMS

ke—who; *kaiche*—how; *vyavahāre*—behaves; *kebā*—who; *kaiche*—how; *khāya*—eats; *ei anusandhāna*—this inquiry; *teṅho*—he; *karaya*—does; *sadāya*—always.

TRANSLATION

"It is Rāmacandra Purī's business to inquire always about how others are eating and conducting their daily affairs.

TEXT 77

শাস্ত্রে যেই দুই ধর্ম কৈরাছে বর্জন ।
সেই কর্ম নিরন্তর ইঁহার করণ ॥ ৭৭ ॥

śāstre yei dui dharma kairāche varjana
sei karma nirantara iṅhāra karaṇa

SYNONYMS

śāstre—in the revealed scriptures; *yei*—which; *dui*—two; *dharma*—activities; *kairāche varjana*—are rejected; *sei*—those; *karma*—activities; *nirantara*—always; *iṅhāra*—his; *karaṇa*—action.

TRANSLATION

"The two kinds of activity rejected in the revealed scriptures constitute his daily affairs.

TEXT 78

পরস্বভাবকর্মাণি ন প্রশংসেন্ন গর্হয়েৎ ।
বিশ্বমেকাত্মকং পশ্যন্ প্রকৃত্যা পুরুষেণ চ ॥ ৭৮ ॥

para-svabhāva-karmāṇi
na praśaṁsen na garhayet
viśvam ekātmakaṁ paśyan
prakṛtyā puruṣeṇa ca

SYNONYMS

para-svabhāva-karmāṇi—the characteristics or activities of others; *na*—not; *praśaṁset*—one should praise; *na*—not; *garhayet*—should criticize; *viśvam*—the universe; *eka-ātmakam*—as one; *paśyan*—seeing; *prakṛtyā*—by nature; *puruṣeṇa*—by the living entity; *ca*—and.

TRANSLATION

" 'One should see that because of the meeting of material nature and the living entity, the universe is acting uniformly. Thus one should neither praise nor criticize the characteristics or activities of others.'

PURPORT

This verse from *Śrīmad-Bhāgavatam* (11.28.1) was spoken by Lord Kṛṣṇa to Uddhava.

TEXT 79

তার মধ্যে পূর্ববিধি 'প্রশংসা' ছাড়িয়া।
পরবিধি 'নিন্দা' করে 'বলিষ্ঠ' জানিয়া ॥ ৭৯ ॥

tāra madhye pūrva-vidhi 'praśaṁsā' chāḍiyā
para-vidhi 'nindā' kare 'baliṣṭha' jāniyā

SYNONYMS

tāra madhye—between the two; *pūrva-vidhi*—the former rule; *praśaṁsā*—praising; *chāḍiyā*—giving up; *para-vidhi*—the other rule; *nindā*—criticizing; *kare*—does; *baliṣṭha jāniyā*—knowing it to be more prominent.

TRANSLATION

"Of the two rules, Rāmacandra Purī obeys the first by abandoning praise, but although he knows that the second is more prominent, he neglects it by criticizing others.

PURPORT

The above-mentioned verse from *Śrīmad-Bhāgavatam* gives two injunctions. The first, called *pūrva-vidhi,* is that one should not praise, and the second, *para-vidhi,* is that one should not criticize. As will be apparent from the following verse, the injunction against praise is less important than the injunction against blasphemy. One should carefully observe the *para-vidhi,* although one may neglect the *pūrva-vidhi.* Thus the actual injunction is that one may praise but should not criticize. This is called *śleṣokti,* or a statement having two meanings. Rāmacandra Purī, however, acted in just the opposite way, for he neglected the *para-vidhi* but strictly observed the *pūrva-vidhi.* Since he avoided following the principle of not criticizing, Rāmacandra Purī broke both the rules.

TEXT 80

পূর্বপরয়োর্মধ্যে পরবিধির্বলবান্ ॥ ৮০ ॥

pūrva-parayor madhye para-vidhir balavān

SYNONYMS

pūrva-parayoḥ—the former and the latter; *madhye*—between; *para-vidhiḥ*—the latter rule; *balavān*—more prominent.

TRANSLATION

" 'Between the former rule and the latter rule, the latter is more important.'

PURPORT

This is a verse from the *nyāya* literatures.

TEXT 81

যাহাঁ গুণ শত আছে, তাহা না করে গ্রহণ।
গুণমধ্যে ছলে করে দোষ-আরোপণ ॥ ৮১ ॥

yāhāṅ guṇa śata āche, tāhā nā kare grahaṇa
guṇa-madhye chale kare doṣa-āropaṇa

SYNONYMS

yāhāṅ—where; *guṇa*—good attributes; *śata*—hundreds; *āche*—there are; *tāhā*—them; *nā kare grahaṇa*—he does not accept; *guṇa-madhye*—in such good attributes; *chale*—by tricks; *kare*—does; *doṣa-āropaṇa*—attributing faults.

TRANSLATION

"Even where there are hundreds of good qualities, a critic does not consider them. Rather, he attempts by some trick to point out a fault in those attributes.

TEXT 82

ইঁহার স্বভাব ইহাঁ করিতে না যুয়ায়।
তথাপি কহিয়ে কিছু মর্ম-দুঃখ পায় ॥ ৮২ ॥

iṅhāra svabhāva ihāṅ karite nā yuyāya
tathāpi kahiye kichu marma-duḥkha pāya

SYNONYMS

iṅhāra sva-bhāva—his characteristics; *ihāṅ*—here; *karite nā yuyāya*—one should not follow; *tathāpi*—still; *kahiye*—I say; *kichu*—something; *marma-duḥkha*—unhappiness within the heart; *pāya*—get.

TRANSLATION

"One should not, therefore, follow the principles of Rāmacandra Purī. Nevertheless, I have to say something against him because he is making our hearts unhappy.

TEXT 83

ইঁহার বচনে কেনে অন্ন ত্যাগ কর ?
পূর্ববৎ নিমন্ত্রণ মান',—সবার বোল ধর ॥" ৮৩ ॥

iṅhāra vacane kene anna tyāga kara?
pūrvavat nimantraṇa māna', —sabāra bola dhara"

SYNONYMS

iṅhāra vacane—by his words; *kene*—why; *anna*—food; *tyāga kara*—You give up; *pūrva-vat*—as before; *nimantraṇa māna'*—please accept the invitation; *sabāra*—of everyone; *bola*—the words; *dhara*—accept.

TRANSLATION

"Why have you given up proper eating due to the criticism of Rāmacandra Purī? Please accept invitations as before. This is the request of us all."

TEXT 84

প্রভু কহে,—"সবে কেনে পুরীরে কর রোষ ?
'সহজ' ধর্ম কহে তেঁহো, তাঁর কিবা দোষ ? ৮৪ ॥

prabhu kahe, —"sabe kene purīre kara roṣa?
'sahaja' dharma kahe teṅho, tāṅra kibā doṣa?

SYNONYMS

prabhu kahe—Śrī Caitanya Mahāprabhu replied; *sabe*—all of you; *kene*—why; *purīre*—at Rāmacandra Purī; *kara roṣa*—are angry; *sahaja*—natural; *dharma*—religious principles; *kahe*—speaks; *teṅho*—he; *tāṅra*—of him; *kibā*—what; *doṣa*—fault.

TRANSLATION

Śrī Caitanya Mahāprabhu replied, "Why are all of you angry at Rāmacandra Purī? He is expounding the natural principles of sannyāsa life. Why are you accusing him?

TEXT 85

যতি হঞা জিহ্বা-লাম্পট্য,—অত্যন্ত অন্যায় ।
যতির ধর্ম,—প্রাণ রাখিতে আহারমাত্র খায় ॥" ৮৫ ॥

yati hañā jihvā-lāmpaṭya——atyanta anyāya
yatira dharma, ——prāṇa rākhite āhāra-mātra khāya"

SYNONYMS

yati hañā—being a *sannyāsī; jihvā-lāmpaṭya*—indulging in satisfying the tongue; *atyanta anyāya*—grievous offense; *yatira dharma*—the religious principle of a *sannyāsī; prāṇa rākhite*—to maintain life; *āhāra*—food; *mātra*—only; *khāya*—eats.

TRANSLATION

"For a sannyāsī to indulge in satisfying the tongue is a great offense. The duty of a sannyāsī is to eat only as much as needed to keep body and soul together."

TEXT 86

তবে সবে মেলি' প্রভুরে বহু যত্ন কৈলা ।
সবার আগ্রহে প্রভু অর্দ্ধেক রাখিলা ॥ ৮৬ ॥

tabe sabe meli' prabhure bahu yatna kailā
sabāra āgrahe prabhu ardheka rākhilā

SYNONYMS

tabe—thereafter; *sabe meli'*—when all the devotees came together; *prabhure*—unto Śrī Caitanya Mahāprabhu; *bahu yatna kailā*—requested fervently; *sabāra āgrahe*—due to the eagerness of all of them; *prabhu*—Śrī Caitanya Mahāprabhu; *ardheḳa rākhilā*—accepted half.

TRANSLATION

When they all requested very fervently that Śrī Caitanya Mahāprabhu take a full meal, He still would not do so. Instead, He responded to their request by accepting half as much as usual.

TEXT 87

দুইপণ কৌড়ি লাগে প্রভুর নিমন্ত্রণে ।
কভু দুইজন ভোক্তা, কভু তিনজনে ॥ ৮৭ ॥

dui-paṇa kauḍi lāge prabhura nimantraṇe
kabhu dui-jana bhoktā, kabhu tina-jane

SYNONYMS

dui-paṇa kauḍi—two *paṇas* of *kauḍis* (160 small conchshells); *lāge*—costs; *prabhura nimantraṇe*—to invite Śrī Caitanya Mahāprabhu; *kabhu*—sometimes; *dui-jana*—two men; *bhoktā*—eating; *kabhu*—sometimes; *tina-jane*—three men.

TRANSLATION

The cost for the food needed to invite Śrī Caitanya Mahāprabhu was fixed at two paṇas of kauḍis [160 conchshells], and that food would be taken by two men and sometimes three.

TEXT 88

অভোজ্যান্ন বিপ্র যদি করেন নিমন্ত্রণ ।
প্রসাদ-মূল্য লইতে লাগে কৌড়ি দুইপণ ॥ ৮৮ ॥

abhojyānna vipra yadi karena nimantraṇa
prasāda-mūlya la-ite lāge kauḍi dui-paṇa

SYNONYMS

abhojya-anna vipra—a *brāhmaṇa* at whose place an invitation cannot be accepted; *yadi*—if; *karena nimantraṇa*—he invites; *prasāda-mūlya*—the price of the *prasāda; la-ite*—to bear; *lāge*—costs; *kauḍi dui-paṇa*—two *paṇas* of *kauḍis.*

TRANSLATION

When a brāhmaṇa at whose home an invitation could not be accepted invited the Lord, he would pay two paṇas of conchshells to purchase the prasāda.

TEXT 89

ভোজ্যান্ন বিপ্র যদি নিমন্ত্রণ করে ।
কিছু 'প্রসাদ' আনে, কিছু পাক করে ঘরে ॥ ৮৯ ॥

bhojyānna vipra yadi nimantraṇa kare
kichu 'prasāda' āne, kichu pāka kare ghare

SYNONYMS

bhojya-anna vipra—a *brāhmaṇa* at whose place an invitation could be accepted; *yadi*—if; *nimantraṇa kare*—invites; *kichu*—some; *prasāda*—*prasāda; āne*—brings; *kichu*—some; *pāka kare*—cooks; *ghare*—at home.

TRANSLATION

When a brāhmaṇa at whose home an invitation could be accepted invited Him, the brāhmaṇa would purchase part of the prasāda and cook the rest at home.

TEXTS 90-91

পণ্ডিত-গোসাঞি, ভগবান্‌-আচার্য, সার্বভৌম।
নিমন্ত্রণের দিনে যদি করে নিমন্ত্রণ ॥ ৯০ ॥
তাঁ-সবার ইচ্ছায় প্রভু করেন ভোজন।
তাহাঁ প্রভুর স্বাতন্ত্র্য নাই, যৈছে তাঁর মন ॥ ৯১ ॥

paṇḍita-gosāñi, bhagavān-ācārya, sārvabhauma
nimantraṇera dine yadi kare nimantraṇa

tāṅ-sabāra icchāya prabhu karena bhojana
tāhāṅ prabhura svātantrya nāi, yaiche tāṅra mana

SYNONYMS

paṇḍita-gosāñi—Gadādhara Paṇḍita; *bhagavān-ācārya*—Bhagavān Ācārya; *sārvabhauma*—Sārvabhauma Bhaṭṭācārya; *nimantraṇera dine*—on the day on which Lord Caitanya was invited by others; *yadi*—if; *kare nimantraṇa*—they would invite; *tāṅ-sabāra*—of all of them; *icchāya*—by the desire; *prabhu*—Śrī Caitanya Mahāprabhu; *karena bhojana*—would accept His meal; *tāhāṅ*—in that case; *prabhura*—of Lord Caitanya; *svātantrya nāi*—there was no independence; *yaiche*—as; *tāṅra*—of them; *mana*—the mind.

TRANSLATION

Even on a day when Śrī Caitanya Mahāprabhu was invited to dine by others, if Gadādhara Paṇḍita, Bhagavān Ācārya or Sārvabhauma Bhaṭṭācārya invited Him, Śrī Caitanya Mahāprabhu had no independence. He would accept their invitations as they desired.

TEXT 92

ভক্তগণে সুখ দিতে প্রভুর 'অবতার'।
যাহাঁ যৈছে যোগ্য, তাহাঁ করেন ব্যবহার ॥ ৯২ ॥

bhakta-gaṇe sukha dite prabhura 'avatāra'
yāhāṅ yaiche yogya, tāhāṅ karena vyavahāra

SYNONYMS

bhakta-gaṇe—to His devotees; *sukha dite*—to give happiness; *prabhura*—of Śrī Caitanya Mahāprabhu; *avatāra*—incarnation; *yāhāṅ yaiche yogya*—whatever was fitting according to the time and circumstances; *tāhāṅ karena vyavahāra*—He behaved in that way.

TRANSLATION

Śrī Caitanya Mahāprabhu actually descended to give happiness to the devotees. Thus He behaved in whatever way fit the time and circumstances.

TEXT 93

কভু লৌকিক রীতি,—যেন 'ইতর' জন ।
কভু স্বতন্ত্র, করেন 'ঐশ্বর্য' প্রকটন ॥ ৯৩ ॥

kabhu laukika rīti, —yena 'itara' jana
kabhu svatantra, karena 'aiśvarya' prakaṭana

SYNONYMS

kabhu—sometimes; *laukika rīti*—common behavior; *yena*—as; *itara jana*—a common man; *kabhu*—sometimes; *svatantra*—fully independent; *karena*—does; *aiśvarya prakaṭana*—manifestation of godly opulence.

TRANSLATION

Because of His full independence, Śrī Caitanya Mahāprabhu sometimes behaved like a common man and sometimes manifested His godly opulence.

TEXT 94

কভু রামচন্দ্রপুরীর হয় ভৃত্যপ্রায় ।
কভু তারে নাহি মানে, দেখে তৃণ-প্রায় ॥ ৯৪ ॥

kabhu rāmacandra-purīra haya bhṛtya-prāya
kabhu tāre nāhi māne, dekhe tṛṇa-prāya

SYNONYMS

kabhu—sometimes; *rāmacandra-purīra*—of Rāmacandra Purī; *haya*—was; *bhṛtya-prāya*—exactly like a servant; *kabhu*—sometimes; *tāre*—for him; *nāhi māne*—He did not care; *dekhe*—sees; *tṛṇa-prāya*—just like a straw.

TRANSLATION

Śrī Caitanya Mahāprabhu sometimes accepted Rāmacandra Purī as His master and considered Himself a servant, and sometimes the Lord, not caring for him, would see him as being just like a straw.

TEXT 95

ঈশ্বর-চরিত্র প্রভুর— বুদ্ধির অগোচর।
যবে যেই করেন, সেই সব—মনোহর ॥ ৯৫ ॥

īśvara-caritra prabhura——buddhira agocara
yabe yei karena, sei saba——manohara

SYNONYMS

īśvara-caritra—character exactly like that of the Supreme Personality of Godhead; *prabhura*—of Śrī Caitanya Mahāprabhu; *buddhira agocara*—beyond one's intelligence; *yabe*—when; *yei*—whatever; *karena*—He did; *sei*—that; *saba*—all; *manohara*—very beautiful.

TRANSLATION

Śrī Caitanya Mahāprabhu behaved exactly like the Supreme Personality of Godhead, beyond the restriction of anyone's intelligence. Whatever He liked He did, but all His activities were very beautiful.

TEXT 96

এইমত রামচন্দ্রপুরী নীলাচলে।
দিন কত রহি' গেলা 'তীর্থ' করিবারে ॥ ৯৬ ॥

ei-mata rāmacandra-purī nīlācale
dina kata rahi' gelā 'tīrtha' karibāre

SYNONYMS

ei-mata—in this way; *rāmacandra-purī*—Rāmacandra Purī; *nīlācale*—at Jagannātha Purī; *dina kata*—for some days; *rahi'*—staying; *gelā*—left; *tīrtha karibāre*—to visit holy places.

TRANSLATION

Thus Rāmacandra Purī stayed for some days at Nīlācala [Jagannātha Purī]. Then he left to visit various holy places of pilgrimage.

TEXT 97

তেঁহো গেলে প্রভুর গণ হৈল হরষিত।
শিরের পাথর যেন পড়িল আচম্বিত ॥ ৯৭ ॥

teṅho gele prabhura gaṇa haila haraṣita
śirera pāthara yena paḍila ācambita

SYNONYMS

teṅho gele—when he left; *prabhura gaṇa*—the associates of Śrī Caitanya Mahāprabhu; *haila haraṣita*—became very, very happy; *śirera*—on the head; *pāthara*—a stone; *yena*—as if; *paḍila*—fell down; *ācambita*—suddenly.

TRANSLATION

The devotees considered Rāmacandra Purī to be like a great burden on their heads. When he left Jagannātha Purī, everyone felt extremely happy, as if a great stone burden had suddenly fallen from their heads to the ground.

TEXT 98

স্বচ্ছন্দে নিমন্ত্রণ, প্রভুর কীর্তন-নর্তন।
স্বচ্ছন্দে করেন সবে প্রসাদ ভোজন ॥ ৯৮ ॥

svacchande nimantraṇa, prabhura kīrtana-nartana
svacchande karena sabe prasāda bhojana

SYNONYMS

svacchande—freely; *nimantraṇa*—invitation; *prabhura*—of Śrī Caitanya Mahāprabhu; *kīrtana-nartana*—chanting and dancing; *svacchande*—in full independence; *karena sabe*—everyone did; *prasāda bhojana*—accepting *prasāda.*

TRANSLATION

After his departure, everything was happy once again. Śrī Caitanya Mahāprabhu accepted invitations as usual and led congregational chanting and dancing. Everyone else also accepted prasāda without hindrances.

TEXT 99

গুরু উপেক্ষা কৈলে, ঐছে ফল হয়।
ক্রমে ঈশ্বরপর্যন্ত অপরাধে ঠেকয় ॥ ৯৯ ॥

guru upekṣā kaile, aiche phala haya
krame īśvara-paryanta aparādhe ṭhekaya

SYNONYMS

guru upekṣā kaile—if one's spiritual master rejects him; *aiche*—such; *phala*—result; *haya*—there is; *krame*—gradually; *īśvara-paryanta*—up to the point of the Personality of Godhead; *aparādhe ṭhekaya*—commits offenses.

TRANSLATION

If one's spiritual master rejects him, one becomes so fallen that he, like Rāmacandra Purī, commits offenses even to the Supreme Personality of Godhead.

TEXT 100

যদ্যপি গুরুবুদ্ধ্যে প্রভু তার দোষ না লইল ।
তার ফলদ্বারা লোকে শিক্ষা করাইল ॥ ১০০ ॥

yadyapi guru-buddhye prabhu tāra doṣa nā la-ila
tāra phala-dvārā loke śikṣā karāila

SYNONYMS

yadyapi—although; *guru-buddhye*—due to considering him a spiritual master; *prabhu*—Śrī Caitanya Mahāprabhu; *tāra*—his; *doṣa*—offense; *nā la-ila*—did not accept; *tāra*—his; *phala*—result; *dvārā*—by; *loke*—the general populace; *śikṣā karāila*—He instructed.

TRANSLATION

Śrī Caitanya Mahāprabhu did not consider the offenses of Rāmacandra Purī, for the Lord considered him His spiritual master. However, his character instructed everyone about the result of offending the spiritual master.

TEXT 101

চৈতন্যচরিত্র—যেন অমৃতের পূর ।
শুনিতে শ্রবণে মনে লাগয়ে মধুর ॥ ১০১ ॥

caitanya-caritra——yena amṛtera pūra
śunite śravaṇe mane lāgaye madhura

SYNONYMS

caitanya-caritra—the character of Śrī Caitanya Mahāprabhu; *yena*—as if; *amṛtera pūra*—filled with nectar; *śunite*—hearing; *śravaṇe*—to the ear; *mane*—to the mind; *lāgaye*—feels; *madhura*—pleasing.

TRANSLATION

The character of Śrī Caitanya Mahāprabhu is full of nectar. Hearing about it is pleasing to the ear and mind.

TEXT 102

চৈতন্যচরিত্র লিখি, শুন একমনে ।
অনায়াসে পাবে প্রেম শ্রীকৃষ্ণচরণে ॥ ১০২ ॥

caitanya-caritra likhi, śuna eka-mane
anāyāse pābe prema śrī-kṛṣṇa-caraṇe

SYNONYMS

caitanya-caritra—the character of Śrī Caitanya Mahāprabhu; *likhi*—I write; *śuna*—please hear; *eka-mane*—with attention; *anāyāse*—easily; *pābe*—you will get; *prema*—ecstatic love; *śrī-kṛṣṇa-caraṇe*—at the lotus feet of Lord Śrī Kṛṣṇa.

TRANSLATION

I write about the character of Śrī Caitanya Mahāprabhu. O readers, please hear with attention, for thus you will easily receive ecstatic love for the lotus feet of Lord Śrī Kṛṣṇa.

TEXT 103

শ্রীরূপ-রঘুনাথ-পদে যার আশ ।
চৈতন্যচরিতামৃত কহে কৃষ্ণদাস ॥ ১০৩ ॥

śrī-rūpa-raghunātha-pade yāra āśa
caitanya-caritāmṛta kahe kṛṣṇadāsa

SYNONYMS

śrī-rūpa—Śrīla Rūpa Gosvāmī; *raghunātha*—Śrīla Raghunātha dāsa Gosvāmī; *pade*—at the lotus feet; *yāra*—whose; *āśa*—expectation; *caitanya-caritāmṛta*—the book named *Caitanya-caritāmṛta; kahe*—describes; *kṛṣṇadāsa*—Śrīla Kṛṣṇadāsa Kavirāja Gosvāmī.

TRANSLATION

Praying at the lotus feet of Śrī Rūpa and Śrī Raghunātha, always desiring their mercy, I, Kṛṣṇadāsa, narrate Śrī Caitanya-caritāmṛta, following in their footsteps.

Thus end the Bhaktivedanta purports to the Śrī Caitanya-caritāmṛta, Antya-līlā, *Eighth Chapter, describing how the Lord reduced His eating in fear of the criticism of Rāmacandra Purī.*

CHAPTER 9

The Deliverance of Gopīnātha Paṭṭanāyaka

This Ninth Chapter is summarized as follows. Gopīnātha Paṭṭanāyaka, the son of Bhavānanda Rāya, was engaged in the service of the government, but he misappropriated some funds from the treasury. Therefore the *baḍa-jānā,* the eldest son of King Pratāparudra, ordered that he be punished by death. Thus Gopīnātha Paṭṭanāyaka was raised on the *cāṅga* to be killed, but by the mercy of Śrī Caitanya Mahāprabhu he was delivered. Moreover, he was even promoted to a higher post.

TEXT 1

অগণ্যধন্যচৈতন্যগণানাং প্রেমবন্যয়া।
নিন্যেঽধন্যজনস্বান্তমরুঃ শশ্বদনূপতাম্॥ ১ ॥

agaṇya-dhanya-caitanya-
gaṇānāṁ prema-vanyayā
ninye 'dhanya-jana-svānta-
maruḥ śaśvad anūpatām

SYNONYMS

agaṇya—innumerable; *dhanya*—glorious; *caitanya-gaṇānām*—of the associates of Śrī Caitanya Mahāprabhu; *prema-vanyayā*—by the inundation of ecstatic love; *ninye*—was brought; *adhanya-jana*—of unfortunate persons; *svānta-maruḥ*—the desert of the heart; *śaśvat*—always; *anūpatām*—to the state of being filled with water.

TRANSLATION

The innumerable, glorious followers of Śrī Caitanya Mahāprabhu brought a constant flood to the desertlike hearts of the unfortunate with an inundation of ecstatic love.

TEXT 2

জয় জয় শ্রীকৃষ্ণচৈতন্য দয়াময়।
জয় জয় নিত্যানন্দ করুণ-হৃদয়॥ ২ ॥

jaya jaya śrī-kṛṣṇa-caitanya dayāmaya
jaya jaya nityānanda karuṇa-hṛdaya

SYNONYMS

jaya jaya—all glories; *śrī-kṛṣṇa-caitanya*—to Śrī Caitanya Mahāprabhu; *dayā-maya*—merciful; *jaya jaya*—all glories; *nityānanda*—to Lord Nityānanda; *karuṇa-hṛdaya*—whose heart is very compassionate.

TRANSLATION

All glories to Śrī Kṛṣṇa Caitanya Mahāprabhu, the most merciful incarnation! All glories to Lord Nityānanda, whose heart is always compassionate!

TEXT 3

জয়াদ্বৈতাচার্য জয় জয় দয়াময় ।
জয় গৌরভক্তগণ সব রসময় ॥ ৩ ॥

jayādvaitācārya jaya jaya dayāmaya
jaya gaura-bhakta-gaṇa saba rasamaya

SYNONYMS

jaya—all glories; *advaita-ācārya*—to Advaita Ācārya; *jaya jaya*—all glories; *dayā-maya*—merciful; *jaya*—all glories; *gaura-bhakta-gaṇa*—to the devotees of Śrī Caitanya Mahāprabhu; *saba*—all; *rasa-maya*—overwhelmed by transcendental bliss.

TRANSLATION

All glories to Advaita Ācārya, who is very merciful! All glories to the devotees of Śrī Caitanya Mahāprabhu, who are always overwhelmed by transcendental bliss!

TEXT 4

এইমত মহাপ্রভু ভক্তগণ-সঙ্গে ।
নীলাচলে বাস করেন কৃষ্ণপ্রেমরঙ্গে ॥ ৪ ॥

ei-mata mahāprabhu bhakta-gaṇa-saṅge
nīlācale vāsa karena kṛṣṇa-prema-raṅge

SYNONYMS

ei-mata—in this way; *mahāprabhu*—Śrī Caitanya Mahāprabhu; *bhakta-gaṇa-saṅge*—along with His devotees; *nīlācale*—at Jagannātha Purī; *vāsa karena*—resides; *kṛṣṇa-prema-raṅge*—overwhelmed by the ecstatic love of Lord Kṛṣṇa.

TRANSLATION

Thus Śrī Caitanya Mahāprabhu lived at Nīlācala [Jagannātha Purī] with His personal devotees, always merged in ecstatic love for Kṛṣṇa.

TEXT 5

অন্তরে-বাহিরে কৃষ্ণবিরহ-তরঙ্গ ।
নানা-ভাবে ব্যাকুল প্রভুর মন আর অঙ্গ ॥ ৫ ॥

antare-bāhire kṛṣṇa-viraha-taraṅga
nānā-bhāve vyākula prabhura mana āra aṅga

SYNONYMS

antare-bāhire—internally and externally; *kṛṣṇa-viraha-taraṅga*—the waves of separation from Kṛṣṇa; *nānā-bhāve*—by various ecstasies; *vyākula*—agitated; *prabhura*—of Śrī Caitanya Mahāprabhu; *mana āra aṅga*—mind and body.

TRANSLATION

Śrī Caitanya Mahāprabhu always felt waves of separation from Kṛṣṇa, externally and internally. His mind and body were agitated by various spiritual transformations.

TEXT 6

দিনে নৃত্য-কীর্তন, জগন্নাথ-দরশন ।
রাত্র্যে রায়-স্বরূপ-সনে রস-আস্বাদন ॥ ৬ ॥

dine nṛtya-kīrtana, jagannātha-daraśana
rātrye rāya-svarūpa-sane rasa-āsvādana

SYNONYMS

dine—during the day; *nṛtya-kīrtana*—dancing and chanting; *jagannātha-daraśana*—seeing Lord Jagannātha; *rātrye*—at night; *rāya-svarūpa-sane*—with Rāmānanda Rāya and Svarūpa Dāmodara; *rasa-āsvādana*—tasting transcendental bliss.

TRANSLATION

During the day He chanted, danced and saw Lord Jagannātha in the temple. At night He tasted transcendental bliss in the company of Rāmānanda Rāya and Svarūpa Dāmodara.

TEXT 7

ত্রিজগতের লোক আসি' করেন দরশন ।
যেই দেখে, সেই পায় কৃষ্ণপ্রেম-ধন ॥ ৭ ॥

trijagatera loka āsi' karena daraśana
yei dekhe, sei pāya kṛṣṇa-prema-dhana

SYNONYMS

tri-jagatera—of the three worlds; *loka*—people; *āsi'*—coming; *karena daraśana*—visited; *yei dekhe*—anyone who saw; *sei pāya*—he got; *kṛṣṇa-prema-dhana*—the transcendental treasure of ecstatic love for Kṛṣṇa.

TRANSLATION

People from the three worlds used to come visit Śrī Caitanya Mahāprabhu. Anyone who saw Him received the transcendental treasure of love for Kṛṣṇa.

TEXT 8

মনুষ্যের বেশে দেব-গন্ধর্ব-কিন্নর ।
সপ্তপাতালের যত দৈত্য বিষধর ॥ ৮ ॥

manuṣyera veśe deva-gandharva-kinnara
sapta-pātālera yata daitya viṣadhara

SYNONYMS

manuṣyera veśe—in the dress of human beings; *deva-gandharva-kinnara*—the demigods, the Gandharvas and the Kinnaras; *sapta-pātālera*—of the seven lower planetary systems; *yata*—all kinds of; *daitya*—demons; *viṣa-dhara*—serpentine living entities.

TRANSLATION

The inhabitants of the seven higher planetary systems—including the demigods, the Gandharvas and the Kinnaras—and the inhabitants of the seven lower planetary systems [Pātālaloka], including the demons and serpentine living entities, all visited Śrī Caitanya Mahāprabhu in the dress of human beings.

TEXT 9

সপ্তদ্বীপে নবখণ্ডে বৈসে যত জন।
নানা-বেশে আসি' করে প্রভুর দরশন ॥ ৯ ॥

sapta-dvīpe nava-khaṇḍe vaise yata jana
nānā-veśe āsi' kare prabhura daraśana

SYNONYMS

sapta-dvīpe—in seven islands; *nava-khaṇḍe*—in nine *khaṇḍas; vaise*—reside; *yata jana*—all persons; *nānā-veśe*—in different dresses; *āsi'*—coming; *kare prabhura daraśana*—visited Śrī Caitanya Mahāprabhu.

TRANSLATION

Dressed in different ways, people from the seven islands and nine khaṇḍas visited Śrī Caitanya Mahāprabhu.

TEXT 10

প্রহ্লাদ, বলি, ব্যাস, শুক আদি মুনিগণ।
আসি' প্রভু দেখি' প্রেমে হয় অচেতন ॥ ১০ ॥

prahlāda, bali, vyāsa, śuka ādi muni-gaṇa
āsi' prabhu dekhi' preme haya acetana

SYNONYMS

prahlāda—Prahlāda Mahārāja; *bali*—Bali Mahārāja; *vyāsa*—Vyāsadeva; *śuka*—Śukadeva Gosvāmī; *ādi*—and so on; *muni-gaṇa*—great sages; *āsi'*—coming; *prabhu dekhi'*—by seeing Śrī Caitanya Mahāprabhu; *preme*—in ecstatic love of Kṛṣṇa; *haya acetana*—became unconscious.

TRANSLATION

Prahlāda Mahārāja, Bali Mahārāja, Vyāsadeva, Śukadeva Gosvāmī and other great sages came to visit Śrī Caitanya Mahāprabhu. Upon seeing Him, they became unconscious in ecstatic love for Kṛṣṇa.

PURPORT

According to the opinion of some historians, Prahlāda Mahārāja was born in Tretā-yuga in the city of Mūlatāna in the state of Punjab. He was born of Hiraṇyakaśipu, a king of the dynasty of Kaśyapa. Prahlāda Mahārāja was a great devotee of Lord Viṣṇu, but his father was very much against Viṣṇu. Because the father and son thus differed in their consciousness, the demon father inflicted all kinds of bodily pain upon Prahlāda. When this torture became intolerable, the Supreme Lord appeared as Nṛsiṁhadeva and killed the great demon Hiraṇyakaśipu.

Bali Mahārāja was the grandson of Prahlāda Mahārāja. The son of Prahlāda Mahārāja was Virocana, and his son was known as Bali. Appearing as Vāmana and begging Bali Mahārāja for three feet of land, the Lord took possession of the entire three worlds. Thus Bali Mahārāja became a great devotee of Lord Vāmana. Bali Mahārāja had one hundred sons, of whom Mahārāja Bāṇa was the eldest and most famous.

Vyāsadeva was the son of the great sage Parāśara. Other names for him are Sātyavateya and Kṛṣṇa-dvaipāyana Bādarāyaṇa Muni. As one of the authorities on the *Vedas,* he divided the original *Veda,* for convenience, into four divisions—*Sāma, Yajur, Ṛg* and *Atharva.* He is the author of eighteen *Purāṇas* as well as the theosophical thesis *Brahma-sūtra* and its natural commentary, *Śrīmad-Bhāgavatam.* He belongs to the Brahma-sampradāya and is a direct disciple of Nārada Muni.

Śukadeva Gosvāmī is the son of Vyāsadeva. He was a *brahmacārī* fully conscious of Brahman realization, but later he became a great devotee of Lord Kṛṣṇa. He narrated *Śrīmad-Bhāgavatam* to Mahārāja Parīkṣit.

TEXT 11

বাহিরে ফুকারে লোক, দর্শন না পাঞা ।
'কৃষ্ণ কহ' বলেন প্রভু বাহিরে আসিয়া ॥ ১১ ॥

bāhire phukāre loka, darśana nā pāñā
'kṛṣṇa kaha' balena prabhu bāhire āsiyā

SYNONYMS

bāhire—outside; *phu-kāre*—with a tumultuous sound; *loka*—people; *darśana nā pāñā*—not being able to see; *kṛṣṇa kaha*—chant Kṛṣṇa; *balena*—says; *prabhu*—Śrī Caitanya Mahāprabhu; *bāhire āsiyā*—coming outside.

TRANSLATION

Being unable to see Śrī Caitanya Mahāprabhu, the populace outside His room would make a tumultuous sound. Thus Śrī Caitanya Mahāprabhu would go outside and tell them, "Chant Hare Kṛṣṇa."

TEXT 12

প্রভুর দর্শনে সব লোক প্রেমে ভাসে ।
এইমত যায় প্রভুর রাত্রি-দিবসে ॥ ১২ ॥

prabhura darśane saba loka preme bhāse
ei-mata yāya prabhura rātri-divase

SYNONYMS

prabhura darśane—by seeing Śrī Caitanya Mahāprabhu; *saba loka*—all the people; *preme bhāse*—became inundated in ecstatic love; *ei-mata*—in this way; *yāya*—passes; *prabhura*—of Śrī Caitanya Mahāprabhu; *rātri-divase*—night and day.

TRANSLATION

All kinds of people would come to see the Lord, and upon seeing Him they would be overwhelmed with ecstatic love for Kṛṣṇa. In this way Śrī Caitanya Mahāprabhu passed His days and nights.

TEXT 13

একদিন লোক আসি' প্রভুরে নিবেদিল।
গোপীনাথেরে 'বড় জানা' চাঙ্গে চড়াইল॥ ১৩॥

eka-dina loka āsi' prabhure nivedila
gopīnāthere 'baḍa jānā' cāṅge caḍāila

SYNONYMS

eka-dina—one day; *loka*—people; *āsi'*—coming; *prabhure*—to Śrī Caitanya Mahāprabhu; *nivedila*—informed; *gopīnāthere*—Gopīnātha Paṭṭanāyaka; *baḍa jānā*—the eldest son of King Pratāparudra; *cāṅge caḍāila*—was raised on the *cāṅga.*

TRANSLATION

One day people suddenly came to Śrī Caitanya Mahāprabhu and informed Him, "Gopīnātha Paṭṭanāyaka, the son of Bhavānanda Rāya, has been condemned to death by the baḍa-jānā, the eldest son of the King, and has been raised on the cāṅga.

PURPORT

The *cāṅga* was a device for killing a condemned person. It consisted of a raised platform on which the condemned was made to stand. Underneath the platform, there were stationary upright swords. The condemned man would be pushed down onto the swords, and in this way he would die. For some reason, Gopīnātha Paṭṭanāyaka had been condemned to death and had therefore been raised upon the *cāṅga.*

TEXT 14

তলে খড়্গ পাতি' তারে উপরে ডারিবে।
প্রভু রক্ষা করেন যবে, তবে নিস্তারিবে ॥ ১৪ ॥

tale khaḍga pāti' tāre upare ḍāribe
prabhu rakṣā karena yabe, tabe nistāribe

SYNONYMS

tale—underneath; *khaḍga*—swords; *pāti'*—setting; *tāre*—him; *upare*—upon; *ḍāribe*—he will throw; *prabhu*—Śrī Caitanya Mahāprabhu; *rakṣā karena*—will protect; *yabe*—when; *tabe*—then; *nistāribe*—he will be saved.

TRANSLATION

"He has placed swords beneath the platform," they said, "and will throw Gopīnātha upon them. O Lord, only if You protect him will he be saved.

TEXT 15

সবংশে তোমার সেবক - ভবানন্দ-রায়।
তাঁর পুত্র—তোমার সেবকে রাখিতে যুয়ায় ॥ ১৫ ॥

savaṁśe tomāra sevaka——bhavānanda-rāya
tāṅra putra——tomāra sevake rākhite yuyāya

SYNONYMS

sa-vaṁśe—with his family; *tomāra*—Your; *sevaka*—servant; *bhavānanda-rāya*—Bhavānanda Rāya; *tāṅra putra*—his son; *tomāra sevake*—Your servant; *rākhite*—to protect; *yuyāya*—is quite fit.

TRANSLATION

"Bhavānanda Rāya and his entire family are your servants. Therefore it is quite fitting for You to save the son of Bhavānanda Rāya."

TEXT 16

প্রভু কহে,—'রাজা কেনে করয়ে তাড়ন?'
তবে সেই লোক কহে সব বিবরণ ॥ ১৬ ॥

prabhu kahe,——'rājā kene karaye tāḍana?'
tabe sei loka kahe saba vivaraṇa

SYNONYMS

prabhu kahe—Śrī Caitanya Mahāprabhu said; *rājā*—the King; *kene*—why; *karaye tāḍana*—punishes; *tabe*—thereupon; *sei loka*—those persons; *kahe*—stated; *saba vivaraṇa*—all of the description.

TRANSLATION

Śrī Caitanya Mahāprabhu inquired, "Why is the King chastising him?" Thereupon the people described the entire incident.

TEXT 17

**"গোপীনাথ-পট্টনায়ক—রামানন্দ-ভাই ।
সর্বকাল হয় তেঁহ রাজবিষয়ী ॥ ১৭ ॥**

"gopīnātha-paṭṭanāyaka——rāmānanda-bhāi
sarva-kāla haya teṅha rāja-viṣayī

SYNONYMS

gopīnātha-paṭṭanāyaka—Gopīnātha Paṭṭanāyaka; *rāmānanda-bhāi*—a brother of Rāmānanda Rāya; *sarva-kāla*—always; *haya*—is; *teṅha*—he; *rāja-viṣayī*—treasurer of the King.

TRANSLATION

They said, "Gopīnātha Paṭṭanāyaka, the brother of Rāmānanda Rāya, has always been a treasurer for the government.

TEXT 18

**'মালজাঠ্যা-দণ্ডপাটে' তার অধিকার ।
সাধি' পাড়ি' আনি' দ্রব্য দিল রাজদ্বার ॥ ১৮ ॥**

'mālajāṭhyā-daṇḍapāṭe' tāra adhikāra
sādhi' pāḍi' āni' dravya dila rāja-dvāra

SYNONYMS

mālajāṭhyā-daṇḍapāṭe—in the place known as Mālajāṭhyā Daṇḍapāta; *tāra*—his; *adhikāra*—authority; *sādhi'*—soliciting; *pāḍi'*—collecting; *āni'*—bringing; *dravya*—the money; *dila*—gave; *rāja-dvāra*—to the door of the King.

TRANSLATION

"He served in the place known as Mālajāṭhyā Daṇḍapāta, soliciting and collecting money there and depositing it in the government treasury.

TEXT 19

দুইলক্ষ কাহন তার ঠাঞি বাকী হইল ।
দুইলক্ষ কাহন কৌড়ি রাজা ত' মাগিল ॥ ১৯ ॥

dui-lakṣa kāhana tāra ṭhāñi bākī ha-ila
dui-lakṣa kāhana kauḍi rājā ta' māgila

SYNONYMS

dui-lakṣa kāhana—200,000 *kāhanas* of *kauḍis* (one *kāhana* equals 1280 *kauḍis*); *tāra ṭhāñi*—from him; *bākī ha-ila*—there was a balance due; *dui-lakṣa kāhana*—200,000 *kāhanas; kauḍi*—conchshells; *rājā*—the King; *ta'*—certainly; *māgila*—demanded.

TRANSLATION

"Once when he deposited the collection, however, a balance of 200,000 kāhanas of conchshells was due from him. Therefore the King demanded this sum.

TEXT 20

তেঁহ কহে,—"স্থূলদ্রব্য নাহি যে গণি' দিব ।
ক্রমে-ক্রমে বেচি' কিনি' দ্রব্য ভরিব ॥ ২০ ॥

teṅha kahe,——"sthūla-dravya nāhi ye gaṇi' diba
krame-krame veci' kini' dravya bhariba

SYNONYMS

teṅha kahe—he replied; *sthūla-dravya*—cash money; *nāhi*—there is not; *ye*—which; *gaṇi'*—counting; *diba*—I can give; *krame-krame*—gradually; *veci' kini'*—purchasing and selling; *dravya*—goods; *bhariba*—I shall fill.

TRANSLATION

"Gopīnātha Paṭṭanāyaka replied, 'There is no money I can immediately give you in cash. Please give me time. Gradually I shall purchase and sell my gross goods and in this way fill your treasury.

TEXT 21

ঘোড়া দশ-বার হয়, লহ' মূল্য করি' ।"
এত বলি' ঘোড়া আনে রাজদ্বারে ধরি' ॥ ২১ ॥

ghoḍā daśa-bāra haya, laha' mūlya kari' "
eta bali' ghoḍā āne rāja-dvāre dhari'

SYNONYMS

ghoḍā—horses; *daśa-bāra*—ten to twelve; *haya*—there are; *laha'*—take; *mūlya kari'*—on the proper value; *eta bali'*—saying this; *ghoḍā āne*—he brought the horses; *rāja-dvāre dhari'*—keeping at the door of the King.

TRANSLATION

" 'There are ten to twelve good horses. Take them immediately for a proper price.' After saying this, he brought all the horses to the door of the King.

TEXT 22

এক রাজপুত্র ঘোড়ার মূল্য ভাল জানে।
তারে পাঠাইল রাজা পাত্র-মিত্র সনে ॥ ২২ ॥

eka rāja-putra ghoḍāra mūlya bhāla jāne
tāre pāṭhāila rājā pātra-mitra sane

SYNONYMS

eka—one; *rāja-putra*—prince; *ghoḍāra mūlya*—the price of horses; *bhāla*—well; *jāne*—knows; *tāre pāṭhāila*—sent for him; *rājā*—the King; *pātra-mitra sane*—accompanied by ministers and friends.

TRANSLATION

"One of the princes knew how to estimate the price of horses very well. Thus the King sent for him to come with his ministers and friends.

TEXT 23

সেই রাজপুত্র মূল্য করে ঘাটাঞা।
গোপীনাথের ক্রোধ হৈল মূল্য শুনিয়া ॥ ২৩ ॥

sei rāja-putra mūlya kare ghāṭāñā
gopīnāthera krodha haila mūlya śuniyā

SYNONYMS

sei—that; *rāja-putra*—prince; *mūlya*—price; *kare*—estimates; *ghāṭāñā*—reducing; *gopīnāthera*—of Gopīnātha; *krodha haila*—there was anger; *mūlya śuniyā*—hearing the price.

TRANSLATION

"The prince, however, purposely gave a reduced estimate for the value of the horses. When Gopīnātha Paṭṭanāyaka heard the price quoted, he was very angry.

TEXT 24

সেই রাজপুত্রের স্বভাব,—গ্রীবা ফিরায়।
ঊর্ধ্বমুখে বারবার ইতি-উতি চায়॥ ২৪॥

sei rāja-putrera svabhāva,——grīvā phirāya
ūrdhva-mukhe bāra-bāra iti-uti cāya

SYNONYMS

sei rāja-putrera—of that prince; *sva-bhāva*—characteristic; *grīvā phirāya*—turns his neck; *ūrdhva-mukhe*—with his face toward the sky; *bāra-bāra*—again and again; *iti-uti*—here and there; *cāya*—looks.

TRANSLATION

"That prince had a personal idiosyncrasy of turning his neck and facing the sky, looking here and there again and again.

TEXT 25

তারে নিন্দা করি' কহে সগর্ব বচনে।
রাজা কৃপা করে তাতে ভয় নাহি মানে॥ ২৫॥

tāre nindā kari' kahe sagarva vacane
rājā kṛpā kare tāte bhaya nāhi māne

SYNONYMS

tāre—him; *nindā kari'*—criticizing; *kahe*—said; *sa-garva vacane*—words full of pride; *rājā*—the King; *kṛpā kare*—was very kind to him; *tāte*—therefore; *bhaya nāhi māne*—he was not afraid.

TRANSLATION

"Gopīnātha Paṭṭanāyaka criticized the prince. He was unafraid of the prince because the King was very kind toward him.

TEXT 26

'আমার ঘোড়া গ্রীবা না ফিরায় ঊর্ধ্বে নাহি চায়।
তাতে ঘোড়ার মূল্য ঘাটি করিতে না যুয়ায়॥' ২৬॥

'āmāra ghoḍā grīvā nā phirāya ūrdhve nāhi cāya
tāte ghoḍāra mūlya ghāṭi karite nā yuyāya'

SYNONYMS

āmāra ghoḍā—my horses; *grīvā*—the neck; *nā phirāya*—do not turn; *ūrdhve*—upward; *nāhi cāya*—do not look; *tāte*—because of this; *ghoḍāra mūlya*—the price of the horse; *ghāṭi karite*—to reduce; *nā yuyāya*—is not proper.

TRANSLATION

"Gopīnātha Paṭṭanāyaka said, 'My horses never turn their necks or look upward. Therefore the price for them should not be reduced.'

TEXT 27

শুনি' রাজপুত্র-মনে ক্রোধ উপজিল।
রাজার ঠাঞি যাই' বহু লাগানি করিল॥ ২৭॥

śuni' rājaputra-mane krodha upajila
rājāra ṭhāñi yāi' bahu lāgāni karila

SYNONYMS

śuni'—hearing; *rāja-putra*—of the prince; *mane*—in the mind; *krodha*—anger; *upajila*—arose; *rājāra ṭhāñi*—before the King; *yāi'*—going; *bahu lāgāni karila*—made many false allegations.

TRANSLATION

"Hearing this criticism, the prince became very angry. Going before the King, he made some false allegations against Gopīnātha Paṭṭanāyaka.

TEXT 28

"কৌড়ি নাহি দিবে এই, বেড়ায় ছদ্ম করি'।
আজ্ঞা দেহ যদি,—'চাঙ্গে চড়াঞা লই কৌড়ি' ॥২৮॥

"kauḍi nāhi dibe ei, beḍāya chadma kari'
ājñā deha yadi,——'cāṅge caḍāñā la-i kauḍi'

SYNONYMS

kauḍi—the money; *nāhi dibe*—will not pay; *ei*—this man; *beḍāya*—wanders; *chadma kari'*—on some pretext; *ājñā deha yadi*—if you order; *cāṅge caḍāñā*—raising on the *cāṅga; la-i kauḍi*—I shall get the money.

TRANSLATION

" 'This Gopīnātha Paṭṭanāyaka,' he said, 'is unwilling to pay the money due. Instead, he is squandering it under some pretext. If you issue an order, I can put him on the cāṅga and thus realize the money.'

TEXT 29

রাজা বলে,—"যেই ভাল, সেই কর যায়।
যে উপায়ে কৌড়ি পাই, কর সে উপায়॥" ২৯ ॥

rājā bale,——"yei bhāla, sei kara yāya
ye upāye kauḍi pāi, kara se upāya"

SYNONYMS

rājā bale—the King said; *yei bhāla*—whatever is best; *sei kara*—do that; *yāya*—going; *ye upāye*—by whatever means; *kauḍi pāi*—I can get back our money; *kara*—do; *se upāya*—such means.

TRANSLATION

"The King replied, 'You can adopt whatever means you think best. Any device by which you can somehow or other realize the money is all right.'

TEXT 30

রাজপুত্র আসি' তারে চাঙ্গে চড়াইল।
খড়্গ-উপরে ফেলাইতে তলে খড়্গ পাতিল॥"৩০ ॥

rāja-putra āsi' tāre cāṅge caḍāila
khaḍaga-upare phelāite tale khaḍaga pātila"

SYNONYMS

rāja-putra—the prince; *āsi'*—coming; *tāre*—him; *cāṅge*—on the *cāṅga; caḍāila*—raised; *khaḍaga-upare*—upon the swords; *phelāite*—to throw; *tale*—below; *khaḍaga pātila*—he spread swords.

TRANSLATION

"Thus the prince went back, raised Gopīnātha Paṭṭanāyaka onto the platform of the cāṅga and spread swords below upon which to throw him."

TEXT 31

শুনি' প্রভু কহে কিছু করি' প্রণয়-রোষ।
"রাজ-কৌড়ি দিতে নারে, রাজার কিবা দোষ ? ৩১॥

śuni' prabhu kahe kichu kari' praṇaya-roṣa
"rāja-kauḍi dite nāre, rājāra kibā doṣa?

SYNONYMS

śuni'—hearing; *prabhu kahe*—Śrī Caitanya Mahāprabhu said; *kichu*—some; *kari' praṇaya-roṣa*—displaying anger in affection; *rāja-kauḍi*—money due the government; *dite nāre*—does not wish to pay; *rājāra*—of the King; *kibā doṣa*—what is the fault.

TRANSLATION

After hearing this explanation, Śrī Caitanya Mahāprabhu replied with affectionate anger. "Gopīnātha Paṭṭanāyaka does not want to pay dues to the King," the Lord said. "How then is the King at fault in punishing him?

TEXT 32

রাজ-বিলাত্ সাধি' খায়, নাহি রাজ-ভয়।
দারী-নাটুয়ারে দিয়া করে নানা ব্যয় ॥ ৩২ ॥

rāja-bilāt sādhi' khāya, nāhi rāja-bhaya
dārī-nāṭuyāre diyā kare nānā vyaya

SYNONYMS

rāja-bilāt—money due the King; *sādhi'*—collecting; *khāya*—he uses; *nāhi rāja-bhaya*—without fear of the King; *dārī-nāṭuyāre*—to dancing girls; *diyā*—giving; *kare*—makes; *nānā*—various; *vyaya*—expenditures.

TRANSLATION

"Gopīnātha Paṭṭanāyaka is in charge of collecting money on behalf of the government, but he misappropriates it. Not fearing the King, he squanders it to see dancing girls.

TEXT 33

যেই চতুর, সেই করুক রাজ-বিষয় ।
রাজ-দ্রব্য শোধি' পায়, তার করুক ব্যয় ॥"৩৩॥

yei catura, sei kuruka rāja-viṣaya
rāja-dravya śodhi' pāya, tāra karuka vyaya"

SYNONYMS

yei—one who; *catura*—intelligent; *sei*—such a person; *kuruka*—let him do; *rāja-viṣaya*—government service; *rāja-dravya śodhi'*—after paying the dues of the government; *pāya*—whatever he gets; *tāra karuka vyaya*—let him spend that.

TRANSLATION

"If one is intelligent, let him perform service to the government, and after paying the government, he can spend whatever money is left."

TEXT 34

হেন-কালে আর লোক আইল ধাঞা ।
'বাণীনাথাদি সবংশে লঞা গেল বান্ধিয়া' ॥ ৩৪ ॥

hena-kāle āra loka āila dhāñā
'vāṇīnāthādi savaṁśe lañā gela bāndhiyā'

SYNONYMS

hena-kāle—at this time; *āra*—another; *loka*—person; *āila*—came; *dhāñā*—in great haste; *vāṇīnātha-ādi*—beginning with Vāṇīnātha; *sa-vaṁśe lañā*—with his family; *gela bāndhiyā*—was arrested.

TRANSLATION

At that time another person came there in great haste, bringing the news that Vāṇīnātha Rāya and his entire family had been arrested.

TEXT 35

প্রভু কহে,—"রাজা আপনে লেখার দ্রব্য লইব ।
আমি—বিরক্ত সন্ন্যাসী, তাহে কি করিব ?" ৩৫ ॥

prabhu kahe,——"rājā āpane lekhāra dravya la-iba
āmi——virakta sannyāsī, tāhe ki kariba?"

SYNONYMS

prabhu kahe—Lord Śrī Caitanya Mahāprabhu said; *rājā*—the King; *āpane*—personally; *lekhāra dravya*—dues of the proper account; *la-iba*—will take; *āmi*—I; *virakta sannyāsī*—a renounced *sannyāsī; tāhe*—about that; *ki kariba*—what can I do.

TRANSLATION

Śrī Caitanya Mahāprabhu said, "The King must personally realize the dues. I am but a sannyāsī, a member of the renounced order. What can I do?"

TEXT 36

তবে স্বরূপাদি যত প্রভুর ভক্তগণ ।
প্রভুর চরণে সবে কৈলা নিবেদন ॥ ৩৬ ॥

tabe svarūpādi yata prabhura bhakta-gaṇa
prabhura caraṇe sabe kailā nivedana

SYNONYMS

tabe—at that time; *svarūpa-ādi*—beginning with Svarūpa Dāmodara; *yata*—all; *prabhura*—of Śrī Caitanya Mahāprabhu; *bhakta-gaṇa*—devotees; *prabhura caraṇe*—at the lotus feet of the Lord; *sabe*—all of them; *kailā nivedana*—submitted.

TRANSLATION

Then all the devotees, headed by Svarūpa Dāmodara Gosvāmī, fell at the lotus feet of Śrī Caitanya Mahāprabhu and submitted the following plea.

TEXT 37

"রামানন্দ-রায়ের গোষ্ঠী, সব—তোমার 'দাস' ।
তোমার উচিত নহে ঐছন উদাস ॥" ৩৭ ॥

"rāmānanda-rāyera goṣṭhī, saba——tomāra 'dāsa'
tomāra ucita nahe aichana udāsa"

SYNONYMS

rāmānanda-rāyera—of Rāmānanda Rāya; *goṣṭhī*—family; *saba*—all; *tomāra dāsa*—Your servants; *tomāra*—for You; *ucita*—befitting; *nahe*—is not; *aichana*—such; *udāsa*—indifference.

TRANSLATION

"All the members of Rāmānanda Rāya's family are Your eternal servants. Now they are in danger. It is not befitting for You to be indifferent to them in this way."

TEXT 38

শুনি' মহাপ্রভু কহে সক্রোধ বচনে ।
"মোরে আজ্ঞা দেহ' সবে, যাঙ রাজস্থানে ! ৩৮ ॥

śuni' mahāprabhu kahe sakrodha vacane
"more ājñā deha' sabe, yāṅa rāja-sthāne!

SYNONYMS

śuni'—hearing; *mahāprabhu*—Lord Śrī Caitanya Mahāprabhu; *kahe*—says; *sa-krodha vacane*—angry words; *more*—Me; *ājñā deha'*—you order; *sabe*—all; *yāṅa*—I shall go; *rāja-sthāne*—to the place of the King.

TRANSLATION

After hearing this, Śrī Caitanya Mahāprabhu spoke in an angry mood. "You want to order Me to go to the King," He said.

TEXT 39

তোমা-সবার এই মত,—রাজ-ঠাঞি যাঞা ।
কৌড়ি মাগি' লঙ্ মুঞি আঁচল পাতিয়া ॥ ৩৯ ॥

tomā-sabāra ei mata,——rāja-ṭhāñi yāñā
kauḍi māgi' laṅ muñi āṅcala pātiyā

SYNONYMS

tomā-sabāra—of all of you; *ei mata*—this is the opinion; *rāja-ṭhāñi yāñā*—going to the King; *kauḍi māgi'*—begging *kauḍis;* *laṅ*—shall take; *muñi*—I; *āṅcala pātiyā*—spreading My cloth.

TRANSLATION

"Your opinion is that I should go to the King's palace and spread My cloth to beg money from him.

TEXT 40

পাঁচগণ্ডার পাত্র হয় সন্ন্যাসী ব্রাহ্মণ ।
মাগিলে বা কেনে দিবে দুইলক্ষ কাহন ?" ৪০ ॥

pāñca-gaṇḍāra pātra haya sannyāsī brāhmaṇa
māgile vā kene dibe dui-lakṣa kāhana?"

SYNONYMS

pāñca-gaṇḍāra—of five *gaṇḍās; pātra*—due recipients; *haya*—are; *sannyāsī brāhmaṇa*—*sannyāsīs* and *brāhmaṇas; māgile*—by begging; *vā*—or; *kene*—why; *dibe*—shall give; *dui-lakṣa kāhana*—200,000 *kāhanas* of *kauḍis.*

TRANSLATION

"Of course, a sannyāsī or brāhmaṇa may beg for up to five gaṇḍās, but why should he be granted the inappropriate sum of 200,000 kāhanas of conch-shells?"

TEXT 41

হেনকালে আর লোক আইল ধাঞা ।
খড়েগর উপরে গোপীনাথে দিতেছে ডারিয়া ॥ ৪১ ॥

hena-kāle āra loka āila dhāñā
khaḍegara upare gopīnāthe diteche ḍāriyā

SYNONYMS

hena-kāle—at this time; *āra*—another; *loka*—person; *āila*—came; *dhāñā*—running; *khaḍegara upare*—upon the swords; *gopīnāthe*—Gopīnātha; *diteche ḍāriyā*—they are throwing.

TRANSLATION

Then another person came with the news that Gopīnātha had already been set up to be thrown upon the points of the swords.

TEXT 42

শুনি' প্রভুর গণ প্রভুরে করে অনুনয় ।
প্রভু কহে,—"আমি ভিক্ষুক, আমা হৈতে কিছু নয় ॥

śuni' prabhura gaṇa prabhure kare anunaya
prabhu kahe,—"āmi bhikṣuka, āmā haite kichu naya

SYNONYMS

śuni'—hearing; *prabhura gaṇa*—the devotees of the Lord; *prabhure kare anunaya*—entreated the Lord; *prabhu kahe*—Lord Śrī Caitanya Mahāprabhu said; *āmi bhikṣuka*—I am a beggar; *āmā haite kichu naya*—it is not possible for Me to do anything.

TRANSLATION

Hearing this news, all the devotees again appealed to the Lord, but the Lord replied, "I am a beggar. It is impossible for Me to do anything about this.

TEXT 43

তাতে রক্ষা করিতে যদি হয় সবার মনে ।
সবে মেলি' জানাহ জগন্নাথের চরণে ॥ ৪৩ ॥

tāte rakṣā karite yadi haya sabāra mane
sabe meli' jānāha jagannāthera caraṇe

SYNONYMS

tāte—therefore; *rakṣā karite*—to save; *yadi*—if; *haya*—is; *sabāra*—of all; *mane*—in the mind; *sabe meli'*—all together; *jānāha*—pray; *jagannāthera caraṇe*—at the lotus feet of Lord Jagannātha.

TRANSLATION

"Therefore if you want to save him, you should all pray together at the lotus feet of Jagannātha.

TEXT 44

ঈশ্বর জগন্নাথ,—যাঁর হাতে সর্ব 'অর্থ' ।
কর্তুমকর্তুমন্যথা করিতে সমর্থ ॥" ৪৪ ॥

īśvara jagannātha,——yāṅra hāte sarva 'artha'
kartum akartum anyathā karite samartha"

SYNONYMS

īśvara—the Supreme Personality of Godhead; *jagannātha*—Lord Jagannātha; *yāṅra hāte*—within His hands; *sarva artha*—all potencies; *kartum*—to do; *akartum*—not to do; *anyathā*—and otherwise; *karite*—to do; *samartha*—able.

TRANSLATION

"Lord Jagannātha is the Supreme Personality of Godhead. He possesses all potencies. Therefore He is able to act freely and can do and undo whatever He likes."

TEXT 45

ইহাঁ যদি মহাপ্রভু এতেক কহিলা ।
হরিচন্দন-পাত্র যাই' রাজারে কহিলা ॥ ৪৫ ॥

ihāṅ yadi mahāprabhu eteka kahilā
haricandana-pātra yāi' rājāre kahilā

SYNONYMS

ihāṅ—here; *yadi*—when; *mahāprabhu*—Śrī Caitanya Mahāprabhu; *eteka kahilā*—spoke like this; *haricandana-pātra*—the officer named Haricandana Pātra; *yāi'*—going; *rājāre kahilā*—informed the King.

TRANSLATION

When Śrī Caitanya Mahāprabhu replied in this way, an officer named Haricandana Pātra went to the King and spoke with him.

TEXT 46

"গোপীনাথ-পট্টনায়ক—সেবক তোমার ।
সেবকের প্রাণদণ্ড নহে ব্যবহার ॥ ৪৬ ॥

"gopīnātha-paṭṭanāyaka——sevaka tomāra
sevakera prāṇa-daṇḍa nahe vyavahāra

SYNONYMS

gopīnātha-paṭṭanāyaka—Gopīnātha Paṭṭanāyaka; *sevaka tomāra*—your servant; *sevakera prāṇa-daṇḍa*—to condemn a servant to death; *nahe*—is not; *vyavahāra*—good behavior.

TRANSLATION

"After all," he said, "Gopīnātha Paṭṭanāyaka is your faithful servant. To condemn a servant to death is not good behavior.

TEXT 47

বিশেষ তাহার ঠাঞি কৌড়ি বাকী হয়।
প্রাণ নিলে কিবা লাভ? নিজ ধনক্ষয় ॥ ৪৭ ॥

viśeṣa tāhāra ṭhāñi kauḍi bākī haya
prāṇa nile kibā lābha? nija dhana-kṣaya

SYNONYMS

viśeṣa—particular; *tāhāra ṭhāñi*—from him; *kauḍi*—of *kauḍis; bākī*—debt; *haya*—there is; *prāṇa nile*—if he is killed; *kibā*—what; *lābha*—profit; *nija*—own; *dhana*—wealth; *kṣaya*—loss.

TRANSLATION

"His only fault is that he owes some money to the government. If he is killed, however, what profit will there be? The government will be the loser, for it will not get the money.

TEXT 48

যথার্থ মূল্যে ঘোড়া লহ, যেবা বাকী হয়।
ক্রমে ক্রমে দিবে, ব্যর্থ প্রাণ কেনে লয়॥" ৪৮ ॥

yathārtha mūlye ghoḍā laha, yebā bākī haya
krame krame dibe, vyartha prāṇa kene laya"

SYNONYMS

yathā-artha mūlye—for the proper price; *ghoḍā laha*—accept the horses; *yebā*—whatever; *bākī haya*—balance is due; *krame krame*—gradually; *dibe*—he will give; *vyartha*—unnecessarily; *prāṇa*—his life; *kene*—why; *laya*—are you taking.

TRANSLATION

"It would be better to take the horses for a proper price and let him gradually repay the balance. Why are you killing him unnecessarily?"

TEXT 49

রাজা কহে,—"এই বাত্ আমি নাহি জানি।
প্রাণ কেনে লইব, তার দ্রব্য চাহি আমি ॥ ৪৯ ॥

rājā kahe,——"ei vāt āmi nāhi jāni
prāṇa kene la-iba, tāra dravya cāhi āmi

SYNONYMS

rājā kahe—the King replied; *ei vāt*—this news; *āmi*—I; *nāhi jāni*—do not know; *prāṇa*—his life; *kene*—why; *la-iba*—should I take; *tāra*—his; *dravya*—money; *cāhi āmi*—I want.

TRANSLATION

The King answered in surprise, "I did not know about all this. Why should his life be taken? I only want the money from him.

TEXT 50

তুমি যাই' কর তাহাঁ সর্ব সমাধান ।
দ্রব্য যৈছে আইসে, আর রহে তার প্রাণ ॥"৫০ ॥

tumi yāi' kara tāhāṅ sarva samādhāna
dravya yaiche āise, āra rahe tāra prāṇa"

SYNONYMS

tumi—you; *yāi'*—going; *kara*—make; *tāhāṅ*—there; *sarva samādhāna*—all adjustments; *dravya*—goods; *yaiche*—so that; *āise*—come; *āra*—and; *rahe*—keeps; *tāra*—his; *prāṇa*—life.

TRANSLATION

"Go there and adjust everything. I want only the payment, not his life."

TEXT 51

তবে হরিচন্দন আসি' জানারে কহিল ।
চাঙ্গে হৈতে গোপীনাথে শীঘ্র নামাইল ॥ ৫১ ॥

tabe haricandana āsi' jānāre kahila
cāṅge haite gopīnāthe śīghra nāmāila

SYNONYMS

tabe—at that time; *haricandana*—Haricandana Pātra; *āsi'*—coming; *jānāre kahila*—informed the prince; *cāṅge haite*—from the *cāṅga* platform; *gopīnāthe*—Gopīnātha; *śīghra*—very soon; *nāmāila*—took down.

TRANSLATION

Haricandana then returned and informed the prince of the King's desire, and immediately Gopīnātha Paṭṭanāyaka was taken down from the *cāṅga*.

TEXT 52

'দ্রব্য দেহ' রাজা মাগে –উপায় পুছিল ।
'যথার্থ-মূল্যে ঘোড়া লহ', তেঁহ ত' কহিল ॥ ৫২ ॥

'dravya deha' rājā māge——upāya puchila
'yathārtha-mūlye ghoḍā laha', teṅha ta' kahila

SYNONYMS

dravya deha—pay the dues; *rājā māge*—the King asks; *upāya*—the means; *puchila*—inquired; *yathā-artha-mūlye*—at a proper price; *ghoḍā laha*—take the horses; *teṅha ta' kahila*—he replied.

TRANSLATION

Then he was told that the King demanded the money due him and asked what means he would adopt to pay it. "Kindly take my horses," he replied, "for a proper price.

TEXT 53

'ক্রমে ক্রমে দিমু, আর যত কিছু পারি ।
অবিচারে প্রাণ লহ,–কি বলিতে পারি ?' ৫৩ ॥

'krame krame dimu, āra yata kichu pāri
avicāre prāṇa laha,——ki balite pāri?'

SYNONYMS

krame krame—gradually; *dimu*—I shall pay; *āra*—more; *yata*—as much; *kichu*—any; *pāri*—I can; *avicāre*—without consideration; *prāṇa laha*—you take my life; *ki balite pāri*—what can I say.

TRANSLATION

"I shall gradually pay the balance as I can. Without consideration, however, you were going to take my life. What can I say?"

TEXT 54

যথার্থ মূল্য করি' তবে সব ঘোড়া লইল ।
আর দ্রব্যের মুদ্দতী করি' ঘরে পাঠাইল ॥ ৫৪ ॥

yathārtha mūlya kari' tabe saba ghoḍā la-ila
āra dravyera muddatī kari' ghare pāṭhāila

SYNONYMS

yathā-artha mūlya kari'—estimating the proper price; *tabe*—then; *saba*—all; *ghoḍā*—horses; *la-ila*—took; *āra dravyera*—of the balance; *muddatī kari'*—setting a time for payment; *ghare pāṭhāila*—sent home.

TRANSLATION

Then the government took all the horses for a proper price, a time was set for payment of the balance, and Gopīnātha Paṭṭanāyaka was released.

TEXT 55

এথা প্রভু সেই মনুষ্যেরে প্রশ্ন কৈল ।
“বাণীনাথ কি করে, যবে বান্ধিয়া আনিল ?” ৫৫ ॥

ethā prabhu sei manuṣyere praśna kaila
"vāṇīnātha ki kare, yabe bāndhiyā ānila?"

SYNONYMS

ethā—here; *prabhu*—Śrī Caitanya Mahāprabhu; *sei manuṣyere*—unto that person who brought the message; *praśna kaila*—inquired; *vāṇīnātha ki kare*—what was Vāṇīnātha doing; *yabe*—when; *bāndhiyā ānila*—he was arrested and brought there.

TRANSLATION

Śrī Caitanya Mahāprabhu inquired from the messenger, "What was Vāṇīnātha doing when he was arrested and brought there?"

TEXT 56

সে কহে—“বাণীনাথ নির্ভয়ে লয় কৃষ্ণনাম ।
‘হরে কৃষ্ণ, হরে কৃষ্ণ’ কহে অবিশ্রাম ॥ ৫৬ ॥

se kahe——"vāṇīnātha nirbhaye laya kṛṣṇa-nāma
'hare kṛṣṇa, hare kṛṣṇa' kahe aviśrāma

SYNONYMS

se kahe—he replied; *vāṇīnātha*—Vāṇīnātha; *nirbhaye*—without fear; *laya kṛṣṇa-nāma*—was chanting the Hare Kṛṣṇa *mahā-mantra; hare kṛṣṇa, hare kṛṣṇa*—Hare Kṛṣṇa, Hare Kṛṣṇa; *kahe aviśrāma*—was chanting incessantly.

TRANSLATION

The messenger replied, "He was fearlessly, incessantly chanting the mahā-mantra—Hare Kṛṣṇa, Hare Kṛṣṇa, Kṛṣṇa Kṛṣṇa, Hare Hare/ Hare Rāma, Hare Rāma, Rāma Rāma, Hare Hare.

TEXT 57

সংখ্যা লাগি' দুই-হাতে অঙ্গুলীতে লেখা ।
সহস্রাদি পূর্ণ হৈলে, অঙ্গে কাটে রেখা ॥" ৫৭ ॥

saṅkhyā lāgi' dui-hāte aṅgulīte lekhā
sahasrādi pūrṇa haile, aṅge kāṭe rekhā"

SYNONYMS

saṅkhyā lāgi'—for counting; *dui-hāte*—in two hands; *aṅgulīte*—on the fingers; *lekhā*—marking; *sahasra-ādi*—one thousand times; *pūrṇa haile*—when finished; *aṅge*—on the body; *kāṭe rekhā*—makes a mark.

TRANSLATION

"He counted the chants on the fingers of both hands, and after he had finished chanting one thousand times, he would make a mark on his body."

TEXT 58

শুনি' মহাপ্রভু হইলা পরম আনন্দ ।
কে বুঝিতে পারে গৌরের কৃপা-ছন্দবন্ধ ? ৫৮ ॥

śuni' mahāprabhu ha-ilā parama ānanda
ke bujhite pāre gaurera kṛpā-chanda-bandha?

SYNONYMS

śuni'—hearing; *mahāprabhu*—Śrī Caitanya Mahāprabhu; *ha-ilā*—became; *parama ānanda*—very pleased; *ke bujhite pāre*—who can understand; *gaurera*—of Lord Śrī Caitanya Mahāprabhu; *kṛpā-chanda-bandha*—mercy upon His devotee.

TRANSLATION

Hearing this news, the Lord was very pleased. Who can understand the mercy of the Lord upon His devotee?

TEXT 59

হেনকালে কাশীমিশ্র আইলা প্রভু-স্থানে।
প্রভু তাঁরে কহে কিছু সোদ্বেগ-বচনে ॥ ৫৯ ॥

hena-kāle kāśī-miśra āilā prabhu-sthāne
prabhu tāṅre kahe kichu sodvega-vacane

SYNONYMS

hena-kāle—at this time; *kāśī-miśra*—Kāśī Miśra; *āilā*—came; *prabhu-sthāne*—to the place of Śrī Caitanya Mahāprabhu; *prabhu*—Śrī Caitanya Mahāprabhu; *tāṅre*—to him; *kahe*—said; *kichu*—some; *sa-udvega*—with anxiety; *vacane*—words.

TRANSLATION

At that time Kāśī Miśra came to the residence of Śrī Caitanya Mahāprabhu, and the Lord talked with him with some agitation.

TEXT 60

"ইহাঁ রহিতে নারি, যামু আলালনাথ।
নানা উপদ্রব ইহাঁ, না পাই সোয়াথ॥"৬০ ॥

"ihāṅ rahite nāri, yāmu ālālanātha
nānā upadrava ihāṅ, nā pāi soyātha"

SYNONYMS

ihāṅ rahite nāri—I cannot stay here; *yāmu ālālanātha*—I shall go to Ālālanātha; *nānā*—various; *upadrava*—disturbances; *ihāṅ*—here; *nā pāi*—I cannot get; *soyātha*—rest.

TRANSLATION

"I cannot stay here any longer," the Lord said. "I shall go to Ālālanātha. There are too many disturbances here, and I cannot get any rest.

TEXT 61

ভবানন্দ-রায়ের গোষ্ঠী করে রাজবিষয়।
নানা-প্রকারে করে তারা রাজদ্রব্য ব্যয় ॥ ৬১ ॥

bhavānanda-rāyera goṣṭhī kare rāja-viṣaya
nānā-prakāre kare tārā rāja-dravya vyaya

SYNONYMS

bhavānanda-rāyera—of Bhavānanda Rāya; *goṣṭhī*—the family; *kare*—engages; *rāja-viṣaya*—in government service; *nānā-prakāre*—in various ways; *kare*—do; *tārā*—all of them; *rāja-dravya vyaya*—spending the government's revenues.

TRANSLATION

"All the family members of Bhavānanda Rāya are engaged in government service, but they spend the government's revenue in various ways.

TEXT 62

রাজার কি দোষ ? রাজা নিজ-দ্রব্য চায় ।
দিতে নারে দ্রব্য, দণ্ড আমারে জানায় ॥ ৬২ ॥

rājāra ki doṣa rājā nija-dravya cāya
dite nāre dravya, daṇḍa āmāre jānāya

SYNONYMS

rājāra—of the King; *ki doṣa*—what is the fault; *rājā*—the King; *nija*—own; *dravya*—money; *cāya*—wants; *dite nāre*—they cannot give; *dravya*—money; *daṇḍa*—punishment; *āmāre*—to Me; *jānāya*—they inform.

TRANSLATION

"What is the fault on the part of the King? He wants the government's money. However, when they are punished for failing to pay the government its due, they come to Me to release them.

TEXT 63

রাজা গোপীনাথে যদি চাঙ্গে চড়াইল ।
চারিবারে লোকে আসি' মোরে জানাইল ॥ ৬৩ ॥

rājā gopīnāthe yadi cāṅge caḍāila
cāri-bāre loke āsi' more jānāila

SYNONYMS

rājā—the King; *gopīnāthe*—Gopīnātha; *yadi*—when; *cāṅge*—on the *cāṅga; caḍāila*—raised; *cāri-bāre*—four times; *loke*—messengers; *āsi'*—coming; *more*—unto Me; *jānāila*—informed.

TRANSLATION

"When the King put Gopīnātha Paṭṭanāyaka on the cāṅga, messengers came four times to inform Me about the incident.

TEXT 64

ভিক্ষুক সন্ন্যাসী আমি নির্জনবাসী ।
আমায় দুঃখ দেয়, নিজ-দুঃখ কহি' আসি' ॥ ৬৪ ॥

bhikṣuka sannyāsī āmi nirjana-vāsī
āmāya duḥkha deya, nija-duḥkha kahi' āsi'

SYNONYMS

bhikṣuka—beggar; *sannyāsī*—mendicant; *āmi*—I; *nirjana-vāsī*—living in a solitary place; *āmāya*—to Me; *duḥkha*—unhappiness; *deya*—they give; *nija-duḥkha*—their own unhappiness; *kahi'*—speaking; *āsi'*—coming.

TRANSLATION

"As a beggar sannyāsī, a mendicant, I wish to live alone in a solitary place, but these people come to tell Me about their unhappiness and disturb Me.

TEXT 65

আজি তারে জগন্নাথ করিলা রক্ষণ ।
কালি কে রাখিবে, যদি না দিবে রাজধন ? ৬৫ ॥

āji tāre jagannātha karilā rakṣaṇa
kāli ke rākhibe, yadi nā dibe rāja-dhana?

SYNONYMS

āji—today; *tāre*—him; *jagannātha*—Lord Jagannātha; *karilā rakṣaṇa*—protected; *kāli*—tomorrow; *ke rākhibe*—who will protect; *yadi*—if; *nā dibe*—he will not pay; *rāja-dhana*—the King's money.

TRANSLATION

"Jagannātha has saved him once from death today, but if tomorrow he again does not pay what he owes the treasury, who will give him protection?

PURPORT

The Supreme Personality of Godhead will certainly protect a devotee who does something sinful accidentally. As the Lord says in *Bhagavad-gītā* (9.30-31):

api cet sudurācāro
bhajate mām ananya-bhāk
sādhur eva sa mantavyaḥ
samyag vyavasito hi saḥ

kṣipraṁ bhavati dharmātmā
śaśvac-chāntiṁ nigacchati
kaunteya pratijānīhi
na me bhaktaḥ praṇaśyati

"Even if one commits the most abominable actions, if he is engaged in devotional service, he is to be considered saintly because he is properly situated. He quickly becomes righteous and attains lasting peace. O son of Kuntī, declare it boldly that My devotee never perishes." However, if a devotee or so-called devotee purposefully commits sinful activities continually in the hope that Kṛṣṇa will give him protection, Kṛṣṇa will not protect him. Therefore Śrī Caitanya Mahāprabhu said, *kāli ke rākhibe, yadi nā dibe rāja-dhana?*: "Jagannātha has saved Gopīnātha Paṭṭanāyaka from being killed by the King today, but if he commits the same offense again, who will give him protection?" Śrī Caitanya Mahāprabhu thus warns all such foolish devotees that Jagannātha will not protect them if they continue to commit offenses.

TEXT 66

বিষয়ীর বার্তা শুনি' ক্ষুব্ধ হয় মন ।
তাতে ইহাঁ রহি' মোর নাহি প্রয়োজন ॥" ৬৬ ॥

viṣayīra vārtā śuni' kṣubdha haya mana
tāte ihāṅ rahi' mora nāhi prayojana"

SYNONYMS

viṣayīra—of materialistic persons; *vārtā*—news; *śuni'*—hearing; *kṣubdha*—agitated; *haya*—becomes; *mana*—mind; *tāte*—therefore; *ihāṅ rahi'*—to stay here; *mora*—My; *nāhi prayojana*—there is no necessity.

TRANSLATION

"If we hear about the activities of materialistic persons, our minds become agitated. There is no need for Me to stay here and be disturbed in that way."

TEXT 67

কাশীমিশ্র কহে প্রভুর ধরিয়া চরণে।
"তুমি কেনে এই বাতে ক্ষোভ কর মনে? ৬৭ ॥

kāśī-miśra kahe prabhura dhariyā caraṇe
"tumi kene ei vāte kṣobha kara mane?

SYNONYMS

kāśī-miśra kahe—Kāśī Miśra said; *prabhura*—of Śrī Caitanya Mahāprabhu; *dhariyā caraṇe*—embracing the lotus feet; *tumi*—You; *kene*—why; *ei vāte*—by these talks; *kṣobha kara*—become agitated; *mane*—within the mind.

TRANSLATION

Kāśī Miśra caught hold of the Lord's lotus feet and said, "Why should You be agitated by these affairs?

TEXT 68

সন্ন্যাসী বিরক্ত তোমার কা-সনে সম্বন্ধ?
ব্যবহার লাগি' তোমা ভজে, সেই জ্ঞান-অন্ধ ॥ ৬৮ ॥

sannyāsī virakta tomāra kā-sane sambandha?
vyavahāra lāgi' tomā bhaje, sei jñāna-andha

SYNONYMS

sannyāsī—a *sannyāsī; virakta*—one who has given up all connections with everyone; *tomāra*—Your; *kā-sane*—with whom; *sambandha*—relationship; *vyavahāra lāgi'*—for some material purpose; *tomā bhaje*—worships You; *sei*—he; *jñāna-andha*—blind to all knowledge.

TRANSLATION

"You are a renounced sannyāsī. What connections do You have? One who worships You for some material purpose is blind to all knowledge."

PURPORT

Becoming a devotee of the Lord to serve material purposes is a great mistake. Many people become showbottle devotees for material profits. Indeed materialistic persons sometimes take to professional devotional service and keep Viṣṇu, the Supreme Personality of Godhead, as a means of livelihood. None of this, however, is approved. In the book known as *Sapta-śatī,* as mentioned by Śrīla

Bhaktisiddhānta Sarasvatī Ṭhākura, one can discover how a person worshiping the goddess Durgā begs her for different varieties of material profit. Such activities are very popular among people in general, but they are the attempts of foolish, blind people (*sei jñāna-andha*).

A materialist does not actually know why one should become a devotee. A devotee's only concern is to satisfy the Supreme Personality of Godhead. Pure devotional service is defined by Śrīla Rūpa Gosvāmī:

anyābhilāṣitā-śūnyaṁ
jñāna-karmādy-anāvṛtam
ānukūlyena kṛṣṇānu-
śīlanaṁ bhaktir uttamā

One should be completely free from all material desires and should serve Kṛṣṇa simply to please Him. When people become interested in their own sense gratification (*bhukti mukti siddhi kāmī*), some of them desire to enjoy the material world to the fullest extent, some of them desire to be liberated and merge into the existence of Brahman, and others want to perform magic through mystic power and thus become incarnations of God. These are all against the principles of devotional service. One must be free from all material desires. The desire of the impersonalist to merge into the existence of Brahman is also material because such an impersonalist wants to gratify his senses by merging into the existence of Kṛṣṇa instead of serving His lotus feet. Even if such a person merges into the Brahman effulgence, he falls down again into material existence. As stated in *Śrīmad-Bhāgavatam* (10.2.32):

āruhya kṛcchreṇa paraṁ padaṁ tataḥ
patanty adho 'nādṛta-yuṣmad-aṅghrayaḥ

Because Māyāvādī philosophers have no information regarding the transcendental service of the Lord, even after attaining liberation from material activities and merging in the Brahman effulgence, they must come down again to this material world.

TEXT 69

তোমার ভজন-ফলে তোমাতে 'প্রেমধন'।
বিষয় লাগি' তোমায় ভজে, সেই মূর্খ জন ॥ ৬৯ ॥

tomāra bhajana-phale tomāte 'prema-dhana'
viṣaya lāgi' tomāya bhaje, sei mūrkha jana

SYNONYMS

tomāra—Your; *bhajana*—devotional service; *phale*—by the result of; *tomāte*—unto You; *prema-dhana*—wealth of love; *viṣaya lāgi'*—for material profit; *tomāya bhaje*—one engages in Your service; *sei*—he; *mūrkha jana*—a fool.

TRANSLATION

Kāśī Miśra continued, "If one engages in devotional service for Your satisfaction, this will result in his increasingly awakening his dormant love for You. But if one engages in Your devotional service for material purposes, he should be considered a number-one fool.

PURPORT

Śrīla Bhaktisiddhānta Sarasvatī Ṭhākura comments that there are many materialistic persons who become preachers, *gurus,* religionists or philosophers only for the sake of maintaining a high standard of living and sense gratification for themselves and their families. Sometimes they adopt the dress of a *sannyāsī* or preacher. They train some of their family members as lawyers and continually seek help from a high court to acquire riches on the plea of maintaining temples. Although such persons may call themselves preachers, live in Vṛndāvana or Navadvīpa, and also print many religious books, it is all for the same purpose, namely to earn a living to maintain their wives and children. They may also professionally recite the *Bhāgavatam* or other scriptures, worship the Deity in the temple and initiate disciples. Making a show of devotional paraphernalia, they may also collect money from the public and use it to cure the disease of some family member or near relative. Sometimes they become *bābājīs* or collect money on the plea of worshiping the poor, whom they call *daridra-nārāyaṇa,* or for social and political upliftment. Thus they spread a network of business schemes to collect money for sense gratification by cheating people in general who have no knowledge of pure devotional service. Such cheaters cannot understand that by offering devotional service to the Supreme Personality of Godhead, one can be elevated to a position of eternal servitude to the Lord, which is even greater than the position of Brahmā and other demigods. Unfortunately, fools have no understanding of the perpetual pleasure of devotional service.

TEXT 70

তোমা লাগি' রামানন্দ রাজ্য ত্যাগ কৈলা ।
তোমা লাগি' সনাতন 'বিষয়' ছাড়িলা ॥ ৭০ ॥

tomā lāgi' rāmānanda rājya tyāga kailā
tomā lāgi' sanātana 'viṣaya' chāḍilā

SYNONYMS

tomā lāgi'—for Your sake; *rāmānanda*—Rāmānanda Rāya; *rājya*—the kingdom; *tyāga kailā*—gave up; *tomā lāgi'*—for Your sake; *sanātana*—Sanātana Gosvāmī; *viṣaya*—material life; *chāḍilā*—gave up.

TRANSLATION

"It is only for Your sake that Rāmānanda Rāya resigned from the governorship of South India and Sanātana Gosvāmī gave up his post as minister.

TEXT 71

তোমা লাগি' রঘুনাথ সকল ছাড়িল ।
হেথায় তাহার পিতা বিষয় পাঠাইল ॥ ৭১ ॥

tomā lāgi' raghunātha sakala chāḍila
hethāya tāhāra pitā viṣaya pāṭhāila

SYNONYMS

tomā lāgi'—for Your sake; *raghunātha*—Raghunātha dāsa; *sakala chāḍila*—gave up everything; *hethāya*—here; *tāhāra pitā*—his father; *viṣaya pāṭhāila*—sent money.

TRANSLATION

"It is for Your sake that Raghunātha dāsa gave up all his family relationships. His father sent money and men here to serve him.

TEXT 72

তোমার চরণ-কৃপা হঞাছে তাহারে ।
ছত্রে মাগি' খায়, 'বিষয়' স্পর্শ নাহি করে ॥ ৭২ ॥

tomāra caraṇa-kṛpā hañāche tāhāre
chatre māgi' khāya, 'viṣaya' sparśa nāhi kare

SYNONYMS

tomāra caraṇa—of Your lotus feet; *kṛpā*—the mercy; *hañāche*—has been; *tāhāre*—upon him; *chatre*—from centers for the distribution of food; *māgi'*—begging; *khāya*—he eats; *viṣaya*—money; *sparśa nāhi kare*—he does not touch.

TRANSLATION

"However, because he has received the mercy of Your lotus feet, he does not even accept his father's money. Instead he eats by begging alms from centers for the distribution of food.

TEXT 73

রামানন্দের ভাই গোপীনাথ-মহাশয় ।
তোমা হৈতে বিষয়-বাঞ্ছা, তার ইচ্ছা নয় ॥ ৭৩ ॥

rāmānandera bhāi gopīnātha-mahāśaya
tomā haite viṣaya-vāñchā, tāra icchā naya

SYNONYMS

rāmānandera—of Rāmānanda; *bhāi*—brother; *gopīnātha*—Gopīnātha Paṭṭanāyaka; *mahāśaya*—a great gentleman; *tomā haite*—from You; *viṣaya-vāñchā*—desire for material advantage; *tāra icchā*—his desire; *naya*—is not.

TRANSLATION

"Gopīnātha Paṭṭanāyaka is a good gentleman. He does not desire material benefits from You.

TEXT 74

তার দুঃখ দেখি' তার সেবকাদিগণ ।
তোমারে জানাইল,—যাতে 'অনন্যশরণ' ॥ ৭৪ ॥

tāra duḥkha dekhi' tāra sevakādi-gaṇa
tomāre jānāila,——yāte 'ananya-śaraṇa'

SYNONYMS

tāra—his; *duḥkha*—distressed condition; *dekhi'*—seeing; *tāra*—his; *sevaka-ādi-gaṇa*—servants and friends; *tomāre jānāila*—informed You; *yāte*—because; *ananya*—no other; *śaraṇa*—shelter.

TRANSLATION

"It is not Gopīnātha who sent all those men so that You would release him from his plight. Rather, his friends and servants, seeing his distressed condition, informed You because they all knew that Gopīnātha is a soul surrendered unto You.

TEXT 75

সেই 'শুদ্ধভক্ত', যে তোমা ভজে তোমা লাগি'।
আপনার সুখ-দুঃখে হয় ভোগ-ভোগী' ॥ ৭৫ ॥

sei 'śuddha-bhakta', ye tomā bhaje tomā lāgi'
āpanāra sukha-duḥkhe haya bhoga-bhogī'

SYNONYMS

sei—he; *śuddha-bhakta*—a pure devotee; *ye*—who; *tomā bhaje*—worships You; *tomā lāgi'*—for Your satisfaction; *āpanāra sukha-duḥkhe*—for personal happiness and distress; *haya*—is; *bhoga-bhogī*—one who wants to enjoy this material world.

TRANSLATION

"Gopīnātha Paṭṭanāyaka is a pure devotee who worships You only for Your satisfaction. He does not care about his personal happiness or distress, for that is the business of a materialist.

TEXT 76

তোমার অনুকম্পা চাহে, ভজে অনুক্ষণ।
অচিরাৎ মিলে তাঁরে তোমার চরণ ॥ ৭৬ ॥

tomāra anukampā cāhe, bhaje anukṣaṇa
acirāt mile tāṅre tomāra caraṇa

SYNONYMS

tomāra—Your; *anukampā*—mercy; *cāhe*—desires; *bhaje anukṣaṇa*—engages in devotional service twenty-four hours a day; *acirāt*—very soon; *mile*—meet; *tāṅre*—him; *tomāra caraṇa*—Your lotus feet.

TRANSLATION

"One who engages in Your devotional service twenty-four hours a day, desiring only Your mercy, will very soon attain shelter at Your lotus feet.

TEXT 77

তত্তেঽনুকম্পাং সুসমীক্ষমাণো
ভুঞ্জান এবাত্মকৃতং বিপাকম্।

হৃদ্বাগ্বপুর্ভির্বিদধন্নমস্তে
জীবেত যো মুক্তিপদে স দায়ভাক্ ॥ ৭৭ ॥

tat te 'nukampāṁ susamīkṣamāṇo
bhuñjāna evātma-kṛtaṁ vipākam
hṛd-vāg-vapurbhir vidadhan namas te
jīveta yo mukti-pade sa dāya-bhāk

SYNONYMS

tat—therefore; *te*—Your; *anukampām*—compassion; *su-samīkṣamāṇaḥ*—hoping for; *bhuñjānaḥ*—enduring; *eva*—certainly; *ātma-kṛtam*—done by himself; *vipākam*—fruitive results; *hṛt*—with the heart; *vāk*—words; *vapurbhiḥ*—and body; *vidadhat*—offering; *namaḥ*—obeisances; *te*—unto You; *jīveta*—may live; *yaḥ*—anyone who; *mukti-pade*—in devotional service; *saḥ*—he; *dāya-bhāk*—a bona fide candidate.

TRANSLATION

" 'One who seeks Your compassion and thus tolerates all kinds of adverse conditions due to the karma of his past deeds, who engages always in Your devotional service with his mind, words and body, and who always offers obeisances unto You is certainly a bona fide candidate for becoming Your unalloyed devotee.'

PURPORT

This is a verse from *Śrīmad-Bhāgavatam* (10.14.8).

TEXT 78

এথা তুমি বসি' রহ, কেনে যাবে আলালনাথ ?
কেহ তোমা না শুনাবে বিষয়ীর বাত্ ॥ ৭৮ ॥

ethā tumi vasi' raha, kene yābe ālālanātha?
keha tomā nā śunābe viṣayīra vāt

SYNONYMS

ethā—here; *tumi*—You; *vasi'*—residing; *raha*—kindly stay; *kene*—why; *yābe*—shall You go; *ālālanātha*—to Ālālanātha; *keha tomā nā śunābe*—no one will inform You; *viṣayīra vāt*—about the affairs of materialistic persons.

TRANSLATION

"Kindly stay here at Jagannātha Purī. Why should You go to Ālālanātha? Henceforward, no one will approach You about material affairs."

TEXT 79

যদি বা তোমার তারে রাখিতে হয় মন ।
আজি যে রাখিল, সেই করিবে রক্ষণ ॥" ৭৯ ॥

yadi vā tomāra tāre rākhite haya mana
āji ye rākhila, sei karibe rakṣaṇa"

SYNONYMS

yadi vā—if somehow or other; *tomāra*—of You; *tāre*—him; *rākhite*—to protect; *haya*—is; *mana*—mind; *āji*—today; *ye*—He who; *rākhila*—protected; *sei*—he; *karibe rakṣaṇa*—will give protection.

TRANSLATION

Finally Kāśī Miśra told the Lord, "If You want to give protection to Gopīnātha, then Lord Jagannātha, who protected him today, will also protect him in the future."

TEXT 80

এত বলি' কাশীমিশ্র গেলা স্ব-মন্দিরে ।
মধ্যাহ্নে প্রতাপরুদ্র আইলা তাঁর ঘরে ॥ ৮০ ॥

eta bali' kāśī-miśra gelā sva-mandire
madhyāhne pratāparudra āilā tāṅra ghare

SYNONYMS

eta bali'—saying this; *kāśī-miśra*—Kāśī Miśra; *gelā*—went; *sva-mandire*—to his own temple; *madhyāhne*—at noon; *pratāparudra*—King Pratāparudra; *āilā*—came; *tāṅra ghare*—to his home.

TRANSLATION

After saying this, Kāśī Miśra left the abode of Śrī Caitanya Mahāprabhu and returned to his own temple. At noon King Pratāparudra came to Kaśī Miśra's home.

TEXT 81

প্রতাপরুদ্রের এক আছয়ে নিয়মে ।
যত দিন রহে তেঁহ শ্রীপুরুষোত্তমে ॥ ৮১ ॥

pratāparudrera eka āchaye niyame
yata dina rahe teṅha śrī-puruṣottame

SYNONYMS

pratāparudrera—of King Pratāparudra; *eka*—one; *āchaye*—is; *niyame*—a regular duty; *yata dina*—as long as; *rahe*—remained; *teṅha*—he; *śrī-puruṣottame*—at Jagannātha Purī.

TRANSLATION

As long as King Pratāparudra stayed in his capital, Puruṣottama, he performed one regular duty.

TEXT 82

নিত্য আসি' করে মিশ্রের পাদ সম্বাহন ।
জগন্নাথ-সেবার করে ভিয়ান শ্রবণ ॥ ৮২ ॥

nitya āsi' kare miśrera pāda saṁvāhana
jagannātha-sevāra kare bhiyāna śravaṇa

SYNONYMS

nitya āsi'—coming daily; *kare*—performs; *miśrera*—of Kāśī Miśra; *pāda*—the feet; *saṁvāhana*—massaging; *jagannātha-sevāra*—for the service of Lord Jagannātha; *kare*—does; *bhiyāna*—arrangements; *śravaṇa*—hearing.

TRANSLATION

He would come daily to the house of Kāśī Miśra to massage his lotus feet. The King would also hear from him about how opulently Lord Jagannātha was served.

TEXT 83

রাজা মিশ্রের চরণ যবে চাপিতে লাগিলা ।
তবে মিশ্র তাঁরে কিছু ভঙ্গীতে কহিলা ॥ ৮৩ ॥

rājā miśrera caraṇa yabe cāpite lāgilā
tabe miśra tāṅre kichu bhaṅgīte kahilā

SYNONYMS

rāja—the King; *miśrera*—of Kāśī Miśra; *caraṇa*—the lotus feet; *yabe*—when; *cāpite lāgilā*—began to press; *tabe*—at that opportunity; *miśra*—Kāśī Miśra; *tāṅre*—unto him; *kichu*—something; *bhaṅgīte*—by a hint; *kahilā*—informed.

TRANSLATION

When the King began pressing his lotus feet, Kāśī Miśra informed him about something through hints.

TEXT 84

"দেব, শুন আর এক অপরূপ বাত্ !
মহাপ্রভু ক্ষেত্র ছাড়ি' যাবেন আলালনাথ !"৮৪ ॥

"deva, śuna āra eka aparūpa vāt!
mahāprabhu kṣetra chāḍi' yābena ālālanātha!"

SYNONYMS

deva—my dear King; *śuna*—hear; *āra*—another; *eka*—one; *aparūpa*—uncommon; *vāt*—news; *mahāprabhu*—Śrī Caitanya Mahāprabhu; *kṣetra chāḍi'*—leaving Jagannātha Purī; *yābena*—will go; *ālālanātha*—to Ālālanātha.

TRANSLATION

"My dear King," he said, "please hear one uncommon item of news. Śrī Caitanya Mahāprabhu wants to leave Jagannātha Purī and go to Ālālanātha."

TEXT 85

শুনি রাজা দুঃখী হৈলা, পুছিলেন কারণ ।
তবে মিশ্র কহে তাঁরে সব বিবরণ ॥ ৮৫ ॥

śuni rājā duḥkhī hailā, puchilena kāraṇa
tabe miśra kahe tāṅre ṣaba vivaraṇa

SYNONYMS

śuni—hearing; *rājā*—the King; *duḥkhī hailā*—became very unhappy; *puchilena*—inquired; *kāraṇa*—the reason; *tabe*—at that time; *miśra kahe*—Miśra said; *tāṅre*—to him; *saba*—all; *vivaraṇa*—details.

TRANSLATION

When the King heard that Śrī Caitanya Mahāprabhu was going to Ālālanātha, he was very unhappy and inquired about the reason. Then Kāśī Miśra informed him of all the details.

TEXT 86

"গোপীনাথ-পট্টনায়কে যবে চাঙ্গে চড়াইলা ।
তার সেবক সব আসি' প্রভুরে কহিলা ॥ ৮৬ ॥

"gopīnātha-paṭṭanāyake yabe cāṅge caḍāilā
tāra sevaka saba āsi' prabhure kahilā

SYNONYMS

gopīnātha-paṭṭanāyake—Gopīnātha Paṭṭanāyaka; *yabe*—when; *cāṅge*—on the *cāṅga; caḍāilā*—they lifted; *tāra sevaka*—his servants; *saba*—all; *āsi'*—coming; *prabhure kahilā*—informed Śrī Caitanya Mahāprabhu.

TRANSLATION

"When Gopīnātha Paṭṭanāyaka was lifted onto the cāṅga," he said, "all his servants went to inform Śrī Caitanya Mahāprabhu.

TEXT 87

শুনিয়া ক্ষোভিত হৈল মহাপ্রভুর মন ।
ক্রোধে গোপীনাথে কৈলা বহুত ভর্ৎসন ॥ ৮৭ ॥

śuniyā kṣobhita haila mahāprabhura mana
krodhe gopīnāthe kailā bahuta bhartsana

SYNONYMS

śuniyā—hearing; *kṣobhita haila*—became agitated; *mahāprabhura mana*—Śrī Caitanya Mahāprabhu's mind; *krodhe*—in anger; *gopīnāthe*—unto Gopīnātha Paṭṭanāyaka; *kailā*—did; *bahuta bhartsana*—much chastisement.

TRANSLATION

"Hearing about this, Śrī Caitanya Mahāprabhu was extremely sorry at heart, and in anger He chastised Gopīnātha Paṭṭanāyaka.

TEXT 88

'অজিতেন্দ্রিয় হঞা করে রাজবিষয় ।
নানা অসৎপথে করে রাজদ্রব্য ব্যয় ॥ ৮৮ ॥

'ajitendriya hañā kare rāja-viṣaya
nānā asat-pathe kare rāja-dravya vyaya

SYNONYMS

ajitendriya hañā—being mad after sense gratification; *kare rāja-viṣaya*—serves the government; *nānā asat-pathe*—in various sinful activities; *kare rāja-dravya vyaya*—spends the revenue of government.

TRANSLATION

" 'Because he is mad after sense gratification,' the Lord said, 'he acts as a government servant but spends the government's revenue for various sinful activities.

TEXT 89

ব্রহ্মস্ব-অধিক এই হয় রাজধন ।
তাহা হরি' ভোগ করে মহাপাপী জন ॥ ৮৯ ॥

brahmasva-adhika ei haya rāja-dhana
tāhā hari' bhoga kare mahā-pāpī jana

SYNONYMS

brahmasva—a *brāhmaṇa's* property; *adhika*—more than; *ei*—this; *haya*—is; *rāja-dhana*—the revenue of the government; *tāhā hari'*—stealing that; *bhoga kare*—enjoys sense gratification; *mahā-pāpī jana*—a most sinful person.

TRANSLATION

" 'The revenue of the government is more sacred than the property of a brāhmaṇa. One who misappropriates the government's money and uses it to enjoy sense gratification is most sinful.

TEXT 90

রাজার বর্তন খায়, আর চুরি করে ।
রাজদণ্ড্য হয় সেই শাস্ত্রের বিচারে ॥ ৯০ ॥

rājāra vartana khāya, āra curi kare
rāja-daṇḍya haya sei śāstrera vicāre

SYNONYMS

rājāra vartana—the salary of the King; *khāya*—he takes; *āra*—and; *curi kare*—steals; *rāja-daṇḍya*—liable to be punished by the King; *haya*—is; *sei*—he; *śāstrera vicāre*—the verdict of the revealed scripture.

TRANSLATION

" 'One who serves the government but misappropriates the government's revenue is liable to be punished by the king. That is the verdict of all revealed scriptures.

TEXT 91

নিজ-কৌড়ি মাগে, রাজা নাহি করে দণ্ড ।
রাজা—মহাধার্ম্মিক, এই হয় পাপী ভণ্ড ! ৯১ ॥

nija-kauḍi māge, rājā nāhi kare daṇḍa
rājā——mahā-dhārmika, ei haya pāpī bhaṇḍa!

SYNONYMS

nija-kauḍi—his own money; *māge*—demands; *rājā*—the King; *nāhi kare daṇḍa*—does not punish; *rājā*—the King; *mahā-dhārmika*—very religious; *ei*—this man; *haya*—is; *pāpī*—sinful; *bhaṇḍa*—cheat.

TRANSLATION

" 'The King wanted his revenue paid and did not want to enforce punishment. Therefore the King is certainly very religious. But Gopīnātha Paṭṭanāyaka is a great cheat.

TEXT 92

রাজ-কড়ি না দেয়, আমারে ফুকারে ।
এই মহাদুঃখ ইহাঁ কে সহিতে পারে ? ৯২ ॥

rājā-kaḍi nā deya, āmāre phukāre
ei mahā-duḥkha ihāṅ ke sahite pāre?

SYNONYMS

rājā-kaḍi—the revenue of the King; *nā deya*—does not pay; *āmāre*—to Me; *phu-kāre*—cries; *ei*—this; *mahā-duḥkha*—great unhappiness; *ihāṅ*—here; *ke sahite pāre*—who can tolerate.

TRANSLATION

" 'He does not pay the revenue to the King, but he wants My help for release. This is a greatly sinful affair. I cannot tolerate it here.

TEXT 93

আলালনাথ যাই' তাহাঁ নিশ্চিন্তে রহিমু ।
বিষয়ীর ভাল মন্দ বার্তা না শুনিমু'॥" ৯৩ ॥

ālālanātha yāi' tāhāṅ niścinte rahimu
viṣayīra bhāla manda vārtā nā śunimu' "

SYNONYMS

ālālanātha yāi'—going to Ālālanātha; *tāhāṅ*—there; *niścinte rahimu*—I shall live peacefully; *viṣayīra*—of materialistic persons; *bhāla manda*—good and bad; *vārtā*—news; *nā śunimu*—I shall not hear.

TRANSLATION

" 'Therefore I shall leave Jagannātha Purī and go to Ālālanātha, where I shall live peacefully and not hear about all these affairs of materialistic people.' "

TEXT 94

এত শুনি' কহে রাজা পাঞা মনে ব্যথা ।
"সব দ্রব্য ছাড়োঁ, যদি প্রভু রহেন এথা ॥ ৯৪ ॥

eta śuni' kahe rājā pāñā mane vyathā
"saba dravya chāḍoṅ, yadi prabhu rahena ethā

SYNONYMS

eta śuni'—hearing all these details; *kahe rājā*—the King said; *pāñā*—getting; *mane vyathā*—pain in his mind; *saba dravya chāḍoṅ*—I shall give up all the dues; *yadi*—if; *prabhu*—Śrī Caitanya Mahāprabhu; *rahena ethā*—remains here.

TRANSLATION

When King Pratāparudra heard all these details, he felt great pain in his mind. "I shall give up all that is due from Gopīnātha Paṭṭanāyaka," he said, "if Śrī Caitanya Mahāprabhu stays here at Jagannātha Purī.

TEXT 95

এককক্ষণ প্রভুর যদি পাইয়ে দরশন ।
কোটিচিন্তামণি-লাভ নহে তার সম ॥ ৯৫ ॥

eka-kṣaṇa prabhura yadi pāiye daraśana
koṭi-cintāmaṇi-lābha nahe tāra sama

SYNONYMS

eka-kṣaṇa—for a moment; *prabhura*—of Śrī Caitanya Mahāprabhu; *yadi*—if; *pāiye*—I get; *daraśana*—an interview; *koṭi-cintāmaṇi-lābha*—obtaining millions of *cintāmaṇi* stones; *nahe*—is not; *tāra sama*—equal to that.

TRANSLATION

"If even for a moment I could get an interview with Lord Śrī Caitanya Mahāprabhu, I would not care for the profit of millions of cintāmaṇi stones.

TEXT 96

কোন্ ছার পদার্থ এই দুইলক্ষ কাহন ?
প্রাণ-রাজ্য করোঁ প্রভুপদে নির্মঞ্ছন ॥" ৯৬ ॥

kon chāra padārtha ei dui-lakṣa kāhana?
prāṇa-rājya karoṅ prabhu-pade nirmañchana"

SYNONYMS

kon—what; *chāra*—little; *padārtha*—matter; *ei*—this; *dui-lakṣa kāhana*—200,000 *kāhanas; prāṇa*—life; *rājya*—kingdom; *karoṅ*—I do; *prabhu-pade*—at the lotus feet of Śrī Caitanya Mahāprabhu; *nirmañchana*—sacrificing.

TRANSLATION

"I do not care about this small sum of 200,000 kāhanas. Not to speak of this, I would indeed sacrifice everything at the lotus feet of the Lord, including my life and kingdom."

TEXT 97

মিশ্র কহে, "কৌড়ি ছাড়িবা,—নহে প্রভুর মন ।
তারা দুঃখ পায়,—এই না যায় সহন ॥" ৯৭ ॥

miśra kahe, "kauḍi chāḍibā, ——nahe prabhura mana
tārā duḥkha pāya, ——ei nā yāya sahana"

SYNONYMS

miśra kahe—Kāśī Miśra said; *kauḍi chāḍibā*—you shall abandon the money; *nahe*—is not; *prabhura mana*—the desire of Śrī Caitanya Mahāprabhu; *tārā*—they; *duḥkha pāya*—get unhappiness; *ei*—this; *nā yāya sahana*—is intolerable.

TRANSLATION

Kāśī Miśra hinted to the King, "It is not the Lord's desire that you forfeit the payment. He is unhappy only because the whole family is troubled."

TEXT 98

রাজা কহে,—"তারে আমি দুঃখ নাহি দিয়ে ।
চাঙ্গে চড়া, খড়্গে ডারা,—আমি না জানিয়ে ॥ ৯৮ ॥

rājā kahe, ——"tāre āmi duḥkha nāhi diye
cāṅge caḍā, khaḍge ḍārā, ——āmi nā jāniye

SYNONYMS

rājā kahe—the King replied; *tāre*—to him; *āmi*—I; *duḥkha*—unhappiness; *nāhi diye*—have no desire to give; *cāṅge caḍā*—the raising on the *cāṅga; khaḍge*—on the swords; *ḍārā*—the throwing; *āmi*—I; *nā jāniye*—did not know.

TRANSLATION

The King replied, "I have no desire to give pain to Gopīnātha Paṭṭanāyaka and his family, nor did I know about his being lifted on the cāṅga to be thrown on the swords and killed.

TEXT 99

পুরুষোত্তম-জানারে তেঁহ কৈল পরিহাস ।
সেই 'জানা' তারে দেখাইল মিথ্যা ত্রাস ॥ ৯৯ ॥

puruṣottama-jānāre teṅha kaila parihāsa
sei 'jānā' tāre dekhāila mithyā trāsa

SYNONYMS

puruṣottama-jānāre—at Puruṣottama Jānā, the prince; *teṅha*—he; *kaila parihāsa*—made a joke; *sei jānā*—that prince; *tāre*—unto him; *dekhāila*—showed; *mithyā*—false; *trāsa*—scare.

TRANSLATION

"He sneered at Puruṣottama Jānā. Therefore the prince tried to scare him as a punishment.

TEXT 100

তুমি যাহ, প্রভুরে রাখহ যত্ন করি' ।
এই মুই তাহারে ছাড়িনু সব কৌড়ি ॥" ১০০ ॥

tumi yāha, prabhure rākhaha yatna kari'
ei mui tāhāre chāḍinu saba kauḍi"

SYNONYMS

tumi—you; *yāha*—go; *prabhure*—Śrī Caitanya Mahāprabhu; *rākhaha*—keep; *yatna kari'*—with great attention; *ei mui*—as far as I am concerned; *tāhāre*—unto him; *chāḍinu*—I abandon; *saba kauḍi*—all dues.

TRANSLATION

"Go personally to Śrī Caitanya Mahāprabhu and keep Him at Jagannātha Purī with great attention. I shall excuse Gopīnātha Paṭṭanāyaka from all his debts."

TEXT 101

মিশ্র কহে, "কৌড়ি ছাড়িবা,—নহে প্রভুর মনে ।
কৌড়ি ছাড়িলে প্রভু কদাচিৎ দুঃখ মানে ॥"১০১ ॥

miśra kahe, "kauḍi chāḍibā, —nahe prabhura mane
kauḍi chāḍile prabhu kadācit duḥkha māne"

SYNONYMS

miśra kahe—Kāśī Miśra said; *kauḍi chāḍibā*—you will excuse all dues; *nahe*—is not; *prabhura mane*—the thought of Śrī Caitanya Mahāprabhu; *kauḍi chāḍile*—if you excuse all the dues; *prabhu*—Śrī Caitanya Mahāprabhu; *kadācit*—certainly; *duḥkha māne*—will be sorry.

TRANSLATION

Kāśī Miśra said, "Excusing Gopīnātha Paṭṭanāyaka of all his debts will not make the Lord happy, for that is not His intention."

TEXT 102

রাজা কহে, "কৌড়ি ছাড়িমু,—ইহা না কহিবা ।
সহজে মোর প্রিয় তা'রা,—ইহা জানাইবা ॥ ১০২ ॥

rājā kahe, "kauḍi chāḍimu, ——ihā nā kahibā
sahaje mora priya tā'rā, ——ihā jānāibā

SYNONYMS

rājā kahe—the King said; *kauḍi chāḍimu*—I shall excuse all the dues; *ihā*—this; *nā kahibā*—do not speak; *sahaje*—naturally; *mora priya*—my dear friends; *tā'rā*—they; *ihā*—this; *jānāibā*—let Him know.

TRANSLATION

The King said, "I shall absolve Gopīnātha Paṭṭanāyaka of all his debts, but don't speak of this to the Lord. Simply let Him know that all the family members of Bhavānanda Rāya and Gopīnātha Paṭṭanāyaka are naturally my dear friends.

TEXT 103

ভবানন্দ-রায়—আমার পূজ্য-গর্বিত ।
তাঁর পুত্রগণে আমার সহজেই প্রীত ॥"১০৩ ॥

bhavānanda-rāya——āmāra pūjya-garvita
tāṅra putra-gaṇe āmāra sahajei prīta"

SYNONYMS

bhavānanda rāya—Bhavānanda Rāya; *āmāra*—by me; *pūjya*—worshipable; *garvita*—honorable; *tāṅra*—his; *putra-gaṇe*—unto sons; *āmāra*—my; *sahajei*—naturally; *prīta*—affection.

TRANSLATION

"Bhavānanda Rāya is worthy of my worship and respect. Therefore I am always naturally affectionate to his sons."

TEXT 104

এত বলি' মিশ্রে নমস্করি' রাজা ঘরে গেলা ।
গোপীনাথে 'বড় জানায়' ডাকিয়া আনিলা ॥ ১০৪ ॥

eta bali' miśre namaskari' rājā ghare gelā
gopīnāthe 'baḍa jānāya' ḍākiyā ānilā

SYNONYMS

eta bali'—saying this; *miśre namaskari'*—after offering obeisances to Kāśī Miśra; *rājā*—the King; *ghare gelā*—returned to his palace; *gopīnāthe*—Gopīnātha Paṭṭanāyaka; *baḍa jānāya*—the eldest prince; *ḍākiyā ānilā*—called forth.

TRANSLATION

After offering obeisances to Kāśī Miśra, the King returned to his palace and called for both Gopīnātha and the eldest prince.

TEXT 105

রাজা কহে,—"সব কৌড়ি তোমারে ছাড়িলুঁ ।
সেই মালজাঠ্যা দণ্ড পাট তোমারে ত' দিলুঁ ॥১০৫॥

rājā kahe, —"saba kauḍi tomāre chāḍiluṅ
sei mālajāṭhyā daṇḍa pāṭa tomāre ta' diluṅ

SYNONYMS

rājā kahe—the King said; *saba*—all; *kauḍi*—money; *tomāre*—unto you; *chāḍiluṅ*—I excuse; *sei mālajāṭhyā daṇḍa pāṭa*—the place called Mālajāṭhyā Daṇḍapāṭa; *tomāre*—to you; *ta'*—certainly; *diluṅ*—I give.

TRANSLATION

The King told Gopīnātha Paṭṭanāyaka, "You are excused for all the money you owe the treasury, and the place known as Mālajāṭhyā Daṇḍapāṭa is again given to you for collections.

TEXT 106

আর বার ঐছে না খাইহ রাজধন ।
আজি হৈতে দিলুঁ তোমায় দ্বিগুণ বর্তন ॥"১০৬ ॥

āra bāra aiche nā khāiha rāja-dhana
āji haite diluṅ tomāya dviguṇa vartana"

SYNONYMS

āra bāra—another time; *aiche*—like this; *nā khāiha*—do not misappropriate; *rāja-dhana*—government revenue; *āji haite*—from today; *diluṅ*—I award; *tomāya*—unto you; *dvi-guṇa vartana*—twice the salary.

TRANSLATION

"Do not again misappropriate the revenue of the government. In case you think your salary insufficient, henceforward it will be doubled."

TEXT 107

এত বলি' 'নেতধটী' তারে পরাইল ।
"প্রভু-আজ্ঞা লঞা যাহ, বিদায় তোমা দিল" ॥১০৭॥

eta bali' 'neta-dhaṭī' tāre parāila
"prabhu-ājñā lañā yāha, vidāya tomā dila"

SYNONYMS

eta bali'—saying this; *neta-dhaṭī*—silken wrapper; *tāre parāila*—put on him; *prabhu-ājñā lañā*—after taking permission from Śrī Caitanya Mahāprabhu; *yāha*—go; *vidāya*—farewell; *tomā*—to you; *dila*—I give.

TRANSLATION

After saying this, the King appointed him by offering him a silken wrapper for his body. "Go to Śrī Caitanya Mahāprabhu," he said. "After taking permission from Him, go to your home. I bid you farewell. Now you may go."

TEXT 108

পরমার্থে প্রভুর কৃপা, সেহ রহু দূরে ।
অনন্ত তাহার ফল, কে বলিতে পারে ? ১০৮ ॥

paramārthe prabhura kṛpā, seha rahu dūre
ananta tāhāra phala, ke balite pāre?

SYNONYMS

paramārthe—for spiritual advancement; *prabhura kṛpā*—mercy of Śrī Caitanya Mahāprabhu; *seha*—that; *rahu dūre*—let alone; *ananta*—unlimited; *tāhāra*—of that; *phala*—result; *ke*—who; *balite pāre*—can estimate.

TRANSLATION

By the mercy of Śrī Caitanya Mahāprabhu, one can certainly become spiritually advanced. Indeed, no one can estimate the results of His mercy.

TEXT 109

'রাজ্য-বিষয়'-ফল এই—কৃপার 'আভাসে' !
তাহার গণনা কারো মনে নাহি আইসে ! ১০৯ ॥

'rājya-viṣaya'-phala ei——kṛpāra 'ābhāse'!
tāhāra gaṇanā kāro mane nāhi āise!

SYNONYMS

rājya-viṣaya—kingly opulence; *phala*—result; *ei*—this; *kṛpāra ābhāse*—by only a glimpse of such mercy; *tāhāra*—of that; *gaṇanā*—calculation; *kāro*—of anyone; *mane*—within the mind; *nāhi āise*—does not come.

TRANSLATION

Gopīnātha Paṭṭanāyaka achieved the result of kingly opulence due to but a glimpse of the Lord's mercy. Therefore no one can calculate the full value of His mercy.

TEXT 110

কাহাঁ চাঙ্গে চড়াঞা লয় ধন-প্রাণ !
কাহাঁ সব ছাড়ি' সেই রাজ্যাদি-প্রদান ! ১১০ ॥

kāhāṅ cāṅge caḍāñā laya dhana-prāṇa!
kāhāṅ saba chāḍi' sei rājyādi-pradāna!

SYNONYMS

kāhāṅ—on one hand; *cāṅge*—on the *cāṅga; caḍāñā*—raising; *laya*—takes; *dhana*—wealth; *prāṇa*—life; *kāhāṅ*—on the other hand; *saba*—all; *chāḍi'*—excusing; *sei*—he; *rājya-ādi-pradāna*—awarding the same government post and so on.

TRANSLATION

Gopīnātha Paṭṭanāyaka was lifted onto the cāṅga to be killed, and all his money was taken away, but instead his debts were excused, and he was appointed collector in the same place.

TEXT 111

কাহাঁ সর্বস্ব বেচি' লয়, দেয়া না যায় কৌড়ি !
কাহাঁ দ্বিগুণ বর্তন, পরায় নেতধড়ি ! ১১১ ॥

kāhāṅ sarvasva veci' laya, deyā nā yāya kauḍi!
kāhāṅ dviguṇa vartana, parāya neta-dhaḍi!

SYNONYMS

kāhāṅ—on one hand; *sarvasva*—all possessions; *veci'*—selling; *laya*—takes; *deyā nā yāya*—cannot be paid; *kauḍi*—the debt; *kāhāṅ*—on the other hand; *dvi-guṇa vartana*—twice the salary; *parāya*—puts on; *neta-dhaḍi*—the silken cover.

TRANSLATION

On one hand Gopīnātha Paṭṭanāyaka was unable to clear his debt even by selling all his possessions, but on the other his salary was doubled, and he was honored with the silken wrapper.

TEXT 112

প্রভুর ইচ্ছা নাহি, তারে কৌড়ি ছাড়াইবে ।
দ্বিগুণ বর্তন করি' পুনঃ 'বিষয়' দিবে ॥ ১১২ ॥

prabhura icchā nāhi, tāre kauḍi chāḍāibe
dviguṇa vartana kari' punaḥ 'viṣaya' dibe

SYNONYMS

prabhura icchā—the wish of the Lord; *nāhi*—was not; *tāre kauḍi chāḍāibe*—he be excused from the dues; *dvi-guṇa*—twice as much; *vartana kari'*—increasing the salary; *punaḥ*—again; *viṣaya dibe*—he should be appointed to the post.

TRANSLATION

It was not the desire of Lord Caitanya Mahāprabhu that Gopīnātha Paṭṭanāyaka be excused of his debt to the government, nor was it His desire that his salary be doubled or that he be reappointed collector at the same place.

TEXT 113

তথাপি তার সেবক আসি' কৈল নিবেদন।
তাতে ক্ষুব্ধ হৈল যবে মহাপ্রভুর মন ॥ ১১৩ ॥

tathāpi tāra sevaka āsi' kaila nivedana
tāte kṣubdha haila yabe mahāprabhura mana

SYNONYMS

tathāpi—still; *tāra sevaka*—his servant; *āsi'*—coming; *kaila nivedana*—submitted; *tāte*—by that; *kṣubdha haila*—was agitated; *yabe*—when; *mahāprabhura mana*—Śrī Caitanya Mahāprabhu's mind.

TRANSLATION

When Gopīnātha Paṭṭanāyaka's servant went to Śrī Caitanya Mahāprabhu and informed the Lord of his plight, the Lord was somewhat agitated and dissatisfied.

TEXT 114

বিষয়-সুখ দিতে প্রভুর নাহি মনোবল।
নিবেদন-প্রভাবেহ তবু ফলে এত ফল ॥ ১১৪ ॥

viṣaya-sukha dite prabhura nāhi manobala
nivedana-prabhāveha tabu phale eta phala

SYNONYMS

viṣaya—of material opulence; *sukha*—happiness; *dite*—award; *prabhura*—of Śrī Caitanya Mahāprabhu; *nāhi*—is not; *manobala*—desire; *nivedana-prabhāveha*—simply because He was informed about it; *tabu*—still; *phale eta phala*—so much of a result was obtained.

TRANSLATION

The Lord had no intention to award His devotee the happiness of material opulence, yet simply because of His being informed, such a great result was obtained.

TEXT 115

কে কহিতে পারে গৌরের আশ্চর্য স্বভাব ?
ব্রহ্মা-শিব আদি যাঁর না পায় অন্তর্ভাব ॥ ১১৫ ॥

ke kahite pāre gaurera āścarya svabhāva?
brahmā-śiva ādi yāṅra nā pāya antarbhāva

SYNONYMS

ke—who; *kahite pāre*—can estimate; *gaurera*—of Śrī Caitanya Mahāprabhu; *āścarya svabhāva*—wonderful characteristics; *brahmā-śiva*—Lord Brahmā, Lord Śiva; *ādi*—and others; *yāṅra*—whose; *nā pāya*—cannot understand; *antarbhāva*—the intention.

TRANSLATION

No one can estimate the wonderful characteristics of Śrī Caitanya Mahāprabhu. Even Lord Brahmā and Lord Śiva cannot understand the intentions of the Lord.

TEXT 116

এথা কাশীমিশ্র আসি' প্রভুর চরণে ।
রাজার চরিত্র সব কৈলা নিবেদনে ॥ ১১৬ ॥

ethā kāśī-miśra āsi' prabhura caraṇe
rājāra caritra saba kailā nivedane

SYNONYMS

ethā—here; *kāśī-miśra*—Kāśī Miśra; *āsi'*—coming; *prabhura*—of Śrī Caitanya Mahāprabhu; *caraṇe*—to the feet; *rājāra*—of the King; *caritra saba*—all the behavior; *kailā nivedane*—informed.

TRANSLATION

Kāśī Miśra went to Śrī Caitanya Mahāprabhu and informed Him in detail of all the King's intentions.

TEXT 117

প্রভু কহে,—"কাশীমিশ্র, কি তুমি করিলা ?
রাজ-প্রতিগ্রহ তুমি আমা' করাইলা ?" ১১৭ ॥

prabhu kahe, —"kāśī-miśra, ki tumi karilā?
rāja-pratigraha tumi āmā' karāilā?"

SYNONYMS

prabhu kahe—Śrī Caitanya Mahāprabhu said; *kāśī-miśra*—My dear Kāśī Miśra; *ki*—what; *tumi karilā*—have you done; *rāja-pratigraha*—taking from the King; *tumi*—you; *āmā'*—me; *karāilā*—have made to do.

TRANSLATION

Upon hearing about Kāśī Miśra's tactics with the King, Śrī Caitanya Mahāprabhu said, "Kāśī Miśra, what have you done? You have made Me indirectly take help from the King."

PURPORT

When the King heard the details of Gopīnātha Paṭṭanāyaka's unfortunate condemnation, he was induced to excuse his debt, in particular because he felt that Śrī Caitanya Mahāprabhu was very sorry about this incident. The Lord did not like the idea that the money forfeited to Gopīnātha Paṭṭanāyaka was indirectly a contribution to Him. Therefore He immediately protested.

TEXT 118

মিশ্র কহে,—"শুন, প্রভু, রাজার বচনে ।
অকপটে রাজা এই কৈলা নিবেদনে ॥ ১১৮ ॥

miśra kahe, —"śuna, prabhu, rājāra vacane
akapaṭe rājā ei kailā nivedane

SYNONYMS

miśra kahe—Kāśī Miśra said; *śuna*—kindly hear; *prabhu*—my dear Lord; *rājāra vacane*—to the statement of the King; *akapaṭe*—without duplicity; *rājā*—the King; *ei*—this; *kailā nivedane*—has submitted.

TRANSLATION

Kāśī Miśra said, "My dear Lord, the King has done this without reservations. Kindly hear his statement.

TEXT 119

'প্রভু যেন নাহি জানেন,—রাজা আমার লাগিয়া ।
দুইলক্ষ কাহন কৌড়ি দিলেক ছাড়িয়া ॥ ১১৯ ॥

'prabhu yena nāhi jānena, —rājā āmāra lāgiyā
dui-lakṣa kāhana kauḍi dileka chāḍiyā

SYNONYMS

prabhu—Śrī Caitanya Mahāprabhu; *yena*—so that; *nāhi jānena*—may not think; *rājā*—the King; *āmāra lāgiyā*—for Me; *dui-lakṣa kāhana kauḍi*—200,000 *kāhanas* of *kauḍis; dileka chāḍiyā*—has remitted.

TRANSLATION

"The King said, 'Speak to the Lord in such a way that He will not think, "For My sake the King has forfeited 200,000 kāhanas of kauḍis."

PURPORT

The *kauḍi* is like an American cent or Japanese yen. In the old medium of exchange, the first unit of currency was a small conchshell called a *kauḍi*. Four *kauḍis* made one *gaṇḍā,* twenty *gaṇḍās* made one *paṇa,* and sixteen *paṇas* made one *kāhana*. Gopīnātha Paṭṭanāyaka owed the government 200,000 *kāhanas*. The King absolved him of this debt, reappointed him to his post and doubled his salary.

TEXT 120

ভবানন্দের পুত্র সব—মোর প্রিয়তম।
ইঁহা-সবাকারে আমি দেখি আত্মসম ॥ ১২০ ॥

bhavānandera putra saba——mora priyatama
iṅhā-sabākāre āmi dekhi ātma-sama

SYNONYMS

bhavānandera—of Bhavānanda Rāya; *putra saba*—all the sons; *mora*—to me; *priyatama*—very dear; *iṅhā-sabākāre*—all of them; *āmi*—I; *dekhi*—see; *ātma-sama*—as my relatives.

TRANSLATION

" 'Inform Śrī Caitanya Mahāprabhu that all the sons of Bhavānanda Rāya are especially dear to me. I consider them like members of my family.

TEXT 121

অতএব যাহাঁ যাহাঁ দেই অধিকার।
খায়, পিয়ে, লুটে, বিলায়, না করোঁ বিচার ॥ ১২১ ॥

ataeva yāhāṅ yāhāṅ dei adhikāra
khāya, piye, luṭe, vilāya, nā karoṅ vicāra

SYNONYMS

ataeva—therefore; *yāhāṅ yāhāṅ*—wherever; *dei adhikāra*—I appoint them; *khāya*—they eat; *piye*—drink; *luṭe*—plunder; *vilāya*—distribute; *nā karoṅ vicāra*—I do not consider.

TRANSLATION

" 'Therefore I have appointed them collectors in various places, and although they spend the government's money, eat, drink, plunder and distribute it as they like, I do not take them very seriously.

TEXT 122

রাজমহিন্দার 'রাজা' কৈনু রাম-রায়।
যে খাইল, যেবা দিল, নাহি লেখা-দায় ॥ ১২২ ॥

rājamahindāra 'rājā' kainu rāma-rāya
ye khāila, yebā dila, nāhi lekhā-dāya

SYNONYMS

rājamahindāra—of the place known as Rājamahendrī; *rājā*—governor; *kainu*—I made; *rāma-rāya*—Rāmānanda Rāya; *ye khāila*—whatever money he took; *yebā*—whatever; *dila*—distributed; *nāhi lekhā-dāya*—there is no account.

TRANSLATION

" 'I made Rāmānanda Rāya the governor of Rājamahendrī. There is practically no account of whatever money he took and distributed in that position.

PURPORT

Near Rājamahendrī is a famous railway station. Śrīla Bhaktisiddhānta Sarasvatī notes that the present Rājamahendrī City is located on the northern bank of the Godāvarī. At the time when Rāmānanda Rāya was governor, however, the state capital, which was known as Vidyānagara or Vidyāpura, was located on the southern side of the Godāvarī, at the confluence of the Godāvarī and the sea. That was the part of the country which at that time was known as Rājamahendrī. North of Kaliṅga-deśa is Utkaliṅga, or the state of Orissa. The capital of southern Orissa was known as Rājamahendrī, but now the location of Rājamahendrī has changed.

TEXT 123

গোপীনাথ এইমত 'বিষয়' করিয়া।
দুইচারি-লক্ষ কাহন রহে ত' খাঞা ॥ ১২৩ ॥

gopīnātha ei-mata 'viṣaya' kariyā
dui-cāri-lakṣa kāhana rahe ta' khāñā

SYNONYMS

gopīnātha—Gopīnātha; *ei-mata*—in this way; *viṣaya kariyā*—doing business; *dui-cāri-lakṣa kāhana*—two to four hundred thousand *kāhanas; rahe ta' khāñā*—spends as he likes.

TRANSLATION

" 'Having been appointed collector, Gopīnātha, in the same way, also generally spends two to four hundred thousand kāhanas as he likes.

TEXT 124

কিছু দেয়, কিছু না দেয়, না করি বিচার।
'জানা'-সহিত অপ্রীত্যে দুঃখ পাইল এইবার ॥ ১২৪ ॥

kichu deya, kichu nā deya, nā kari vicāra
'jānā'-sahita aprītye duḥkha pāila ei-bāra

SYNONYMS

kichu—some; *deya*—he pays; *kichu*—some; *nā deya*—he does not pay; *nā kari vicāra*—I do not consider; *jānā sahita*—with the prince; *aprītye*—due to some unfriendliness; *duḥkha pāila*—has gotten so much trouble; *ei-bāra*—this time.

TRANSLATION

" 'Gopīnātha Paṭṭanāyaka would collect some and pay some, spending it at will, but I would not consider this very seriously. This time, however, he was put in trouble because of a misunderstanding with the prince.

TEXT 125

'জানা' এত কৈলা,—ইহা মুই নাহি জানোঁ।
ভবানন্দের পুত্র-সবে আত্মসম মানোঁ ॥ ১২৫ ॥

'jānā' eta kailā, ——ihā mui nāhi jānoṅ
bhavānandera putra-sabe ātma-sama mānoṅ

SYNONYMS

jānā—the prince; *eta*—such; *kailā*—has done; *ihā*—this; *mui*—I; *nāhi jānoṅ*—did not know; *bhavānandera putra*—the sons of Bhavānanda Rāya; *sabe*—all; *ātma-sama mānoṅ*—I considered like my relatives.

TRANSLATION

" 'The prince created this situation without my knowledge, but actually I consider all the sons of Bhavānanda Rāya to be like my relatives.

TEXT 126

তাঁহা লাগি' দ্রব্য ছাড়ি,—ইহা মাৎ জানে ।
'সহজেই মোর প্রীতি হয় তাহা-সনে' ॥"১২৬ ॥

tāṅhā lāgi' dravya chāḍi'——ihā māt jāne
'sahajei mora prīti haya tāhā-sane' "

SYNONYMS

tāṅhā lāgi'—for them; *dravya chāḍi'*—I remit the debt; *ihā*—this; *māt jāne*—He does not know; *sahajei*—naturally; *mora prīti*—my affection; *haya*—is; *tāhā-sane*—with them all.

TRANSLATION

" 'Because of my intimate relationship with them, I have absolved Gopīnātha Paṭṭanāyaka of all his debts. Śrī Caitanya Mahāprabhu does not know this fact. Whatever I have done is because of my intimate relationship with the family of Bhavānanda Rāya.' "

TEXT 127

শুনিয়া রাজার বিনয় প্রভুর আনন্দ ।
হেনকালে আইলা তথা রায় ভবানন্দ ॥ ১২৭ ॥

śuniyā rājāra vinaya prabhura ānanda
hena-kāle āilā tathā rāya bhavānanda

SYNONYMS

śuniyā—hearing; *rājāra*—of the King; *vinaya*—submission; *prabhura ānanda*—Śrī Caitanya Mahāprabhu became very happy; *hena-kāle*—at this time; *āilā*—arrived; *tathā*—there; *rāya bhavānanda*—Bhavānanda Rāya.

TRANSLATION

Having heard from Kāśī Miśra all these statements concerning the King's mentality, Śrī Caitanya Mahāprabhu was very happy. At that time, Bhavānanda Rāya also arrived there.

TEXT 128

পঞ্চপুত্র-সহিতে আসি' পড়িলা চরণে ।
উঠাঞা প্রভু তাঁরে কৈলা আলিঙ্গনে ॥ ১২৮ ॥

pañca-putra-sahite āsi' paḍilā caraṇe
uṭhāñā prabhu tāṅre kailā āliṅgane

SYNONYMS

pañca-putra-sahite—with five sons; *āsi'*—coming; *paḍilā caraṇe*—fell down at the lotus feet of Śrī Caitanya Mahāprabhu; *uṭhāñā*—getting him up; *prabhu*—Śrī Caitanya Mahāprabhu; *tāṅre*—him; *kailā āliṅgane*—embraced.

TRANSLATION

Bhavānanda Rāya, along with his five sons, fell at the lotus feet of Śrī Caitanya Mahāprabhu, who lifted him up and embraced him.

TEXT 129

রামানন্দ-রায় আদি সবাই মিলিলা ।
ভবানন্দ-রায় তবে বলিতে লাগিলা ॥ ১২৯ ॥

rāmānanda-rāya ādi sabāi mililā
bhavānanda-rāya tabe balite lāgilā

SYNONYMS

rāmānanda-rāya ādi—Rāmānanda Rāya and other brothers; *sabāi*—all; *mililā*—met; *bhavānanda-rāya*—Bhavānanda Rāya; *tabe*—then; *balite lāgilā*—began to speak.

TRANSLATION

Thus Rāmānanda Rāya, all his brothers, and their father met Śrī Caitanya Mahāprabhu. Then Bhavānanda Rāya began speaking.

TEXT 130

"তোমার কিঙ্কর এই সব মোর কুল ।
এ বিপদে রাখি' প্রভু, পুনঃ নিলা মূল ॥ ১৩০ ॥

"tomāra kiṅkara ei saba mora kula
e vipade rākhi' prabhu, punaḥ nilā mūla

SYNONYMS

tomāra kiṅkara—your servants; *ei saba*—all these; *mora kula*—my family; *e vipade*—in this great danger; *rākhi'*—by saving; *prabhu*—my Lord; *punaḥ*—again; *nilā mūla*—have purchased.

TRANSLATION

"All these members of my family," he said, "are Your eternal servants. You have saved us from this great danger. Therefore You have purchased us for a proper price.

TEXT 131

ভক্তবাৎসল্য এবে প্রকট করিলা ।
পূর্বে যেন পঞ্চপাণ্ডবে বিপদে তারিলা ॥" ১৩১ ॥

bhakta-vātsalya ebe prakaṭa karilā
pūrve yena pañca-pāṇḍave vipade tārilā"

SYNONYMS

bhakta-vātsalya—love for Your devotees; *ebe*—now; *prakaṭa karilā*—You have demonstrated; *pūrve*—previously; *yena*—as; *pañca-pāṇḍave*—the five Pāṇḍavas; *vipade*—from danger; *tārilā*—You saved.

TRANSLATION

"You have now demonstrated Your love for Your devotees, just as when You previously saved the five Pāṇḍavas from great danger."

TEXT 132

'নেতধটী'-মাথে গোপীনাথ চরণে পড়িলা ।
রাজার কৃপা-বৃত্তান্ত সকল কহিলা ॥ ১৩২ ॥

'netadhaṭī'-māthe gopīnātha caraṇe paḍilā
rājāra kṛpā-vṛttānta sakala kahilā

SYNONYMS

netadhaṭī-māthe—with the silken cover on the head; *gopīnātha*—Gopīnātha Paṭṭanāyaka; *caraṇe paḍilā*—fell down at the lotus feet; *rājāra*—of the King; *kṛpā-vṛttānta*—story of the mercy; *sakala*—all; *kahilā*—narrated.

TRANSLATION

Gopīnātha Paṭṭanāyaka, his head covered with the silken wrapper, fell at the lotus feet of Śrī Caitanya Mahāprabhu and described in detail the King's mercy toward him.

TEXT 133

"বাকী-কৌড়ি বাদ, আর দ্বিগুণ বর্তন কৈলা।
পুনঃ 'বিষয়' দিয়া 'নেতধটী' পরাইলা॥ ১৩৩॥

"bākī-kauḍi bāda, āra dviguṇa vartana kailā
punaḥ 'viṣaya' diyā 'neta-dhaṭī' parāilā

SYNONYMS

bākī-kauḍi bāda—excusing the balance due; *āra*—and; *dvi-guṇa*—double; *vartana kailā*—made the salary; *punaḥ*—again; *viṣaya diyā*—giving the post; *neta-dhaṭī parāilā*—decorated with the silken cloth.

TRANSLATION

"The King has excused me for the balance due," he said. "He has reappointed me to my post by honoring me with this silken cloth and has doubled my salary.

TEXT 134

কাহাঁ চাঙ্গের উপর সেই মরণ-প্রমাদ!
কাহাঁ 'নেতধটী' পুনঃ,—এসব প্রসাদ! ১৩৪॥

kāhāṅ cāṅgera upara sei maraṇa-pramāda!
kāhāṅ 'neta-dhaṭī' punaḥ, ——e-saba prasāda!

SYNONYMS

kāhāṅ—on one hand; *cāṅgera upara*—on the *cāṅga; sei*—that; *maraṇa-pramāda*—danger of death; *kāhāṅ*—on the other hand; *neta-dhaṭī*—the silken cloth; *punaḥ*—again; *e-saba*—all this; *prasāda*—mercy.

TRANSLATION

"I was lifted upon the cāṅga to be killed, but on the contrary I was honored with this silken cloth. This is all Your mercy.

TEXT 135

চাঙ্গের উপরে তোমার চরণ ধ্যান কৈলুঁ ।
চরণ-স্মরণ-প্রভাবে এই ফল পাইলুঁ ॥ ১৩৫ ॥

cāṅgera upare tomāra caraṇa dhyāna kailuṅ
caraṇa-smaraṇa-prabhāve ei phala pāiluṅ

SYNONYMS

cāṅgera upare—on the *cāṅga; tomāra caraṇa*—on Your lotus feet; *dhyāna kailuṅ*—I meditated; *caraṇa-smaraṇa-prabhāve*—by the power of remembering Your lotus feet; *ei phala*—these results; *pāiluṅ*—I have got.

TRANSLATION

"On the cāṅga I began meditating upon Your lotus feet, and the power of that remembrance has yielded all these results.

TEXT 136

লোকে চমৎকার মোর এ সব দেখিয়া ।
প্রশংসে তোমার কৃপা-মহিমা গাঞা ॥ ১৩৬ ॥

loke camatkāra mora e saba dekhiyā
praśaṁse tomāra kṛpā-mahimā gāñā

SYNONYMS

loke—among the people; *camatkāra*—great wonder; *mora*—my; *e saba*—all these; *dekhiyā*—by seeing; *praśaṁse*—they glorify; *tomāra*—Your; *kṛpā*—of mercy; *mahimā*—greatness; *gāñā*—chanting.

TRANSLATION

"Struck with wonder by my affairs, the populace is glorifying the greatness of Your mercy.

TEXT 137

কিন্তু তোমার স্মরণের নহে এই 'মুখ্যফল' ।
'ফলাভাস' এই,—যাতে 'বিষয়' চঞ্চল ॥ ১৩৭ ॥

kintu tomāra smaraṇera nahe ei 'mukhya-phala'
'phalābhāsa' ei, ——yāte 'viṣaya' cañcala

SYNONYMS

kintu—but; *tomāra*—Your; *smaraṇera*—of remembrance; *nahe*—not; *ei*—this; *mukhya-phala*—chief result; *phala-ābhāsa*—a glimpse of the result; *ei*—this; *yāte*—because; *viṣaya*—material opulence; *cañcala*—flickering.

TRANSLATION

"However, my Lord, these are not the principal results of meditating upon Your lotus feet. Material opulence is very flickering. Therefore it is simply a glimpse of the result of Your mercy.

PURPORT

One can achieve the highest perfection of life simply by meditating upon the lotus feet of Śrī Caitanya Mahāprabhu. Generally people are concerned with the four religious principles, namely religion, material opulence, sense gratification and liberation. However, as indicated in *Śrīmad-Bhāgavatam* (*dharmaḥ projjhita-kaitavo 'tra*), success in these four kinds of material and spiritual gain are not the true results of devotional service. The true result of devotional service is the actual development of one's dormant love for Kṛṣṇa in every circumstance. By the mercy of Śrī Caitanya Mahāprabhu, Gopīnātha Paṭṭanāyaka could understand that the material benefits he had achieved were not the ultimate result of meditating upon His lotus feet. The true result comes when one is detached from material opulences. Therefore Gopīnātha Paṭṭanāyaka prayed to the Lord for such detachment.

TEXT 138

রাম-রায়ে, বাণীনাথে কৈলা 'নির্বিষয়'।
সেই কৃপা মোতে নাহি, যাতে ঐছে হয়! ১৩৮

rāma-rāye, vāṇīnāthe kailā 'nirviṣaya'
sei kṛpā mote nāhi, yāte aiche haya!

SYNONYMS

rāma-rāye—Rāmānanda Rāya; *vāṇīnāthe*—Vāṇīnātha; *kailā*—You have made; *nirviṣaya*—free from all material attachment; *sei kṛpā*—that mercy; *mote nāhi*—I have not received; *yāte*—by which; *aiche*—such; *haya*—is.

TRANSLATION

"Your real mercy has been granted to Rāmānanda Rāya and Vāṇīnātha Rāya, for You have detached them from all material opulence. I think that I have not been favored by such mercy.

TEXT 139

শুদ্ধ কৃপা কর, গোসাঞি, ঘুচাহ 'বিষয়'।
নির্বিণ্ণ হইনু, মোতে 'বিষয়' না হয়॥" ১৩৯॥

śuddha kṛpā kara, gosāñi, ghucāha 'viṣaya'
nirviṇṇa ha-inu, mote 'viṣaya' nā haya"

SYNONYMS

śuddha kṛpā—pure mercy; *kara*—kindly bestow; *gosāñi*—my Lord; *ghucāha viṣaya*—let me be free from all these material opulences; *nirviṇṇa*—detached; *ha-inu*—I have become; *mote viṣaya nā haya*—I am no longer interested in material opulences.

TRANSLATION

"Kindly bestow upon me Your pure mercy so that I may also become renounced. I am no longer interested in material enjoyment."

TEXT 140

প্রভু কহে,—সন্ন্যাসী যবে হইবা পঞ্চজন।
কুটুম্ব-বাহুল্য তোমার কে করে ভরণ? ১৪০॥

prabhu kahe, —sannyāsī yabe ha-ibā pañca-jana
kuṭumba-bāhulya tomāra ke kare bharaṇa?

SYNONYMS

prabhu kahe—Lord Śrī Caitanya Mahāprabhu said; *sannyāsī—sannyāsīs; yabe*—when; *ha-ibā*—will be; *pañca-jana*—five persons; *kuṭumba-bāhulya*—the many members of the family; *tomāra*—your; *ke*—who; *kare bharaṇa*—will maintain.

TRANSLATION

Śrī Caitanya Mahāprabhu said, "If you all adopt the renounced order and lose interest in dealing with pounds, shillings and pence, who will take charge of maintaining your large family?

TEXT 141

মহাবিষয় কর, কিবা বিরক্ত উদাস।
জন্মে-জন্মে তুমি পঞ্চ—মোর 'নিজদাস'॥ ১৪১॥

mahā-viṣaya kara, kibā virakta udāsa
janme-janme tumi pañca——mora 'nija-dāsa'

SYNONYMS

mahā-viṣaya—great material engagements; *kara*—you perform; *kibā*—or; *virakta*—renounced; *udāsa*—free from attachment; *janme-janme*—birth after birth; *tumi pañca*—you five; *mora*—My; *nija-dāsa*—own servants.

TRANSLATION

"Whether you are involved in material activities or become completely renounced, you five brothers are all My eternal servants, birth after birth.

PURPORT

Śrīla Bhaktisiddhānta Sarasvatī Ṭhākura comments that one should remember that he is eternally a servant of Kṛṣṇa. Whether one is engaged in material activity involving pounds, shillings and pence or is in the renounced order, he should always think that he is an eternal servant of God, for that is the real position of the living being. Taking *sannyāsa* and dealing in pounds, shillings and pence are both external affairs. One should always consider how to please and satisfy Kṛṣṇa. Thus even if one is involved in great material affairs, he will not become attached. As soon as one forgets that he is an eternal servant of Kṛṣṇa, he becomes involved in material attachments. However, if one is always conscious that Kṛṣṇa is always the supreme master and that he is an eternal servant of Kṛṣṇa, he is a liberated person in any condition. Entangling material activities will not affect him.

TEXT 142

কিন্তু মোর করিহ এক 'আজ্ঞা' পালন ।
'ব্যয় না করিহ কিছু রাজার মূলধন' ॥ ১৪২ ॥

kintu mora kariha eka 'ājñā' pālana
'vyaya nā kariha kichu rājāra mūla-dhana'

SYNONYMS

kintu—but; *mora*—My; *kariha*—just carry out; *eka*—one; *ājñā*—order; *pālana*—obedience to; *vyaya nā kariha*—never spend; *kichu*—any; *rājāra mūla-dhana*—capital of the King.

TRANSLATION

"However, just obey one order from Me. Do not spend any of the King's revenue.

PURPORT

When a person forgets his position as an eternal servant of Kṛṣṇa, he commits many sinful activities, but one who maintains his position as an eternal servant of Kṛṣṇa cannot deviate from the path of morality, religion and ethics. At the present, people all over the world, especially in India, have forgotten their relationship with the Supreme Personality of Godhead and His eternal servants. Therefore the principles of morality, religion and ethics have almost disappeared. This situation is most unprofitable for human society. Therefore everyone should try to accept Kṛṣṇa consciousness and follow the principles of Śrī Caitanya Mahāprabhu.

TEXT 143

**রাজার মূলধন দিয়া যে কিছু লভ্য হয় ।
সেই ধন করিহ নানা ধর্মে-কর্মে ব্যয় ॥ ১৪৩ ।**

rājāra mūla-dhana diyā ye kichu labhya haya
sei dhana kariha nānā dharme-karme vyaya

SYNONYMS

rājāra—of the King; *mūla-dhana*—revenue; *diyā*—after paying; *ye kichu labhya haya*—whatever is obtained; *sei*—that; *dhana*—money; *kariha nānā dharme-karme vyaya*—spend in various types of religious and fruitive activities.

TRANSLATION

"First you should pay the revenue due the King, and then you may spend the balance for religious and fruitive activities.

TEXT 144

**অসদ্ব্যয় না করিহ,—যাতে দুইলোক যায় ।"
এত বলি' সবাকারে দিলেন বিদায় ॥ ১৪৪ ॥**

asad-vyaya nā kariha, ——yāte dui-loka yāya"
eta bali' sabākāre dilena vidāya

SYNONYMS

asat-vyaya nā kariha—do not spend for sinful activities; *yāte*—by which; *dui-loka yāya*—one loses this life and the next; *eta bali'*—saying this; *sabākāre*—to all of them; *dilena vidāya*—bade farewell.

TRANSLATION

"Don't spend a farthing for sinful activities for which you will be the loser both in this life and the next." After saying this, Śrī Caitanya Mahāprabhu bade them farewell.

TEXT 145

রায়ের ঘরে প্রভুর 'কৃপা-বিবর্ত' কহিল।
ভক্তবাৎসল্য-গুণ যাতে ব্যক্ত হৈল ॥ ১৪৫ ॥

rāyera ghare prabhura 'kṛpā-vivarta' kahila
bhakta-vātsalya-guṇa yāte vyakta haila

SYNONYMS

rāyera—of Bhavānanda Rāya; *ghare*—at the home; *prabhura*—of Śrī Caitanya Mahāprabhu; *kṛpā-vivarta*—mercy appearing as something else; *kahila*—spoke; *bhakta-vātsalya-guṇa*—the quality of being very affectionate to the devotees; *yāte*—in which; *vyakta haila*—was revealed.

TRANSLATION

Thus the mercy of Śrī Caitanya Mahāprabhu was spoken of in the family of Bhavānanda Rāya. That mercy was clearly demonstrated, although it appeared to be something different.

PURPORT

The result of advancement in spiritual knowledge is not material improvement, but Śrī Caitanya Mahāprabhu advised Gopīnātha Paṭṭanāyaka how to use material opulence without incurring reactions to sinful life. From this advice, it appeared that the Lord encouraged Gopīnātha Paṭṭanāyaka to enhance his material condition. Actually, however, He did not. In fact, this was but a manifestation of His great affection for His devotee.

TEXT 146

সবায় আলিঙ্গিয়া প্রভু বিদায় যবে দিলা।
হরিধ্বনি করি' সব ভক্ত উঠি' গেলা ॥ ১৪৬ ॥

sabāya āliṅgiyā prabhu vidāya yabe dilā
hari-dhvani kari' saba bhakta uṭhi' gelā

SYNONYMS

sabāya—all of them; *āliṅgiyā*—embracing; *prabhu*—Śrī Caitanya Mahāprabhu; *vidāya*—farewell; *yabe dilā*—when He gave; *hari-dhvani kari'*—chanting the holy name of Hari; *saba bhakta*—all devotees; *uṭhi'*—getting up; *gelā*—left.

TRANSLATION

Śrī Caitanya Mahāprabhu embraced them all and bade them farewell. Then all the devotees got up and left, loudly chanting the holy name of Hari.

TEXT 147

প্রভুর কৃপা দেখি' সবার হৈল চমৎকার ।
তাহারা বুঝিতে নারে প্রভুর ব্যবহার ॥ ১৪৭ ॥

prabhura kṛpā dekhi' sabāra haila camatkāra
tāhārā bujhite nāre prabhura vyavahāra

SYNONYMS

prabhura—of Śrī Caitanya Mahāprabhu; *kṛpā*—mercy; *dekhi'*—seeing; *sabāra haila camatkāra*—everyone became struck with wonder; *tāhārā*—they; *bujhite nāre*—could not understand; *prabhura vyavahāra*—the behavior of Śrī Caitanya Mahāprabhu.

TRANSLATION

Seeing the extraordinary mercy the Lord granted to the family of Bhavānanda Rāya, everyone was struck with wonder. They could not understand the behavior of Śrī Caitanya Mahāprabhu.

TEXT 148

তারা সবে যদি কৃপা করিতে সাধিল ।
'আমা' হৈতে কিছু নহে—প্রভু তবে কহিল ॥ ১৪৮ ॥

tārā sabe yadi kṛpā karite sādhila
'āmā' haite kichu nahe——prabhu tabe kahila

SYNONYMS

tārā—they; *sabe*—all; *yadi*—when; *kṛpā karite*—to show mercy; *sādhila*—requested; *āmā haite kichu nahe*—I cannot do anything; *prabhu*—Lord Caitanya; *tabe*—then; *kahila*—replied.

TRANSLATION

Indeed, when all the devotees had requested the Lord to bestow His mercy upon Gopīnātha Paṭṭanāyaka, the Lord had replied that He could do nothing.

PURPORT

When a person is sinful, he loses both the chance for spiritual advancement and the chance for material opulence. If one enjoys the material world for sense gratification, he is certainly doomed. Advancement in material opulence is not the direct mercy of the Supreme Personality of Godhead; nevertheless, it indicates the indirect mercy of the Lord, for even a person too attached to material prosperity can gradually be detached and raised to the spiritual platform. Then he can offer causeless, purified service to the Lord. When Śrī Caitanya said, *āmā haite kichu nahe* ("It is not My business to do anything"), He set the ideal example for a person in the renounced order. If a *sannyāsī* takes the side of a *viṣayī,* a person engaged in material activities, his character will be criticized. A person in the renounced order should not take interest in material activities, but if he does so out of affection for a particular person, that should be considered his special mercy.

TEXT 149

গোপীনাথের নিন্দা, আর আপন-নির্বেদ ।
এইমাত্র কহিল—ইহার না বুঝিবে ভেদ ॥ ১৪৯ ॥

gopīnāthera nindā, āra āpana-nirveda
ei-mātra kahila——ihāra nā bujhibe bheda

SYNONYMS

gopīnāthera nindā—the chastisement of Gopīnātha Paṭṭanāyaka; *āra*—and; *āpana-nirveda*—His indifference; *ei*—this; *mātra*—simply; *kahila*—I have described; *ihāra*—of this; *nā bujhibe bheda*—one cannot understand the depth of meaning.

TRANSLATION

I have simply described the chastisement of Gopīnātha Paṭṭanāyaka and Śrī Caitanya Mahāprabhu's indifference. But the deep meaning of this behavior is very difficult to understand.

TEXT 150

কাশীমিশ্রে না সাধিল, রাজারে না সাধিল ।
উদ্‌যোগ বিনা মহাপ্রভু এত ফল দিল ॥ ১৫০ ॥

kāśī-miśre nā sādhila, rājāre nā sādhila
udyoga vinā mahāprabhu eta phala dila

SYNONYMS

kāśī-miśre—Kāśī Miśra; *nā sādhila*—He did not request; *rājāre*—the King; *nā sādhila*—He did not request; *udyoga vinā*—without endeavor; *mahāprabhu*—Śrī Caitanya Mahāprabhu; *eta*—such; *phala*—result; *dila*—gave.

TRANSLATION

Śrī Caitanya Mahāprabhu gave so much to Gopīnātha Paṭṭanāyaka without directly making requests of either Kāśī Miśra or the King.

TEXT 151

চৈতন্যচরিত্র এই পরম গম্ভীর ।
সেই বুঝে, তাঁর পদে যাঁর মন 'ধীর' ॥ ১৫১ ॥

caitanya-caritra ei parama gambhīra
sei bujhe, tāṅra pade yāṅra mana 'dhīra'

SYNONYMS

caitanya-caritra—behavior of Lord Caitanya; *ei*—this; *parama gambhīra*—very grave; *sei bujhe*—he understands; *tāṅra pade*—upon His lotus feet; *yāṅra*—whose; *mana*—mind; *dhīra*—sober.

TRANSLATION

The intentions of Śrī Caitanya Mahāprabhu are so deep that one can understand them only if he has complete faith in service to the lotus feet of the Lord.

TEXT 152

যেই ইহাঁ শুনে প্রভুর বাৎসল্য-প্রকাশ ।
প্রেমভক্তি পায়, তাঁর বিপদ যায় নাশ ॥ ১৫২ ॥

yei ihāṅ śune prabhura vātsalya-prakāśa
prema-bhakti pāya, tāṅra vipada yāya nāśa

SYNONYMS

yei—one who; *ihāṅ*—this; *śune*—hears; *prabhura*—of Śrī Caitanya Mahāprabhu; *vātsalya-prakāśa*—manifestation of special affection; *prema-bhakti*—loving devotional service; *pāya*—attains; *tāṅra*—his; *vipada*—dangerous condition of life; *yāya nāśa*—is destroyed.

TRANSLATION

Whether or not one understands it, if one hears of this incident concerning Gopīnātha Paṭṭanāyaka's activities and Lord Śrī Caitanya Mahāprabhu's causeless mercy upon him, certainly he will be promoted to the platform of ecstatic love for the Lord, and for him all dangers will be nullified.

TEXT 153

শ্রীরূপ-রঘুনাথ-পদে যার আশ ।
চৈতন্যচরিতামৃত কহে কৃষ্ণদাস ॥ ১৫৩ ॥

śrī-rūpa-raghunātha pade yāra āśa
śrī-caitanya-caritāmṛta kahe kṛṣṇadāsa

SYNONYMS

śrī-rūpa—Śrīla Rūpa Gosvāmī; *raghunātha*—Śrīla Raghunātha dāsa Gosvāmī; *pade*—at the lotus feet; *yāra*—whose; *āśa*—expectation; *caitanya-caritāmṛta*—the book named *Caitanya-caritāmṛta; kahe*—describes; *kṛṣṇadāsa*—Śrīla Kṛṣṇadāsa Kavirāja Gosvāmī.

TRANSLATION

Praying at the lotus feet of Śrī Rūpa and Śrī Raghunātha, always desiring their mercy, I, Kṛṣṇadāsa, narrate Śrī Caitanya-caritāmṛta, following in their footsteps.

Thus end the Bhaktivedanta purports to the Śrī Caitanya-caritāmṛta, Antya-līlā, *Ninth Chapter, describing the deliverance of Gopīnātha Paṭṭanāyaka and the manifestation of Lord Śrī Caitanya Mahāprabhu's causeless mercy to His devotee.*

CHAPTER 10

Śrī Caitanya Mahāprabhu Accepts Prasāda from the Devotees

The following summary of Chapter Ten is given by Bhaktivinoda Ṭhākura in his *Amṛta-pravāha-bhāṣya.* Before the Ratha-yātrā ceremony, all the devotees from Bengal started for Jagannātha Purī as usual. Rāghava Paṇḍita brought with him various kinds of food for Śrī Caitanya Mahāprabhu. The food had been cooked by his sister, whose name was Damayantī, and the stock was generally known as *rāghavera jhāli.* Makaradhvaja Kara, an inhabitant of Pānihāṭi who accompanied Rāghava Paṇḍita, was the secretary in charge of accounting for the *rāghavera jhāli,* the bags of food carried by Rāghava Paṇḍita.

The day when all the devotees arrived at Jagannātha Purī, Lord Govinda was enjoying sporting pastimes in the water of Narendra-sarovara. Śrī Caitanya Mahāprabhu also enjoyed the ceremony in the water with His devotees. As previously, Śrī Caitanya Mahāprabhu performed the cleansing ceremony at Guṇḍicā and chanted the famous verse *jagamohana-pari-muṇḍā yāu.* After *kīrtana* ended, He distributed *prasāda* to all the devotees and also took some Himself. Then He lay down at the door of the Gambhīrā to take rest. Somehow or other Govinda came by and massaged His feet. Govinda could not go out that day, however, and therefore he was unable to accept *prasāda.* From the character of Govinda it is to be learned that we may sometimes commit offenses for the service of the Lord, but not for sense gratification.

Govinda, the personal servant of Śrī Caitanya Mahāprabhu, induced the Lord to eat all the food delivered by the devotees of Bengal for His service. All the Vaiṣṇavas used to invite Śrī Caitanya Mahāprabhu to their homes. The Lord accepted the invitation of Caitanya dāsa, the son of Śivānanda Sena, and ate rice and yogurt there.

TEXT 1

বন্দে শ্রীকৃষ্ণচৈতন্যং ভক্তানুগ্রহকাতরম্ ।
যেন কেনাপি সন্তুষ্টং ভক্তদত্তেন শ্রদ্ধয়া ॥ ১ ॥

vande śrī-kṛṣṇa-caitanyaṁ
bhaktānugraha-kātaram

yena kenāpi santuṣṭaṁ
bhakta-dattena śraddhayā

SYNONYMS

vande—I offer my respectful obeisances; *śrī-kṛṣṇa-caitanyam*—to Lord Śrī Caitanya Mahāprabhu; *bhakta*—to His devotees; *anugraha-kātaram*—eager to show mercy; *yena kenāpi*—by anything; *santuṣṭam*—pleased; *bhakta*—by His devotees; *dattena*—offered; *śraddhayā*—with faith and love.

TRANSLATION

Let me offer my respectful obeisances unto Lord Śrī Caitanya Mahāprabhu, who is always pleased to accept anything given with faith and love by His devotees and is always ready to bestow mercy upon them.

TEXT 2

জয় জয় গৌরচন্দ্র জয় নিত্যানন্দ ।
জয়াদ্বৈতচন্দ্র জয় গৌরভক্তবৃন্দ ॥ ২ ॥

jaya jaya gauracandra jaya nityānanda
jayādvaita-candra jaya gaura-bhakta-vṛnda

SYNONYMS

jaya jaya—all glories; *gauracandra*—to Śrī Caitanya Mahāprabhu; *jaya*—all glories; *nityānanda*—to Lord Nityānanda; *jaya*—all glories; *advaita-candra*—to Advaita Ācārya; *jaya*—all glories; *gaura-bhakta-vṛnda*—to the devotees of Lord Gaurāṅga.

TRANSLATION

All glories to Śrī Caitanya Mahāprabhu! All glories to Lord Nityānanda Prabhu! All glories to Advaitacandra! All glories to all the devotees of Lord Caitanya!

TEXT 3

বর্ষান্তরে সব ভক্ত প্রভুরে দেখিতে ।
পরম-আনন্দে সবে নীলাচল যাইতে ॥ ৩ ॥

varṣāntare saba bhakta prabhure dekhite
parama-ānande sabe nīlācala yāite

SYNONYMS

varṣa-antare—at the next year; *saba bhakta*—all the devotees; *prabhure dekhite*—to see Śrī Caitanya Mahāprabhu; *parama-ānande*—in great happiness; *sabe*—all of them; *nīlācala yāite*—to go to Jagannātha Purī, Nīlācala.

TRANSLATION

The next year, all the devotees were very pleased to go to Jagannātha Purī [Nīlācala] to see Śrī Caitanya Mahāprabhu.

TEXT 4

অদ্বৈতআচার্য-গোসাঞি —সর্ব-অগ্রগণ্য ।
আচার্যরত্ন, আচার্যনিধি, শ্রীবাস আদি ধন্য ॥ ৪ ॥

advaitācārya-gosāñi——sarva-agra-gaṇya
ācāryaratna, ācāryanidhi, śrīvāsa ādi dhanya

SYNONYMS

advaita-ācārya-gosāñi—Advaita Ācārya Gosvāmī; *sarva*—of all; *agra*—the chief; *gaṇya*—to be counted; *ācāryaratna*—Candraśekhara; *ācāryanidhi*—Puṇḍarīka Vidyānidhi; *śrīvāsa*—Śrīvāsa Ṭhākura; *ādi*—and so on; *dhanya*—glorious.

TRANSLATION

Advaita Ācārya Gosāñi led the party from Bengal. He was followed by Ācāryaratna, Ācāryanidhi, Śrīvāsa Ṭhākura and other glorious devotees.

TEXT 5

যদ্যপি প্রভুর আজ্ঞা গৌড়ে রহিতে ।
তথাপি নিত্যানন্দ প্রেমে চলিলা দেখিতে ॥ ৫ ॥

yadyapi prabhura ājñā gauḍe rahite
tathāpi nityānanda preme calilā dekhite

SYNONYMS

yadyapi—although; *prabhura*—of Śrī Caitanya Mahāprabhu; *ājñā*—the order; *gauḍe rahite*—to stay in Bengal; *tathāpi*—still; *nityānanda*—Lord Nityānanda; *preme*—in ecstatic love; *calilā*—went; *dekhite*—to see.

TRANSLATION

Śrī Caitanya Mahāprabhu had ordered Lord Nityānanda to stay in Bengal, but nevertheless, because of ecstatic love, Lord Nityānanda also went to see Him.

TEXT 6

অনুরাগের লক্ষণ এই,—'বিধি' নাহি মানে।
তাঁর আজ্ঞা ভাঙ্গে তাঁর সঙ্গের কারণে ॥ ৬ ॥

anurāgera lakṣaṇa ei,——'vidhi' nāhi māne
tāṅra ājñā bhāṅge tāṅra saṅgera kāraṇe

SYNONYMS

anurāgera—of real affection; *lakṣaṇa*—symptom; *ei*—this; *vidhi*—the regulation; *nāhi māne*—does not care for; *tāṅra*—His; *ājñā*—order; *bhāṅge*—neglects; *tāṅra*—His; *saṅgera*—association; *kāraṇe*—for the purpose of.

TRANSLATION

Indeed, it is a symptom of real affection that one breaks the order of the Supreme Personality of Godhead, not caring for the regulative principles, to associate with Him.

TEXT 7

রাসে যৈছে ঘর যাইতে গোপীরে আজ্ঞা দিলা।
তাঁর আজ্ঞা ভাঙ্গি' তাঁর সঙ্গে সে রহিলা ॥ ৭ ॥

rāse yaiche ghara yāite gopīre ājñā dilā
tāṅra ājñā bhāṅgi' tāṅra saṅge se rahilā

SYNONYMS

rāse—at the time of the *rāsa* dance; *yaiche*—as; *ghara yāite*—to return home; *gopīre*—the *gopīs; ājñā dilā*—Lord Kṛṣṇa ordered; *tāṅra*—His; *ājñā*—order; *bhāṅgi'*—breaking; *tāṅra saṅge*—in His association; *se*—they; *rahilā*—kept themselves.

TRANSLATION

During the rāsa dance, Kṛṣṇa asked all the gopīs to return home, but the gopīs neglected His order and stayed there for His association.

TEXT 8

আজ্ঞা-পালনে কৃষ্ণের যৈছে পরিতোষ।
প্রেমে আজ্ঞা ভাঙ্গিলে হয় কোটিসুখ-পোষ ॥ ৮ ॥

ājñā-pālane kṛṣṇera yaiche paritoṣa
preme ājñā bhāṅgile haya koṭi-sukha-poṣa

SYNONYMS

ājñā-pālane—by carrying out the order; *kṛṣṇera*—of Lord Kṛṣṇa; *yaiche*—as; *paritoṣa*—happiness; *preme*—in ecstatic love; *ājñā bhāṅgile*—when one breaks the order; *haya*—there is; *koṭi-sukha-poṣa*—millions of times more happiness.

TRANSLATION

If one carries out Kṛṣṇa's order, Kṛṣṇa is certainly pleased, but if one sometimes breaks His order due to ecstatic love, that gives Him millions of times greater happiness.

TEXTS 9-11

বাসুদেব-দত্ত, মুরারি-গুপ্ত, গঙ্গাদাস।
শ্রীমান্‌-সেন, শ্রীমান্‌-পণ্ডিত, অকিঞ্চন কৃষ্ণদাস ॥৯॥
মুরারি, গরুড়-পণ্ডিত, বুদ্ধিমন্ত-খাঁন।
সঞ্জয়-পুরুষোত্তম, পণ্ডিত-ভগবান্‌ ॥ ১০ ॥
শুক্লাম্বর, নৃসিংহানন্দ আর যত জন।
সবাই চলিলা, নাম না যায় লিখন ॥ ১১ ॥

vāsudeva-datta, murāri-gupta, gaṅgādāsa
śrīmān-sena, śrīmān-paṇḍita, akiñcana kṛṣṇadāsa

murāri, garuḍa-paṇḍita, buddhimanta-khāṅna
sañjaya-puruṣottama, paṇḍita-bhagavān

śuklāmbara, nṛsiṁhānanda āra yata jana
sabāi calilā, nāma nā yāya likhana

SYNONYMS

vāsudeva-datta—Vāsudeva Datta; *murāri-gupta*—Murāri Gupta; *gaṅgādāsa*—Gaṅgādāsa; *śrīmān-sena*—Śrīmān Sena; *śrīmān-paṇḍita*—Śrīmān Paṇḍita;

akiñcana kṛṣṇadāsa—Akiñcana Kṛṣṇadāsa; *murāri*—Murāri Gupta; *garuḍa-paṇḍita*—Garuḍa Paṇḍita; *buddhimanta-khāṅna*—Buddhimanta Khān; *sañjaya-puruṣottama*—Sañjaya Puruṣottama; *paṇḍita-bhagavān*—Bhagavān Paṇḍita; *śuklāmbara*—Śuklāmbara; *nṛsiṁhānanda*—Nṛsiṁhānanda; *āra*—and; *yata*—as many; *jana*—persons; *sabāi*—all; *calilā*—went; *nāma*—names; *nā yāya likhana*—it is not possible to mention.

TRANSLATION

Vāsudeva Datta, Murāri Gupta, Gaṅgādāsa, Śrīmān Sena, Śrīmān Paṇḍita, Akiñcana Kṛṣṇadāsa, Murāri Gupta, Garuḍa Paṇḍita, Buddhimanta Khān, Sañjaya Puruṣottama, Bhagavān Paṇḍita, Śuklāmbara Brahmacārī, Nṛsiṁhānanda Brahmacārī and many others joined together to go to Jagannātha Purī. It would be impossible to mention the names of them all.

TEXT 12

কুলীনগ্রামী, খণ্ডবাসী মিলিলা আসিয়া ।
শিবানন্দ-সেন চলিলা সবারে লঞা ॥ ১২ ॥

kulīna-grāmī, khaṇḍa-vāsī mililā āsiyā
śivānanda-sena calilā sabāre lañā

SYNONYMS

kulīna-grāmī—the residents of Kulīna-grāma; *khaṇḍa-vāsī*—the residents of Khaṇḍa; *mililā āsiyā*—came and joined; *śivānanda-sena*—Śivānanda Sena; *calilā*—went; *sabāre lañā*—taking all of them.

TRANSLATION

The inhabitants of Kulīna-grāma and Khaṇḍa also came and joined. Śivānanda Sena took the leadership and thus started taking care of them all.

TEXT 13

রাঘব-পণ্ডিত চলে ঝালি সাজাইয়া ।
দময়ন্তী যত দ্রব্য দিয়াছে করিয়া ॥ ১৩ ॥

rāghava-paṇḍita cale jhāli sājāiyā
damayantī yata dravya diyāche kariyā

SYNONYMS

rāghava-paṇḍita—Rāghava Paṇḍita; *cale*—goes; *jhāli sājāiyā*—after preparing his bag of food; *damayantī*—his sister; *yata dravya*—all the goods; *diyāche kariyā*—cooked and prepared.

TRANSLATION

Rāghava Paṇḍita came with bags full of food prepared very nicely by his sister, Damayantī.

TEXT 14

নানা অপূর্ব ভক্ষ্যদ্রব্য প্রভুর যোগ্য ভোগ ।
বৎসরেক প্রভু যাহা করেন উপযোগ ॥ ১৪ ॥

nānā apūrva bhakṣya-dravya prabhura yogya bhoga
vatsareka prabhu yāhā karena upayoga

SYNONYMS

nānā—various; *upūrva*—unparalleled; *bhakṣya-dravya*—eatables; *prabhura*—of Śrī Caitanya Mahāprabhu; *yogya bhoga*—just suitable for the eating; *vatsareka*—for one year; *prabhu*—Śrī Caitanya Mahāprabhu; *yāhā*—which; *karena upayoga*—uses.

TRANSLATION

Damayantī made varieties of unparalleled food just suitable for Lord Śrī Caitanya Mahāprabhu to eat. The Lord ate it continually for one year.

TEXTS 15-16

আম্র-কাশন্দি, আদা-কাশন্দি ঝাল-কাশন্দি নাম ।
নেম্বু-আদা আম্রকোলি বিবিধ বিধান ॥ ১৫ ॥
আম্‌সি, আমখণ্ড, তৈলাম্র, আমসত্তা ।
যত্ন করি' গুণ্ডা করি' পুরাণ সুকুতা ॥ ১৬ ॥

āmra-kāśandi, ādā-kāśandi jhāla-kāśandi nāma
nembu-ādā āmra-koli vividha vidhāna

āmsi, āma-khaṇḍa, tailāmra, āma-sattā
yatna kari' guṇḍā kari' purāṇa sukutā

SYNONYMS

āmra-kāśandi—*āmra-kāśandi; ādā-kāśandi*—*ādā-kāśandi; jhāla-kāśandi*—*jhāla-kāśandi; nāma*—named; *nembu-ādā*—a preparation made with lime and ginger; *āmra-koli*—*āmra-koli; vividha vidhāna*—various preparations; *āmsi*—*āmsi; āma-khaṇḍa*—*āma-khaṇḍa; tailāmra*—mango within mustard oil; *āma-sattā*—*āma-sattā; yatna kari'*—with great attention; *guṇḍā kari'*—making into a powder; *purāṇa sukutā*—dried bitter vegetables such as bitter melon.

TRANSLATION

These are the names of some of the pickles and condiments in the bags of Rāghava Paṇḍita: āmra-kāśandi, ādā-kāśandi, jhāla-kāśandi, nembu-ādā, āmra-koli, āmsi, āma-khaṇḍa, tailāmra and āma-sattā. With great attention, Damayantī also made dried bitter vegetables into a powder.

TEXT 17

'সুকুতা' বলি' অবজ্ঞা না করিহ চিত্তে।
সুকুতায় যে সুখ প্রভুর, তাহা নহে পঞ্চামৃতে ॥ ১৭ ॥

'sukutā' bali' avajñā nā kariha citte
sukutāya ye sukha prabhura, tāhā nahe pañcāmṛte

SYNONYMS

sukutā—*sukutā; bali'*—because; *avajñā*—neglect; *nā kariha*—do not make; *citte*—within the mind; *sukutāya*—from *sukutā; ye*—which; *sukha*—happiness; *prabhura*—of Śrī Caitanya Mahāprabhu; *tāhā*—that; *nahe*—is not; *pañcāmṛte*—in *pañcāmṛta.*

TRANSLATION

Do not neglect sukutā because it is a bitter preparation. Śrī Caitanya Mahāprabhu derived more happiness from eating this sukutā than from drinking pañcāmṛta [a preparation of milk, sugar, ghee, honey and curd].

TEXT 18

ভাবগ্রাহী মহাপ্রভু স্নেহমাত্র লয়।
সুকুতা পাতা কাশন্দিতে মহাসুখ পায় ॥ ১৮ ॥

bhāva-grāhī mahāprabhu sneha-mātra laya
sukutā pātā kāśandite mahā-sukha pāya

SYNONYMS

bhāva-grāhī—one who accepts the purpose; *mahāprabhu*—Śrī Caitanya Mahāprabhu; *sneha*—affection; *mātra*—only; *laya*—accepts; *sukutā pātā*—in leaves of *sukutā; kāśandite*—in *kāśandi; mahā-sukha*—much pleasure; *pāya*—gets.

TRANSLATION

Since Śrī Caitanya Mahāprabhu is the Supreme Personality of Godhead, He extracts the purpose from everything. He accepted Damayantī's affection for Him, and therefore He derived great pleasure even from the dried bitter leaves of sukutā and from kāśandi [a sour condiment].

TEXT 19

'মনুষ্য'-বুদ্ধি দময়ন্তী করে প্রভুর পায়।
গুরু-ভোজনে উদরে কভু 'আম' হঞা যায় ॥ ১৯ ॥

'manuṣya'-buddhi damayantī kare prabhura pāya
guru-bhojane udare kabhu 'āma' hañā yāya

SYNONYMS

manuṣya-buddhi—considering an ordinary human being; *damayantī*—the sister of Rāghava Paṇḍita; *kare*—does; *prabhura pāya*—at the lotus feet of Śrī Caitanya Mahāprabhu; *guru-bhojane*—by overeating; *udare*—in the abdomen; *kabhu*—sometimes; *āma*—mucus; *hañā yāya*—there is.

TRANSLATION

Because of her natural love for Śrī Caitanya Mahāprabhu, Damayantī considered the Lord an ordinary human being. Therefore she thought that He would become sick by overeating and there would be mucus within His abdomen.

PURPORT

Because of pure love, the devotees of Kṛṣṇa in Goloka Vṛndāvana, Vrajabhūmi, loved Kṛṣṇa as an ordinary human being like them. Yet although they considered Kṛṣṇa one of them, their love for Kṛṣṇa knew no bounds. Similarly, because of extreme love, devotees like Rāghava Paṇḍita and his sister, Damayantī, thought of Śrī Caitanya Mahāprabhu as a human being, but their love for Him was boundless. By overeating, an ordinary human being becomes prone to a disease called *amla-pitta,* which is a product of indigestion characterized by acidity of the stomach. Damayantī thought that such a condition would afflict Śrī Caitanya Mahāprabhu.

TEXT 20

সুকুতা খাইলে সেই আম হইবেক নাশ।
এই স্নেহ মনে ভাবি' প্রভুর উল্লাস ॥ ২০ ॥

sukutā khāile sei āma ha-ibeka nāśa
ei sneha mane bhāvi' prabhura ullāsa

SYNONYMS

sukutā khāile—by eating the *sukutā; sei āma*—that mucus; *ha-ibeka nāśa*—will be vanquished; *ei*—this; *sneha*—affection; *mane*—in the mind; *bhāvi'*—thinking of; *prabhura*—of Śrī Caitanya Mahāprabhu; *ullāsa*—delight.

TRANSLATION

Because of sincere affection, she thought that eating this sukutā would cure the Lord's disease. Considering these affectionate thoughts of Damayantī, the Lord was very pleased.

TEXT 21

প্রিয়েণ সংগ্রথ্য বিপক্ষ-সন্নিধা-
বুপাহিতাং বক্ষসি পীবরস্তনী ।
স্রজং ন কাচিদ্বিজহৌ জলাবিলাং
বসন্তি হি প্রেম্ণি গুণা ন বস্তুনি ॥ ২১ ॥

priyeṇa saṅgrathya vipakṣa-sannidhāv
upāhitāṁ vakṣasi pīvara-stanī
srajaṁ na kācid vijahau jalāvilāṁ
vasanti hi premṇi guṇā na vastuni

SYNONYMS

priyeṇa—by the lover; *saṅgrathya*—after stringing; *vipakṣa-sannidhau*—in the presence of an opposite party; *upāhitām*—placed; *vakṣasi*—on the chest; *pīvara-stanī*—having raised breasts; *srajam*—a garland; *na*—not; *kācit*—some beloved; *vijahau*—rejected; *jala-āvilām*—muddy; *vasanti*—reside; *hi*—because; *premṇi*—in love; *guṇāḥ*—attributes; *na*—not; *vastuni*—in the material things.

TRANSLATION

"A dear lover strung a garland and placed it on the shoulder of his beloved in the presence of her co-wives. She had raised breasts and was very beautiful, yet although the garland was tainted with mud, she did not reject it, for its value lay not in material things but in love."

PURPORT

This is a verse from the *Kirātārjunīya* by Bhāravī.

TEXT 22

ধনিয়া-মৌহরীর তণ্ডুল গুণ্ডা করিয়া ।
নাড়ু বান্ধিয়াছে চিনি-পাক করিয়া ॥ ২২ ॥

dhaniyā-mauharīra taṇḍula guṇḍā kariyā
nāḍu bāndhiyāche cini-pāka kariyā

SYNONYMS

dhaniyā—of coriander seeds; *mauharīra*—of anise seeds; *taṇḍula*—grains; *guṇḍā kariyā*—grinding to a powder; *nāḍu bāndhiyāche*—rendered into *laḍḍus; cini-pāka kariyā*—cooking with sugar.

TRANSLATION

Damayantī powdered coriander and anise seeds, cooked them with sugar and made them into small sweetmeats that were shaped like small balls.

TEXT 23

শুণ্ঠিখণ্ড নাড়ু, আর আমপিত্তহর ।
পৃথক্ পৃথক্ বান্ধি' বস্ত্রের কুথলী ভিতর ॥ ২৩ ॥

śuṇṭhi-khaṇḍa nāḍu, āra āma-pitta-hara
pṛthak pṛthak bāndhi' vastrera kuthalī bhitara

SYNONYMS

śuṇṭhi-khaṇḍa nāḍu—sweetmeat balls made with dried ginger; *āra*—and; *āma-pitta-hara*—which removes mucus caused by too much bile; *pṛthak pṛthak*—separately; *bāndhi'*—packaging; *vastrera*—of cloth; *kuthalī*—small bags; *bhitara*—within.

TRANSLATION

She made balls of sweetmeats with dried ginger to remove mucus caused by too much bile. She put all these preparations separately into small cloth bags.

TEXT 24

কোলিশুণ্ঠি, কোলিচূর্ণ, কোলিখণ্ড আর ।
কত নাম লইব, শতপ্রকার 'আচার' ॥ ২৪ ॥

koli-śuṇṭhi, koli-cūrṇa, koli-khaṇḍa āra
kata nāma la-iba, śata-prakāra 'ācāra'

SYNONYMS

koli-śuṇṭhi—dried ginger and berries; *koli-cūrṇa*—powder of berries; *koli-khaṇḍa*—another preparation of berries; *āra*—and; *kata nāma*—how many names; *la-iba*—I shall call; *śata-prakāra*—a hundred varieties; *ācāra*—condiments and pickles.

TRANSLATION

She made a hundred varieties of condiments and pickles. She also made koli-śuṇṭhi, koli-cūrṇa, koli-khaṇḍa and many other preparations. How many should I name?

TEXT 25

নারিকেল-খণ্ড নাড়ু, আর নাড়ু গঙ্গাজল ।
চিরস্থায়ী খণ্ডবিকার করিলা সকল ॥ ২৫ ॥

nārikela-khaṇḍa nāḍu, āra nāḍu gaṅgā-jala
cira-sthāyī khaṇḍa-vikāra karilā sakala

SYNONYMS

nārikela-khaṇḍa nāḍu—sweetmeat balls made with coconut powder; *āra*—and; *nāḍu gaṅgā-jala*—a sweetmeat ball as white as Ganges water; *cira-sthāyī*—long-lasting; *khaṇḍa-vikāra*—modified forms of sugar-candy sweets; *karilā*—made; *sakala*—all.

TRANSLATION

She made many sweetmeats shaped like balls. Some were made with powdered coconut, and others looked as white as the water of the Ganges. In this way she made many varieties of long-lasting sugar confections.

TEXT 26

চিরস্থায়ী ক্ষীরসার, মণ্ডাদি-বিকার ।
অমৃত-কর্পূর আদি অনেক প্রকার ॥ ২৬ ॥

cira-sthāyī kṣīra-sāra, maṇḍādi-vikāra
amṛta-karpūra ādi aneka prakāra

SYNONYMS

cira-sthāyī—long-lasting; *kṣīra-sāra*—cheese; *maṇḍādi-vikāra*—varieties of sweetmeats made from *maṇḍa,* or milk and cream; *amṛta-karpūra*—a preparation made with milk and camphor; *ādi*—and others; *aneka prakāra*—many varieties.

TRANSLATION

She made long-lasting cheese, many varieties of sweetmeats with milk and cream, and many other varied preparations, such as amṛta-karpūra.

TEXT 27

শালিকাচুটি-ধান্যের 'আতপ' চিড়া করি'।
নূতন-বস্ত্রের বড় কুথলী সব ভরি'॥ ২৭॥

śālikācuṭi-dhānyera 'ātapa' ciḍā kari'
nūtana-vastrera baḍa kuthalī saba bhari'

SYNONYMS

śālikācuṭi-dhānyera—of a kind of fine rice; *ātapa*—dried in the sunshine; *ciḍā kari'*—making flat rice; *nūtana-vastrera*—of new cloth; *baḍa kuthalī*—a large bag; *saba*—all; *bhari'*—filling.

TRANSLATION

She made flat rice from fine, unboiled, śāli paddy and filled a large bag made of new cloth.

TEXT 28

কতেক চিড়া হুড়ুম্ করি' ঘৃতেতে ভাজিয়া।
চিনি-পাকে নাড়ু কৈলা কর্পূরাদি দিয়া॥ ২৮॥

kateka ciḍā huḍum kari' ghṛtete bhājiyā
cini-pāke nāḍu kailā karpūrādi diyā

SYNONYMS

kateka ciḍā—some of the flat rice; *huḍum kari'*—making into puffed rice; *ghṛtete bhājiyā*—frying in ghee; *cini-pāke*—by cooking in sugar juice; *nāḍu kailā*—made into round balls; *karpūra-ādi diyā*—mixing with camphor and other ingredients.

TRANSLATION

She made some of the flat rice into puffed rice, fried it in ghee, cooked it in sugar juice, mixed in some camphor and rolled it into balls.

TEXTS 29-30

শালি-ধান্যের তণ্ডুল-ভাজা চূর্ণ করিয়া।
ঘৃতসিক্ত চূর্ণ কৈলা চিনি-পাক দিয়া॥ ২৯॥
কর্পূর, মরিচ, লবঙ্গ, এলাচি, রসবাস।
চূর্ণ দিয়া নাড়ু কৈলা পরম সুবাস॥ ৩০॥

śāli-dhānyera taṇḍula-bhājā cūrṇa kariyā
ghṛta-sikta cūrṇa kailā cini-pāka diyā

karpūra, marica, lavaṅga, elāci, rasavāsa
cūrṇa diyā nāḍu kailā parama suvāsa

SYNONYMS

śāli-dhānyera—of rice of a fine quality; *taṇḍula*—the grains; *bhājā*—being fried; *cūrṇa kariyā*—making it into a powder; *ghṛta-sikta*—moistened with ghee; *cūrṇa*—the powder; *kailā*—made; *cini-pāka diyā*—by cooking with sugar; *karpūra*—camphor; *marica*—black pepper; *lavaṅga*—cloves; *elāci*—cardamom; *rasa-vāsa*—and other spices; *cūrṇa*—to the powder; *diyā*—adding; *nāḍu*—round sweetmeats; *kailā*—made; *parama su-vāsa*—very palatable.

TRANSLATION

She powdered fried grains of fine rice, moistened the powder with ghee and cooked it in a solution of sugar. Then she added camphor, black pepper, cloves, cardamom and other spices and rolled it into balls that were very palatable and aromatic.

TEXT 31

শালি-ধান্যের খই পুনঃ ঘৃতেতে ভাজিয়া ।
চিনি-পাক উখ্ড়া কৈলা কর্পূরাদি দিয়া ॥ ৩১ ॥

śāli-dhānyera kha-i punaḥ ghṛtete bhājiyā
cini-pāka ukhḍā kailā karpūrādi diyā

SYNONYMS

śāli-dhānyera kha-i—parched rice from fine paddy; *punaḥ*—again; *ghṛtete bhājiyā*—frying with ghee; *cini-pāka*—boiling with sugar juice; *ukhḍā*—of the name *ukhḍā; kailā*—made; *karpūra-ādi diyā*—mixing with camphor.

TRANSLATION

She took parched rice from fine paddy, fried it in ghee, cooked it in a sugar solution, mixed in some camphor and thus made a preparation called ukhḍā or muḍki.

TEXT 32

ফুট্কলাই চূর্ণ করি' ঘৃতে ভাজাইল ।
চিনি-পাকে কর্পূরাদি দিয়া নাড়ু কৈল ॥ ৩২ ॥

phuṭkalāi cūrṇa kari' ghṛte bhājāila
cini-pāke karpūrādi diyā nāḍu kaila

SYNONYMS

phuṭkalāi—fused peas fried in ghee and soaked in sugar juice; *cūrṇa kari'*—making into powder; *ghṛte bhājāila*—fried with ghee; *cini-pāke*—cooking with sugar; *karpūra-ādi*—camphor and other ingredients; *diyā*—adding; *nāḍu kaila*—made round sweetmeat balls.

TRANSLATION

Another variety of sweet was made with fused peas that were powdered, fried in ghee and then cooked in sugar juice. Camphor was mixed in, and then the sweet was rolled into a ball.

TEXT 33

কহিতে না জানি নাম এ-জন্মে যাহার ।
ঐছে নানা ভক্ষ্যদ্রব্য সহস্রপ্রকার ॥ ৩৩ ॥

kahite nā jāni nāma e-janme yāhāra
aiche nānā bhakṣya-dravya sahasra-prakāra

SYNONYMS

kahite nā jāni—I cannot speak; *nāma*—the names; *e-janme*—in this life; *yāhāra*—of which; *aiche*—similar; *nānā*—many; *bhakṣya-dravya*—eatables; *sahasra-prakāra*—hundreds and thousands of varieties.

TRANSLATION

I could not mention the names of all these wonderful eatables, even in a lifetime. Damayantī made hundreds and thousands of varieties.

TEXT 34

রাঘবের আজ্ঞা, আর করেন দময়ন্তী ।
দুঁহার প্রভুতে স্নেহ পরম-ভকতি ॥ ৩৪ ॥

rāghavera ājñā, āra karena damayantī
duṅhāra prabhute sneha parama-bhakati

SYNONYMS

rāghavera ājñā—the order of Rāghava Paṇḍita; *āra*—and; *karena*—executes; *damayantī*—Damayantī; *duṅhāra*—of both of them; *prabhute*—unto Śrī Caitanya

Mahāprabhu; *sneha*—affection; *parama-bhakati*—highly developed devotional service.

TRANSLATION

Damayantī made all these preparations following the order of her brother, Rāghava Paṇḍita. Both of them had unlimited affection for Śrī Caitanya Mahāprabhu and were advanced in devotional service.

TEXT 35

গঙ্গা-মৃত্তিকা আনি' বস্ত্রেতে ছানিয়া ।
পাঁপড়ি করিয়া দিলা গন্ধদ্রব্য দিয়া ॥ ৩৫ ॥

gaṅgā-mṛttikā āni' vastrete chāniyā
pāṅpaḍi kariyā dilā gandha-dravya diyā

SYNONYMS

gaṅgā-mṛttikā—dirt from the River Ganges; *āni'*—bringing; *vastrete*—through a cloth; *chāniyā*—pressing; *pāṅpaḍi kariyā dilā*—made into small balls; *gandha-dravya diyā*—mixing with aromatic agents.

TRANSLATION

Damayantī took earth from the Ganges, dried it, powdered it, strained it through a fine cloth, mixed in aromatic ingredients and rolled it into small balls.

TEXT 36

পাতল মৃৎপাত্রে সন্ধানাদি ভরি' ।
আর সব বস্তু ভরে বস্ত্রের কুথলী ॥ ৩৬ ॥

pātala mṛt-pātre sandhānādi bhari'
āra saba vastu bhare vastrera kuthalī

SYNONYMS

pātala—thin; *mṛt-pātre*—in pots of earth; *sandhāna-ādi*—condiments and other items; *bhari'*—filling; *āra*—other; *saba*—all; *vastu*—things; *bhare*—filled; *vastrera kuthalī*—small bags of cloth.

TRANSLATION

The condiments and similar items were put into thin earthen pots, and everything else was put into small cloth bags.

TEXT 37

সামান্য ঝালি হৈতে দ্বিগুণ ঝালি কৈলা।
পারিপাটি করি' সব ঝালি ভরাইলা ॥ ৩৭ ॥

sāmānya jhāli haite dviguṇa jhāli kailā
pāripāṭi kari' saba jhāli bharāilā

SYNONYMS

sāmānya—small; *jhāli*—bags; *haite*—from; *dvi-guṇa*—twice as big; *jhāli*—bags; *kailā*—made; *pāripāṭi kari'*—with great attention; *saba jhāli*—all the bags; *bharāilā*—she filled.

TRANSLATION

From small bags Damayantī made bags that were twice as large. Then with great attention she filled all the large ones with the small ones.

TEXT 38

ঝালি বান্ধি' মোহর দিল আগ্রহ করিয়া।
তিন বোঝারি ঝালি বহে ক্রম করিয়া ॥ ৩৮ ॥

jhāli bāndhi' mohara dila āgraha kariyā
tina bojhāri jhāli vahe krama kariyā

SYNONYMS

jhāli bāndhi'—binding the bags; *mohara dila*—she sealed; *āgraha kariyā*—with great attention; *tina bojhāri*—three carriers; *jhāli vahe*—carried the bags; *krama kariyā*—one after another.

TRANSLATION

She then wrapped and sealed each and every bag with great attention. The bags were carried by three bearers, one after another.

TEXT 39

সংক্ষেপে কহিলুঁ এই ঝালির বিচার।
'রাঘবের ঝালি' বলি' বিখ্যাতি যাহার ॥ ৩৯ ॥

saṅkṣepe kahiluṅ ei jhālira vicāra
'rāghavera jhāli' bali' vikhyāti yāhāra

SYNONYMS

saṅkṣepe—in brief; *kahiluṅ*—I have spoken; *ei jhālira*—of these bags; *vicāra*—the description; *rāghavera jhāli*—the bags of Rāghava; *bali'*—as; *vikhyāti*—the fame; *yāhāra*—of which.

TRANSLATION

Thus I have briefly described the bags that have become famous as rāghavera jhāli.

TEXT 40

ঝালির উপর 'মুন্‌সিব' মকরধ্বজ-কর ।
প্রাণরূপে ঝালি রাখে হঞা তৎপর ॥ ৪০ ॥

jhālira upara 'munsiba' makaradhvaja-kara
prāṇa-rūpe jhāli rākhe hañā tatpara

SYNONYMS

jhālira upara—upon the bags; *munsiba*—the superintendent; *makaradhvaja-kara*—Makaradhvaja Kara; *prāṇa-rūpe*—like his life; *jhāli rākhe*—he keeps the bags; *hañā tatpara*—with great attention.

TRANSLATION

The superintendent for all those bags was Makaradhvaja Kara, who kept them with great attention like his very life.

TEXT 41

এইমতে বৈষ্ণব সব নীলাচলে আইলা ।
দৈবে জগন্নাথের সে দিন জল-লীলা ॥ ৪১ ॥

ei-mate vaiṣṇava saba nīlācale āilā
daive jagannāthera se dina jala-līlā

SYNONYMS

ei-mate—in this way; *vaiṣṇava saba*—all the Vaiṣṇavas; *nīlācale āilā*—came to Nīlācala; *daive*—by chance; *jagannāthera*—of Lord Jagannātha; *se dina*—that day; *jala-līlā*—pastimes in the water.

TRANSLATION

Thus all the Vaiṣṇavas from Bengal went to Jagannātha Purī. By chance, they arrived on the day when Lord Jagannātha performs pastimes in the water.

TEXT 42

**নরেন্দ্রের জলে 'গোবিন্দ' নৌকাতে চড়িয়া ।
জলক্রীড়া করে সব ভক্তগণ লঞা ॥ ৪২ ॥**

*narendrera jale 'govinda' naukāte caḍiyā
jala-krīḍā kare saba bhakta-gaṇa lañā*

SYNONYMS

narendrera jale—upon the water of the lake known as Narendra-sarovara; *govinda*—Lord Govinda; *naukāte caḍiyā*—getting aboard a boat; *jala-krīḍā kare*—displays His water pastimes; *saba bhakta-gaṇa*—all the devotees; *lañā*—taking.

TRANSLATION

Boarding a boat in the waters of Narendra-sarovara, Lord Govinda performed His water pastimes with all the devotees.

TEXT 43

**সেইকালে মহাপ্রভু ভক্তগণ-সঙ্গে ।
নরেন্দ্রে আইলা দেখিতে জলকেলি-রঙ্গে ॥ ৪৩ ॥**

*sei-kāle mahāprabhu bhakta-gaṇa-saṅge
narendre āilā dekhite jala-keli-raṅge*

SYNONYMS

sei-kāle—at that time; *mahāprabhu*—Śrī Caitanya Mahāprabhu; *bhakta-gaṇa-saṅge*—with His devotees; *narendre āilā*—arrived at the Narendra Lake; *dekhite*—to see; *jala-keli*—the pastimes on the water; *raṅge*—in great jubilation.

TRANSLATION

Then Śrī Caitanya Mahāprabhu arrived with His personal associates to see the jubilant pastimes of Lord Jagannātha in the Narendra-sarovara.

TEXT 44

**সেইকালে আইলা সব গৌড়ের ভক্তগণ ।
নরেন্দ্রেতে প্রভু-সঙ্গে হইল মিলন ॥ ৪৪ ॥**

*sei-kāle āilā saba gauḍera bhakta-gaṇa
narendrete prabhu-saṅge ha-ila milana*

SYNONYMS

sei-kāle—at the same time; *āilā*—arrived; *saba*—all; *gauḍera bhakta-gaṇa*—the devotees from Bengal; *narendrete*—at the lake known as Narendra-sarovara; *prabhu-saṅge*—with Lord Śrī Caitanya Mahāprabhu; *ha-ila milana*—there was a meeting.

TRANSLATION

At the same time, all the devotees from Bengal arrived at the lake and had a great meeting with the Lord.

TEXT 45

ভক্তগণ পড়ে আসি' প্রভুর চরণে ।
উঠাঞা প্রভু সবারে কৈলা আলিঙ্গনে ॥ ৪৫ ॥

bhakta-gaṇa paḍe āsi' prabhura caraṇe
uṭhāñā prabhu sabāre kailā āliṅgane

SYNONYMS

bhakta-gaṇa—the devotees; *paḍe*—fell; *āsi'*—coming; *prabhura caraṇe*—at the lotus feet of Śrī Caitanya Mahāprabhu; *uṭhāñā*—getting them up; *prabhu*—Śrī Caitanya Mahāprabhu; *sabāre*—all of them; *kailā āliṅgane*—embraced.

TRANSLATION

All the devotees immediately fell at the lotus feet of Śrī Caitanya Mahāprabhu, and the Lord lifted and embraced every one of them.

TEXT 46

গৌড়ীয়া-সম্প্রদায় সব করেন কীর্তন ।
প্রভুর মিলনে উঠে প্রেমের ক্রন্দন ॥ ৪৬ ॥

gauḍīyā-sampradāya saba karena kīrtana
prabhura milane uṭhe premera krandana

SYNONYMS

gauḍīyā-sampradāya—of the group of Vaiṣṇavas from Bengal; *saba*—all; *karena kīrtana*—perform congregational chanting; *prabhura milane*—upon meeting Śrī Caitanya Mahāprabhu; *uṭhe*—rise; *premera krandana*—crying in ecstatic love.

TRANSLATION

The Gauḍīya-sampradāya, consisting of all the devotees from Bengal, began congregational chanting. When they met the Lord, they began to cry loudly in ecstatic love.

TEXT 47

জলক্রীড়া, বাদ্য, গীত, নর্তন, কীর্তন ।
মহাকোলাহল তীরে, সলিলে খেলন ॥ ৪৭ ॥

jala-krīḍā, vādya, gīta, nartana, kīrtana
mahā-kolāhala tīre, salile khelana

SYNONYMS

jala-krīḍā—the pastimes in the water; *vādya*—musical vibration; *gīta*—singing; *nartana*—dancing; *kīrtana*—chanting; *mahā-kolāhala*—tumultuous sound; *tīre*—on the bank; *salile*—in the water; *khelana*—sporting.

TRANSLATION

Because of the pastimes in the water, there was great jubilation on the shore, with music, singing, chanting, dancing and tumultuous crying.

TEXT 48

গৌড়ীয়া-সঙ্কীর্তনে আর রোদন মিলিয়া ।
মহাকোলাহল হৈল ব্রহ্মাণ্ড ভরিয়া ॥ ৪৮ ॥

gauḍīyā-saṅkīrtane āra rodana miliyā
mahā-kolāhala haila brahmāṇḍa bhariyā

SYNONYMS

gauḍīyā-saṅkīrtane—congregational chanting by the Gauḍīya Vaiṣṇavas; *āra*—and; *rodana*—crying; *miliyā*—mixing; *mahā-kolāhala*—a great, tumultuous sound vibration; *haila*—there was; *brahmāṇḍa*—the universe; *bhariyā*—filling.

TRANSLATION

The chanting and crying of the Gauḍīyā Vaiṣṇavas mixed and created a tumultuous sound vibration that filled the entire universe.

TEXT 49

সব ভক্ত লঞা প্রভু নামিলেন জলে ।
সবা লঞা জলক্রীড়া করেন কুতুহলে ॥ ৪৯ ॥

saba bhakta lañā prabhu nāmilena jale
sabā lañā jala-krīḍā karena kutūhale

SYNONYMS

saba bhakta—all the devotees; *lañā*—taking; *prabhu*—Śrī Caitanya Mahāprabhu; *nāmilena jale*—got down in the water; *sabā lañā*—taking all of them; *jala-krīḍā*—activities in the water; *karena*—performs; *kutūhale*—in great jubilation.

TRANSLATION

Śrī Caitanya Mahāprabhu entered the water with His devotees and began His pastimes with them in great jubilation.

TEXT 50

প্রভুর এই জলক্রীড়া দাস-বৃন্দাবন ।
'চৈতন্যমঙ্গলে' বিস্তারি' করিয়াছেন বর্ণন ॥ ৫০ ॥

prabhura ei jala-krīḍā dāsa-vṛndāvana
'caitanya-maṅgale' vistāri' kariyāchena varṇana

SYNONYMS

prabhura—of Śrī Caitanya Mahāprabhu; *ei*—these; *jala-krīḍā*—activities in the water; *dāsa-vṛndāvana*—Vṛndāvana dāsa Ṭhākura; *caitanya-maṅgale*—in his book *Caitanya-maṅgala,* now known as *Caitanya-bhāgavata; vistāri'*—describing in detail; *kariyāchena varṇana*—has narrated.

TRANSLATION

In his Caitanya-maṅgala [now known as Caitanya-bhāgavata], Vṛndāvana dāsa Ṭhākura has given a detailed description of the activities the Lord performed in the water.

TEXT 51

পুনঃ ইহাঁ বর্ণিলে পুনরুক্তি হয় ।
ব্যর্থ লিখন হয়, আর গ্রন্থ বাড়য় ॥ ৫১ ॥

punaḥ ihāṅ varṇile punarukti haya
vyartha likhana haya, āra grantha bāḍaya

SYNONYMS

punaḥ—again; *ihāṅ*—here; *varṇile*—if I describe; *punaḥ-ukti haya*—it will be repetition; *vyartha*—useless; *likhana*—writing; *haya*—is; *āra*—and; *grantha bāḍaya*—increases the volume of the book.

TRANSLATION

There is no use describing here the activities of the Lord again. It would simply be repetitious and would increase the size of this book.

TEXT 52

জললীলা করি' গোবিন্দ চলিলা আলয় ।
নিজগণ লঞা প্রভু গেলা দেবালয় ॥ ৫২ ॥

jala-līlā kari' govinda calilā ālaya
nija-gaṇa lañā prabhu gelā devālaya

SYNONYMS

jala-līlā kari'—after finishing the pastimes on the water; *govinda*—Lord Jagannātha in His moving form as Govinda; *calilā ālaya*—returned to His place; *nija-gaṇa*—His devotees; *lañā*—taking; *prabhu*—Śrī Caitanya Mahāprabhu; *gelā*—went; *deva-ālaya*—to the temple.

TRANSLATION

After concluding His pastimes in the water, Lord Govinda returned to His residence. Then Śrī Caitanya Mahāprabhu went to the temple, taking all His devotees with Him.

PURPORT

The Deity referred to herein as Govinda is the *vijaya-vigraha* in the temple of Jagannātha. When there is a need to take Jagannātha somewhere, the *vijaya-vigraha* is taken because the body of Jagannātha is very heavy. The *vijaya-vigraha* in the Jagannātha temple is known as Govinda. For the pastimes in the Narendra-sarovara, the *vijaya-vigraha* was carried there instead of Lord Jagannātha.

TEXT 53

জগন্নাথ দেখি' পুনঃ নিজ-ঘরে আইলা ।
প্রসাদ আনাঞা ভক্তগণে খাওয়াইলা ॥ ৫৩ ॥

jagannātha dekhi' punaḥ nija-ghare āilā
prasāda ānāñā bhakta-gaṇe khāoyāilā

SYNONYMS

jagannātha dekhi'—after seeing Lord Jagannātha; *punaḥ*—again; *nija-ghare*—to His residence; *āilā*—returned; *prasāda*—*prasāda;* *ānāñā*—causing to be brought; *bhakta-gaṇe khāoyāilā*—fed the devotees.

TRANSLATION

When Śrī Caitanya Mahāprabhu returned to His residence after visiting the temple of Jagannātha, He asked for a large quantity of Lord Jagannātha's prasāda, which He then distributed among His devotees so that they could eat sumptuously.

TEXT 54

ইষ্টগোষ্ঠী সবা লঞা কতক্ষণ কৈলা ।
নিজ নিজ পূর্ব-বাসায় সবায় পাঠাইলা ॥ ৫৪ ॥

iṣṭa-goṣṭhī sabā lañā kata-kṣaṇa kailā
nija nija pūrva-vāsāya sabāya pāṭhāilā

SYNONYMS

iṣṭa-goṣṭhī—discussion of spiritual matters; *sabā lañā*—taking all the devotees; *kata-kṣaṇa*—for some time; *kailā*—did; *nija nija*—respective; *pūrva-vāsāya*—to the former residences; *sabāya*—all; *pāṭhāilā*—He sent.

TRANSLATION

After talking with all the devotees for some time, Śrī Caitanya Mahāprabhu asked them to occupy the individual residences in which they had lived the previous year.

TEXT 55

গোবিন্দ-ঠাঞি রাঘব ঝালি সমর্পিলা ।
ভোজন-গৃহের কোণে ঝালি গোবিন্দ রাখিলা ॥৫৫॥

govinda-ṭhāñi rāghava jhāli samarpilā
bhojana-gṛhera koṇe jhāli govinda rākhilā

SYNONYMS

govinda-ṭhāñi—in charge of Govinda; *rāghava*—Rāghava Paṇḍita; *jhāli*—the *jhāli,* the bags of eatables; *samarpilā*—delivered; *bhojana-gṛhera*—of the dining room; *koṇe*—in the corner; *jhāli*—the bags; *govinda*—Govinda; *rākhilā*—kept.

TRANSLATION

Rāghava Paṇḍita delivered the bags of eatables to Govinda, who kept them in a corner of the dining room.

TEXT 56

পূর্ব-বৎসরের ঝালি আজাড় করিয়া ।
দ্রব্য ভরিবারে রাখে অন্য গৃহে লঞা ॥ ৫৬ ॥

pūrva-vatsarera jhāli ājāḍa kariyā
dravya bharibāre rākhe anya gṛhe lañā

SYNONYMS

pūrva-vatsarera—of the previous year; *jhāli*—bags; *ājāḍa kariyā*—emptying; *dravya bharibāre*—to fill with goods; *rākhe*—keeps; *anya gṛhe*—to another room; *lañā*—taking.

TRANSLATION

Govinda thoroughly emptied the bags from the previous year and kept them in another room to fill them with other goods.

TEXT 57

আর দিন মহাপ্রভু নিজগণ লঞা ।
জগন্নাথ দেখিলেন শয্যোত্থানে যাঞা ॥ ৫৭ ॥

āra dina mahāprabhu nija-gaṇa lañā
jagannātha dekhilena śayyotthāne yāñā

SYNONYMS

āra dina—the next day; *mahāprabhu*—Śrī Caitanya Mahāprabhu; *nija-gaṇa lañā*—accompanied by His personal devotees; *jagannātha dekhilena*—saw Lord Jagannātha; *śayyā-utthāne*—at the time of rising early from bed; *yāñā*—going.

TRANSLATION

The next day, Śrī Caitanya Mahāprabhu went with His personal devotees to see Lord Jagannātha when Lord Jagannātha arose early in the morning.

TEXT 58

বেড়া-সঙ্কীর্তন তাহাঁ আরম্ভ করিলা ।
সাত-সম্প্রদায় তবে গাইতে লাগিলা ॥ ৫৮ ॥

beḍā-saṅkīrtana tāhāṅ ārambha karilā
sāta-sampradāya tabe gāite lāgilā

SYNONYMS

beḍā-saṅkīrtana—surrounding congregational chanting; *tāhāṅ*—there; *ārambha karilā*—began; *sāta-sampradāya*—seven groups; *tabe*—thereupon; *gāite lāgilā*—began to chant.

TRANSLATION

After seeing Lord Jagannātha, Śrī Caitanya Mahāprabhu began His all-encompassing saṅkīrtana. He formed seven groups, which then began to chant.

PURPORT

For an explanation of the *beḍā-saṅkīrtana,* one may refer to *Madhya-līlā,* Chapter Eleven, verses 215-238.

TEXT 59

সাত-সম্প্রদায়ে নৃত্য করে সাত জন ।
অদ্বৈত আচার্য, আর প্রভু-নিত্যানন্দ ॥ ৫৯ ॥

sāta-sampradāye nṛtya kare sāta jana
advaita ācārya, āra prabhu-nityānanda

SYNONYMS

sāta-sampradāye—in the seven groups; *nṛtya kare*—danced; *sāta jana*—seven persons; *advaita ācārya*—Advaita Ācārya; *āra*—and; *prabhu-nityānanda*—Lord Nityānanda.

TRANSLATION

In each of the seven groups was a principal dancer like Advaita Ācārya and Lord Nityānanda.

TEXT 60

বক্রেশ্বর, অচ্যুতানন্দ, পণ্ডিত-শ্রীবাস ।
সত্যরাজ-খাঁন, আর নরহরিদাস ॥ ৬০ ॥

vakreśvara, acyutānanda, paṇḍita-śrīvāsa
satyarāja-khāṅna, āra narahari-dāsa

SYNONYMS

vakreśvara—Vakreśvara; *acyutānanda*—Acyutānanda; *paṇḍita-śrīvāsa*—Paṇḍita Śrīvāsa; *satyarāja-khāṅna*—Satyarāja Khān; *āra*—and; *narahari-dāsa*—Narahari dāsa.

TRANSLATION

The dancers in the other groups were Vakreśvara Paṇḍita, Acyutānanda, Paṇḍita Śrīvāsa, Satyarāja Khān and Narahari dāsa.

TEXT 61

সাত-সম্প্রদায়ে প্রভু করেন ভ্রমণ ।
'মোর সম্প্রদায়ে প্রভু'—ঐছে সবার মন ॥ ৬১ ॥

sāta-sampradāye prabhu karena bhramaṇa
'mora sampradāye prabhu'——aiche sabāra mana

SYNONYMS

sāta-sampradāye—in the seven groups; *prabhu*—Śrī Caitanya Mahāprabhu; *karena bhramaṇa*—wanders; *mora sampradāye prabhu*—Śrī Caitanya Mahāprabhu is in our group; *aiche*—in this way; *sabāra mana*—everyone was thinking.

TRANSLATION

As Śrī Caitanya Mahāprabhu walked from one group to another inspecting them, the men in each group thought, "The Lord is within our group."

TEXT 62

সঙ্কীর্তন-কোলাহলে আকাশ ভেদিল ।
সব জগন্নাথবাসী দেখিতে আইল ॥ ৬২ ॥

saṅkīrtana-kolāhale ākāśa bhedila
saba jagannātha-vāsī dekhite āila

SYNONYMS

saṅkīrtana-kolāhale—tumultuous roaring of congregational chanting; *ākāśa bhedila*—filled the sky; *saba*—all; *jagannātha-vāsī*—the inhabitants of Jagannātha Purī; *dekhite āila*—came to see.

TRANSLATION

The congregational chanting made a tumultuous roar that filled the sky. All the inhabitants of Jagannātha Purī came to see the kīrtana.

TEXT 63

রাজা আসি' দূরে দেখে নিজগণ লঞা ।
রাজপত্নী সব দেখে অট্টালী চড়িয়া ॥ ৬৩ ॥

rājā āsi' dūre dekhe nija-gaṇa lañā
rāja-patnī saba dekhe aṭṭālī caḍiyā

SYNONYMS

rājā—the King; *āsi'*—coming; *dūre*—from a distant place; *dekhe*—sees; *nija-gaṇa lañā*—accompanied by his personal staff; *rāja-patnī*—the queens; *saba*—all; *dekhe*—see; *aṭṭālī caḍiyā*—going up high in the palace.

TRANSLATION

Accompanied by his personal staff, the King also came there and watched from a distance, and all the queens watched from the elevated parts of the palace.

TEXT 64

কীর্তন-আটোপে পৃথিবী করে টলমল ।
'হরিধ্বনি' করে লোক, হৈল কোলাহল ॥ ৬৪ ॥

kīrtana-āṭope pṛthivī kare ṭalamala
'hari-dhvani' kare loka, haila kolāhala

SYNONYMS

kīrtana-āṭope—by the force of congregational chanting; *pṛthivī*—the whole world; *kare ṭalamala*—trembles; *hari-dhvani kare*—chanted the transcendental sound Hari; *loka*—people in general; *haila*—there was; *kolāhala*—a tumultuous sound.

TRANSLATION

Due to the forceful vibration of kīrtana, the entire world began trembling. When everyone chanted the holy name, they made a tumultuous sound.

TEXT 65

এইমত কতক্ষণ করাইলা কীর্তন ।
আপনে নাচিতে তবে প্রভুর হৈল মন ॥ ৬৫ ॥

ei-mata kata-kṣaṇa karāilā kīrtana
āpane nācite tabe prabhura haila mana

SYNONYMS

ei-mata—in this way; *kata-kṣaṇa*—for some time; *karāilā kīrtana*—caused *kīrtana* to be performed; *āpane*—personally; *nācite*—to dance; *tabe*—then; *prabhura haila mana*—Śrī Caitanya Mahāprabhu desired.

TRANSLATION

In this way the Lord had congregational chanting performed for some time, and then He Himself desired to dance.

TEXT 66

সাত-দিকে সাত-সম্প্রদায় গায়, বাজায় ।
মধ্যে মহাপ্রেমাবেশে নাচে গৌর-রায় ॥ ৬৬ ॥

sāta-dike sāta-sampradāya gāya, bājāya
madhye mahā-premāveśe nāce gaura-rāya

SYNONYMS

sāta-dike—in seven directions; *sāta-sampradāya*—the seven groups; *gāya*—chant; *bājāya*—play on the *mṛdaṅga; madhye*—in the center; *mahā-premāveśe*—in great ecstatic love of Kṛṣṇa; *nāce*—dances; *gaura-rāya*—Śrī Caitanya Mahāprabhu.

TRANSLATION

The seven groups began chanting and beating their drums in seven directions, and Śrī Caitanya Mahāprabhu began dancing in the center in great ecstatic love.

TEXT 67

উড়িয়া-পদ মহাপ্রভুর মনে স্মৃতি হৈল ।
স্বরূপেরে সেই পদ গাইতে আজ্ঞা দিল ॥ ৬৭ ॥

uḍiyā-pada mahāprabhura mane smṛti haila
svarūpere sei pada gāite ājñā dila

SYNONYMS

uḍiyā-pada—a line of a song in the language of Orissa; *mahāprabhura*—of Śrī Caitanya Mahāprabhu; *mane*—in the mind; *smṛti haila*—was remembered; *svarūpere*—unto Svarūpa Dāmodara Gosvāmī; *sei pada*—that special line; *gāite*—to sing; *ājñā dila*—ordered.

TRANSLATION

Śrī Caitanya Mahāprabhu remembered a line in the Orissan language and ordered Svarūpa Dāmodara to sing it.

TEXT 68

"জগমোহন-পরিমুণ্ডা যাউ্" ॥ ৬৮ ॥ ধ্রু ॥

"jagamohana-pari-muṇḍā yāu"

SYNONYMS

jagamohana—the *kīrtana* hall known as Jagamohana; *pari*—in; *muṇḍā*—my head; *yāu*—let it be offered.

TRANSLATION

"Let my head fall at the feet of Jagannātha in the kīrtana hall known as Jagamohana."

TEXT 69

এই পদে নৃত্য করেন পরম-আবেশে ।
সবলোক চৌদিকে প্রভুর প্রেম-জলে ভাসে ॥ ৬৯ ॥

ei pade nṛtya karena parama-āveśe
saba-loka caudike prabhura prema-jale bhāse

SYNONYMS

ei pade—by this line; *nṛtya karena*—dances; *parama-āveśe*—in great ecstatic love; *saba-loka*—all people; *cau-dike*—in all four directions; *prabhura*—of Śrī Caitanya Mahāprabhu; *prema-jale*—in tears of love; *bhāse*—float.

TRANSLATION

Simply because of this line, Śrī Caitanya Mahāprabhu was dancing in greatly ecstatic love. People all around Him floated in the water of His tears.

TEXT 70

'বোল্' 'বোল্' বলেন প্রভু শ্রীবাহু তুলিয়া।
হরিধ্বনি করে লোক আনন্দে ভাসিয়া ॥ ৭০ ॥

'bol' 'bol' balena prabhu śrī-bāhu tuliyā
hari-dhvani kare loka ānande bhāsiyā

SYNONYMS

bol—chant; *bol*—chant; *balena*—said; *prabhu*—the Lord; *śrī-bāhu*—His transcendental arms; *tuliyā*—raising; *hari-dhvani kare*—chanted the holy name Hari; *loka*—people; *ānande bhāsiyā*—floating in transcendental bliss.

TRANSLATION

Raising His two arms, the Lord said, "Chant! Chant!" Floating in transcendental bliss, the people responded by chanting the holy name of Hari.

TEXT 71

প্রভু পড়ি' মূর্চ্ছা যায়, শ্বাস নাহি আর।
আচম্বিতে উঠে প্রভু করিয়া হুঙ্কার ॥ ৭১ ॥

prabhu paḍi' mūrchā yāya, śvāsa nāhi āra
ācambite uṭhe prabhu kariyā huṅkāra

SYNONYMS

prabhu—the Lord; *paḍi'*—falling down; *mūrchā yāya*—became unconscious; *śvāsa nāhi*—there was no breathing; *āra*—and; *ācambite*—suddenly; *uṭhe*—stands up; *prabhu*—Śrī Caitanya Mahāprabhu; *kariyā huṅkāra*—making a loud sound.

TRANSLATION

The Lord fell to the ground unconscious, not even breathing. Then suddenly He stood up, making a loud sound.

TEXT 72

সঘন পুলক,—যেন শিমুলের তরু।
কভু প্রফুল্লিত অঙ্গ, কভু হয় সরু ॥ ৭২ ॥

saghana pulaka,——yena śimulera taru
kabhu praphullita aṅga, kabhu haya saru

SYNONYMS

sa-ghana—constant; *pulaka*—standing of the hairs of the body; *yena*—like; *śimulera taru*—the *śimula* tree; *kabhu*—sometimes; *praphullita*—swollen; *aṅga*—body; *kabhu*—sometimes; *haya*—is; *saru*—lean and thin.

TRANSLATION

The hairs on His body constantly stood up like the thorns on a śimula tree. Sometimes His body was swollen and sometimes lean and thin.

TEXT 73

প্রতি রোম-কূপে হয় প্রস্বেদ, রক্তোদগম ।
'জজ' 'গগ' 'পরি' 'মুমু'— গদ্‌গদ বচন ॥ ৭৩ ॥

prati roma-kūpe haya prasveda, raktodgama
'jaja' 'gaga' 'pari' 'mumu'——gadgada vacana

SYNONYMS

prati roma-kūpe—in every hole of the hair; *haya*—there was; *prasveda*—perspiration; *rakta-udgama*—a profusion of blood; *jaja gaga pari mumu*—the sounds *"jaja gaga pari mumu"*; *gadgada*—faltering; *vacana*—words.

TRANSLATION

He bled and perspired from every pore of His body. His voice faltered. Unable to say the line properly, He uttered only, "jaja gaga pari mumu."

TEXT 74

এক এক দন্ত যেন পৃথক্ পৃথক্ নড়ে ।
ঐছে নড়ে দন্ত,— যেন ভূমে খসি' পড়ে ॥ ৭৪ ॥

eka eka danta yena pṛthak pṛthak naḍe
aiche naḍe danta,——yena bhūme khasi' paḍe

SYNONYMS

eka eka—each and every; *danta*—tooth; *yena*—as if; *pṛthak pṛthak*—separately; *naḍe*—shakes; *aiche*—like that; *naḍe*—shake; *danta*—the teeth; *yena*—as if; *bhūme*—on the ground; *khasi'*—becoming loose; *paḍe*—fall.

TRANSLATION

All His teeth shook, as if each were separate from the others. Indeed, they seemed about to fall to the ground.

TEXT 75

ক্ষণে ক্ষণে বাড়ে প্রভুর আনন্দ-আবেশ ।
তৃতীয় প্রহর হইল, নৃত্য নহে শেষ ॥ ৭৫ ॥

kṣaṇe kṣaṇe bāḍe prabhura ānanda-āveśa
tṛtīya prahara ha-ila, nṛtya nahe śeṣa

SYNONYMS

kṣaṇe kṣaṇe—at every moment; *bāḍe*—increases; *prabhura*—of Śrī Caitanya Mahāprabhu; *ānanda-āveśa*—transcendental bliss; *tṛtīya prahara*—midafternoon; *ha-ila*—there was; *nṛtya*—the dancing; *nahe śeṣa*—did not end.

TRANSLATION

His transcendental bliss increased at every moment. Therefore even by midafternoon the dancing had not ended.

TEXT 76

সব লোকের উথলিল আনন্দ-সাগর ।
সব লোক পাসরিল দেহ-আত্ম-ঘর ॥ ৭৬ ॥

saba lokera uthalila ānanda-sāgara
saba loka pāsarila deha-ātma-ghara

SYNONYMS

saba lokera—of every person; *uthalila*—overflowed; *ānanda-sāgara*—the ocean of transcendental bliss; *saba loka*—every person; *pāsarila*—forgot; *deha*—body; *ātma*—mind; *ghara*—home.

TRANSLATION

The ocean of transcendental bliss overflowed, and everyone present forgot his body, mind and home.

TEXT 77

তবে নিত্যানন্দ প্রভু সৃজিলা উপায় ।
ক্রমে-ক্রমে কীর্তনীয়া রাখিল সবায় ॥ ৭৭ ॥

tabe nityānanda prabhu sṛjilā upāya
krame-krame kīrtanīyā rākhila sabāya

SYNONYMS

tabe—at that time; *nityānanda*—Lord Nityānanda; *prabhu*—the Lord; *sṛjilā upāya*—made a device; *krame-krame*—by and by; *kīrtanīyā*—the chanters; *rākhila*—stopped; *sabāya*—all.

TRANSLATION

Then Lord Nityānanda found a way to end the kīrtana. He gradually stopped all the chanters.

TEXT 78

স্বরূপের সঙ্গে মাত্র এক সম্প্রদায় ।
স্বরূপের সঙ্গে সেহ মন্দস্বর গায় ॥ ৭৮ ॥

svarūpera saṅge mātra eka sampradāya
svarūpera saṅge seha manda-svara gāya

SYNONYMS

svarūpera saṅge—with Svarūpa Dāmodara; *mātra*—only; *eka*—one; *sampradāya*—group; *svarūpera saṅge*—with Svarūpa Dāmodara; *seha*—they; *manda-svara*—very softly; *gāya*—chanted.

TRANSLATION

Thus only one group continued chanting with Svarūpa Dāmodara, and they chanted very softly.

TEXT 79

কোলাহল নাহি, প্রভুর কিছু বাহ্য হৈল ।
তবে নিত্যানন্দ সবার শ্রম জানাইল ॥ ৭৯ ॥

kolāhala nāhi, prabhura kichu bāhya haila
tabe nityānanda sabāra śrama jānāila

SYNONYMS

kolāhala—tumultuous sound; *nāhi*—there was not; *prabhura*—of Śrī Caitanya Mahāprabhu; *kichu*—some; *bāhya*—external consciousness; *haila*—there was; *tabe*—at that time; *nityānanda*—Lord Nityānanda; *sabāra*—of all of them; *śrama*—fatigue; *jānāila*—informed.

TRANSLATION

When there was no longer a tumultuous sound, Śrī Caitanya Mahāprabhu returned to consciousness. Then Nityānanda Prabhu informed Him of the fatigue of the chanters and dancers.

TEXT 80

ভক্তশ্রম জানি' কৈলা কীর্তন সমাপন ।
সবা লঞা আসি' কৈলা সমুদ্রে স্নপন ॥ ৮০ ॥

bhakta-śrama jāni' kailā kīrtana samāpana
sabā lañā āsi' kailā samudre snapana

SYNONYMS

bhakta-śrama—the fatigue of the devotees; *jāni'*—understanding; *kailā*—performed; *kīrtana samāpana*—ending the chanting; *sabā lañā āsi'*—accompanied by all of them; *kailā*—did; *samudre*—in the sea; *snapana*—bathing.

TRANSLATION

Understanding the fatigue of the devotees, Śrī Caitanya Mahāprabhu stopped the congregational chanting. Then He bathed in the sea, accompanied by them all.

TEXT 81

সব লঞা প্রভু কৈলা প্রসাদ ভোজন ।
সবারে বিদায় দিলা করিতে শয়ন ॥ ৮১ ॥

saba lañā prabhu kailā prasāda bhojana
sabāre vidāya dilā karite śayana

SYNONYMS

saba lañā—with all of them; *prabhu*—Śrī Caitanya Mahāprabhu; *kailā*—performed; *prasāda bhojana*—taking *prasāda;* *sabāre*—to everyone; *vidāya dilā*—bade farewell; *karite śayana*—to take rest.

TRANSLATION

Then Śrī Caitanya Mahāprabhu took prasāda with all of them and then asked them to return to their dwellings and take rest.

TEXT 82

গম্ভীরার দ্বারে করেন আপনে শয়ন ।
গোবিন্দ আসিয়া করে পাদ-সম্বাহন ॥ ৮২ ॥

gambhīrāra dvāre karena āpane śayana
govinda āsiyā kare pāda-samvāhana

SYNONYMS

gambhīrāra dvāre—at the door of the Gambhīrā, the small room within the room; *karena*—does; *āpane*—personally; *śayana*—lying down; *govinda*—His personal servant Govinda; *āsiyā*—coming; *kare*—performs; *pāda-samvāhana*—massaging the legs.

TRANSLATION

Śrī Caitanya Mahāprabhu lay down at the door of the Gambhīrā, and Govinda came there to massage His legs.

TEXTS 83-84

সর্বকাল আছে এই সুদৃঢ় 'নিয়ম' ।
'প্রভু যদি প্রসাদ পাঞা করেন শয়ন ॥ ৮৩ ॥
গোবিন্দ আসিয়া করে পাদসম্বাহন ।
তবে যাই' প্রভুর 'শেষ' করেন ভোজন ॥' ৮৪ ॥

sarva-kāla āche ei sudṛḍha 'niyama'
'prabhu yadi prasāda pāñā karena śayana

govinda āsiyā kare pāda-samvāhana
tabe yāi' prabhura 'śeṣa' karena bhojana'

SYNONYMS

sarva-kāla—all the time; *āche*—there is; *ei*—this; *su-dṛḍha*—hard-and-fast; *niyama*—regulation; *prabhu*—Śrī Caitanya Mahāprabhu; *yadi*—when; *prasāda pāñā*—after taking His meals; *karena śayana*—lies down; *govinda*—Govinda; *āsiyā*—coming; *kare*—performs; *pāda-samvāhana*—massaging the legs; *tabe*—

thereafter; *yāi'*—going; *prabhura*—of Śrī Caitanya Mahāprabhu; *śeṣa*—the remnants of food; *karena bhojana*—eats.

TRANSLATION

It was a steady, long-standing rule that Śrī Caitanya Mahāprabhu would lie down to rest after lunch and Govinda would come to massage His legs. Then Govinda would honor the remnants of food left by Śrī Caitanya Mahāprabhu.

TEXT 85

সব দ্বার যুড়ি' প্রভু করিয়াছেন শয়ন ।
ভিতরে যাইতে নারে, গোবিন্দ করে নিবেদন ॥৮৫॥

saba dvāra yuḍi' prabhu kariyāchena śayana
bhitare yāite nāre, govinda kare nivedana

SYNONYMS

saba dvāra—the whole door; *yuḍi'*—occupying the space of; *prabhu*—Śrī Caitanya Mahāprabhu; *kariyāchena śayana*—was lying down; *bhitare*—within; *yāite nāre*—could not go; *govinda*—Govinda; *kare nivedana*—he requested.

TRANSLATION

This time when the Lord lay down, He occupied the entire doorway. Govinda could not enter the room, and therefore he made the following request.

TEXT 86

'একপাশ হও, মোরে দেহ' ভিতর যাইতে' ।
প্রভু কহে,—'শক্তি নাহি অঙ্গ চালাইতে' ॥ ৮৬ ॥

'eka-pāśa hao, more deha' bhitara yāite'
prabhu kahe,——'śakti nāhi aṅga cālāite'

SYNONYMS

eka-pāśa hao—kindly turn on one side; *more*—me; *deha'*—allow; *bhitara*—within; *yāite*—to go; *prabhu kahe*—Śrī Caitanya Mahāprabhu replied; *śakti*—strength; *nāhi*—there is not; *aṅga cālāite*—to move My body.

TRANSLATION

"Kindly turn on one side. Let me pass to enter the room." However, the Lord replied, "I don't have the strength to move My body."

TEXT 87

বার বার গোবিন্দ কহে একদিক্ হইতে।
প্রভু কহে,—'অঙ্গ আমি নারি চালাইতে ॥' ৮৭ ॥

bāra bāra govinda kahe eka-dik ha-ite
prabhu kahe,——'aṅga āmi nāri cālāite'

SYNONYMS

bāra bāra—again and again; *govinda*—Govinda; *kahe*—requests; *eka-dik ha-ite*—to turn on one side; *prabhu kahe*—Śrī Caitanya Mahāprabhu replied; *aṅga*—My body; *āmi*—I; *nāri cālāite*—cannot move.

TRANSLATION

Govinda made his request again and again, but the Lord replied, "I cannot move My body."

TEXT 88

গোবিন্দ কহে,—'করিতে চাহি পাদ-সম্বাহন'।
প্রভু কহে,—'কর বা না কর, যেই লয় তোমার মন' ॥ ৮৮ ॥

govinda kahe,——'karite cāhi pāda-samvāhana'
prabhu kahe,——'kara vā nā kara, yei laya tomāra mana'

SYNONYMS

govinda kahe—Govinda said; *karite*—to do; *cāhi*—I want; *pāda-samvāhana*—massaging Your legs; *prabhu kahe*—the Lord replied; *kara*—do; *vā*—or; *nā kara*—do not do; *yei*—whatever; *laya tomāra mana*—you decide.

TRANSLATION

Govinda repeatedly requested, "I want to massage Your legs," but the Lord said, "Do it or don't do it. It depends upon your mind."

TEXT 89

তবে গোবিন্দ বহির্বাস তাঁর উপরে দিয়া।
ভিতর-ঘরে গেলা মহাপ্রভুরে লঙ্ঘিয়া ॥ ৮৯ ॥

tabe govinda bahirvāsa tāṅra upare diyā
bhitara-ghare gelā mahāprabhure laṅghiyā

SYNONYMS

tabe—then; *govinda*—Govinda; *bahirvāsa*—outward wrapper; *tāṅra upare*—over Him; *diyā*—spreading; *bhitara-ghare*—within the room; *gelā*—went; *mahāprabhure laṅghiyā*—crossing Śrī Caitanya Mahāprabhu.

TRANSLATION

Then Govinda spread the Lord's wrapper over the Lord's body and in this way entered the room by crossing over Him.

TEXT 90

পাদ-সম্বাহন কৈল, কটি-পৃষ্ঠ চাপিল ।
মধুর-মর্দনে প্রভুর পরিশ্রম গেল ॥ ৯০ ॥

pāda-samvāhana kaila, kaṭi-pṛṣṭha cāpila
madhūra-mardane prabhura pariśrama gela

SYNONYMS

pāda-samvāhana—massaging of the legs; *kaila*—he performed; *kaṭi*—waist; *pṛṣṭha*—back; *cāpila*—pressed; *madhūra-mardane*—by mild pressing; *prabhura*—of Śrī Caitanya Mahāprabhu; *pariśrama*—fatigue; *gela*—went away.

TRANSLATION

Govinda massaged the Lord's legs as usual. He pressed the Lord's waist and back very softly, and thus all the Lord's fatigue went away.

TEXT 91

সুখে নিদ্রা হৈল প্রভুর, গোবিন্দ চাপে অঙ্গ ।
দণ্ড-দুই বই প্রভুর হৈলা নিদ্রা-ভঙ্গ ॥ ৯১ ॥

sukhe nidrā haila prabhura, govinda cāpe aṅga
daṇḍa-dui ba-i prabhura hailā nidrā-bhaṅga

SYNONYMS

sukhe—very nicely; *nidrā haila prabhura*—Śrī Caitanya Mahāprabhu slept; *govinda*—Govinda; *cāpe aṅga*—pressed the body; *daṇḍa-dui bāi*—after about forty-five minutes; *prabhura*—of Śrī Caitanya Mahāprabhu; *hailā*—there was; *nidrā-bhaṅga*—breaking of sleep.

TRANSLATION

As Govinda stroked His body, the Lord slept very nicely for about forty-five minutes, and then His sleep broke.

TEXT 92

গোবিন্দে দেখিয়া প্রভু বলে ক্রুদ্ধ হঞা ।
'আজি কেনে এতক্ষণ আছিস্ বসিয়া ? ৯২ ॥

govinde dekhiyā prabhu bale kruddha hañā
'āji kene eta-kṣaṇa āchis vasiyā?

SYNONYMS

govinde dekhiyā—seeing Govinda; *prabhu*—Śrī Caitanya Mahāprabhu; *bale*—said; *kruddha hañā*—in an angry mood; *āji*—today; *kene*—why; *eta-kṣaṇa*—for so long; *āchis*—have you been; *vasiyā*—sitting.

TRANSLATION

When Śrī Caitanya Mahāprabhu saw Govinda sitting by His side, He was somewhat angry. "Why have you been sitting here for so long today?" the Lord asked.

TEXT 93

মোর নিদ্রা হৈলে কেনে না গেলা প্রসাদ খাইতে ?'
গোবিন্দ কহে—'দ্বারে শুইলা, যাইতে নাহি পথে' ॥ ৯৩ ॥

mora nidrā haile kene nā gelā prasāda khāite?'
govinda kahe——'dvāre śuilā, yāite nāhi pathe'

SYNONYMS

mora nidrā haile—when I fell asleep; *kene*—why; *nā gelā*—did you not go; *prasāda khāite*—to take your meal; *govinda kahe*—Govinda said; *dvāre*—the door; *śuilā*—You were blocking; *yāite*—to go; *nāhi pathe*—there is no passage.

TRANSLATION

"Why didn't you go to take your meal after I fell asleep?" the Lord asked. Govinda replied, "You were lying down, blocking the door, and there was no way to go."

TEXT 94

প্রভু কহে,—'ভিতরে তবে আইলা কেমনে ?
তৈছে কেনে প্রসাদ লৈতে না কৈলা গমনে ?' ৯৪ ॥

prabhu kahe,—'bhitare tabe āilā kemane?
taiche kene prasāda laite nā kailā gamane?'

SYNONYMS

prabhu kahe—Śrī Caitanya Mahāprabhu said; *bhitare*—inside; *tabe*—then; *āilā*—you came; *kemane*—how; *taiche*—in the same way; *kene*—why; *prasāda laite*—to take *prasāda; nā kailā gamane*—did you not go.

TRANSLATION

The Lord asked, "How did you enter the room? Why didn't you go out to take your lunch in the same way?"

TEXT 95

গোবিন্দ কহে মনে—"আমার 'সেবা' সে 'নিয়ম'।
অপরাধ হউক, কিবা নরকে গমন ॥ ৯৫ ॥

govinda kahe mane—"āmāra 'sevā' se 'niyama'
aparādha ha-uka, kibā narake gamana

SYNONYMS

govinda kahe—Govinda said; *mane*—within his mind; *āmāra sevā*—my service; *se niyama*—that is the regulation; *aparādha ha-uka*—let there be offenses; *kibā*—or; *narake*—to hell; *gamana*—going.

TRANSLATION

Govinda mentally replied, "My duty is to serve, even if I have to commit offenses or go to hell.

TEXT 96

'সেবা' লাগি' কোটি 'অপরাধ' নাহি গণি।
স্ব-নিমিত্ত 'অপরাধাভাসে' ভয় মানি ॥" ৯৬ ॥

'sevā' lāgi' koṭi 'aparādha' nāhi gaṇi
sva-nimitta 'aparādhābhāse' bhaya māni"

SYNONYMS

sevā lāgi'—for the matter of service; *koṭi aparādha*—ten million offenses; *nāhi gaṇi*—I do not care for; *sva-nimitta*—for my personal self; *aparādha-ābhāse*—by a glimpse of an offense; *bhaya māni*—I am afraid.

TRANSLATION

"I would not mind committing hundreds and thousands of offenses for the service of the Lord, but I greatly fear committing even a glimpse of an offense for my own self."

TEXT 97

এত সব মনে করি' গোবিন্দ রহিলা ।
প্রভু যে পুছিলা, তার উত্তর না দিলা ॥ ৯৭ ॥

eta saba mane kari' govinda rahilā
prabhu ye puchilā, tāra uttara nā dilā

SYNONYMS

eta saba—all this; *mane kari'*—thinking; *govinda rahilā*—Govinda kept silent; *prabhu*—Śrī Caitanya Mahāprabhu; *ye*—what; *puchilā*—inquired; *tāra*—of that; *uttara*—reply; *nā dilā*—did not give.

TRANSLATION

Thinking in this way, Govinda kept silent. He did not reply to the Lord's inquiry.

TEXT 98

প্রত্যহ প্রভুর নিদ্রায় যান প্রসাদ লইতে ।
সে দিবসের শ্রম দেখি' লাগিলা চাপিতে ॥ ৯৮ ॥

pratyaha prabhura nidrāya yāna prasāda la-ite
se divasera śrama dekhi' lāgilā cāpite

SYNONYMS

prati-aha—daily; *prabhura nidrāya*—when the Lord was asleep; *yāna*—he goes; *prasāda la-ite*—to accept his lunch; *se divasera*—of that day; *śrama*—the weariness; *dekhi'*—seeing; *lāgilā cāpite*—began to press.

TRANSLATION

It was Govinda's practice to go take lunch when the Lord was asleep. On that day, however, seeing the Lord's weariness, Govinda continued massaging His body.

TEXT 99

যাইতেহ পথ নাহি, যাইবে কেমনে ?
মহা-অপরাধ হয় প্রভুর লঙ্ঘনে ॥ ৯৯ ॥

yāiteha patha nāhi, yāibe kemane?
mahā-aparādha haya prabhura laṅghane

SYNONYMS

yāiteha—to go; *patha nāhi*—there was no passage; *yāibe kemane*—how would he go away; *mahā-aparādha*—a great offense; *haya*—there would be; *prabhura laṅghane*—to cross over the body of Śrī Caitanya Mahāprabhu.

TRANSLATION

There was no way to go. How could he leave? When he thought of crossing over the Lord's body, he considered it a great offense.

TEXT 100

এই সব হয় ভক্তিশাস্ত্র-সূক্ষ্ম মর্ম ।
চৈতন্যের কৃপায় জানে এই সব ধর্ম ॥ ১০০ ॥

ei saba haya bhakti-śāstra-sūkṣma marma
caitanyera kṛpāya jāne ei saba dharma

SYNONYMS

ei saba—all these; *haya*—are; *bhakti-śāstra*—of the system of devotional service; *sūkṣma marma*—finer principles; *caitanyera kṛpāya*—by the mercy of Śrī Caitanya Mahāprabhu; *jāne*—one can understand; *ei saba*—all these; *dharma*—principles of devotional service.

TRANSLATION

These are some of the finer points of etiquette in devotional service. Only one who has received the mercy of Śrī Caitanya Mahāprabhu can understand these principles.

PURPORT

Karmīs, fruitive workers, cannot understand the finer conclusions of devotional service because they accept only its ritualistic value but do not understand how devotional service satisfies the Supreme Personality of Godhead. The *karmīs* view the formalities as a means of advancing in religion, economic development, sensual satisfaction and liberation. Although these are only material results of following religious principles, the *karmīs* consider them everything. Such ritualistic activities are called *karma. Karmīs* who adopt devotional service very loosely and who therefore remain on the platform of material activities are called *prākṛta-sahajiyās.* They cannot understand how pure devotional service is rendered in paternal and conjugal love, for this can be understood only by the special mercy bestowed by Śrī Caitanya Mahāprabhu upon pure devotees.

TEXT 101

ভক্ত-গুণ প্রকাশিতে প্রভু বড় রঙ্গী ।
এই সব প্রকাশিতে কৈলা এত ভঙ্গী ॥ ১০১ ॥

bhakta-guṇa prakāśite prabhu baḍa raṅgī
ei saba prakāśite kailā eta bhaṅgī

SYNONYMS

bhakta-guṇa—the attributes of the devotee; *prakāśite*—to manifest; *prabhu*—the Lord; *baḍa raṅgī*—very interested; *ei saba*—all these; *prakāśite*—to manifest; *kailā*—He performed; *eta*—such; *bhaṅgī*—incident.

TRANSLATION

The Lord is very interested in manifesting the exalted qualities of His devotees, and that is why He engineered this incident.

TEXT 102

সঙ্ক্ষেপে কহিলুঁ এই পরিমুণ্ডা-নৃত্য ।
অদ্যাপিহ গায় যাহা চৈতন্যের ভৃত্য ॥ ১০২ ॥

saṅkṣepe kahiluṅ ei pari-muṇḍā-nṛtya
adyāpiha gāya yāhā caitanyera bhṛtya

SYNONYMS

saṅkṣepe—in brief; *kahiluṅ*—I have described; *ei*—this; *pari-muṇḍā-nṛtya*—dancing in the dancing hall of Jagannātha's temple; *adyāpiha*—even up-to-dately;

gāya—sing about; *yāhā*—which; *caitanyera bhṛtya*—the servants of Śrī Caitanya Mahāprabhu.

TRANSLATION

Thus I have briefly described Śrī Caitanya Mahāprabhu's dancing in the hall of the Jagannātha temple. The servants of Śrī Caitanya Mahāprabhu sing about this dancing even now.

TEXT 103

এইমত মহাপ্রভু লঞা নিজগণ ।
গুণ্ডিচা-গৃহের কৈলা ক্ষালন, মার্জন ॥ ১০৩ ॥

ei-mata mahāprabhu lañā nija-gaṇa
guṇḍicā-gṛhera kailā kṣālana, mārjana

SYNONYMS

ei-mata—in this way; *mahāprabhu*—Śrī Caitanya Mahāprabhu; *lañā nija-gaṇa*—accompanied by His personal associates; *guṇḍicā-gṛhera*—of the Guṇḍicā temple; *kailā*—performed; *kṣālana*—washing; *mārjana*—cleansing.

TRANSLATION

Accompanied by His personal associates, Śrī Caitanya Mahāprabhu washed and swept the Guṇḍicā temple, cleansing it as usual.

TEXT 104

পূর্ব্ববৎ কৈলা প্রভু কীর্তন, নর্তন ।
পূর্ব্ববৎ টোটায় কৈলা বন্য-ভোজন ॥ ১০৪ ॥

pūrvavat kailā prabhu kīrtana, nartana
pūrvavat ṭoṭāya kailā vanya-bhojana

SYNONYMS

pūrva-vat—as previously; *kailā*—performed; *prabhu*—Śrī Caitanya Mahāprabhu; *kīrtana*—chanting; *nartana*—dancing; *pūrva-vat*—as previously; *ṭoṭāya*—in the garden; *kailā*—performed; *vanya-bhojana*—taking a picnic.

TRANSLATION

The Lord danced and chanted and then enjoyed a picnic in the garden as He had done before.

TEXT 105

পূর্ব্ববৎ রথ-আগে করিলা নর্ত্তন।
হেরাপঞ্চমী-যাত্রা কৈলা দরশন ॥ ১০৫ ॥

pūrvavat ratha-āge karilā nartana
herā-pañcamī-yātrā kailā daraśana

SYNONYMS

pūrva-vat—as previously; *ratha-āge*—in front of the chariot; *karilā nartana*—performed dancing; *herā-pañcamī-yātrā*—the festival of Herā-pañcamī; *kailā daraśana*—He saw.

TRANSLATION

As previously, He danced in front of the Jagannātha cart and observed the festival of Herā-pañcamī.

TEXT 106

চারিমাস বর্ষায় রহিলা সব ভক্তগণ।
জন্মাষ্টমী আদি যাত্রা কৈলা দরশন ॥ ১০৬ ॥

cāri-māsa varṣāya rahilā saba bhakta-gaṇa
janmāṣṭamī ādi yātrā kailā daraśana

SYNONYMS

cāri-māsa—for four months; *varṣāya*—of the rainy season; *rahilā*—stayed; *saba bhakta-gaṇa*—all the devotees; *janmāṣṭamī ādi yātrā*—festivals like Lord Kṛṣṇa's birth ceremony; *kailā daraśana*—observed.

TRANSLATION

All the devotees from Bengal stayed in Jagannātha Purī for the four months of the rainy season and observed many other ceremonies, such as the anniversary of Lord Kṛṣṇa's birth.

TEXT 107

পূর্বে যদি গৌড় হইতে ভক্তগণ আইল।
প্রভুরে কিছু খাওয়াইতে সবার ইচ্ছা হৈল ॥ ১০৭ ॥

pūrve yadi gauḍa ha-ite bhakta-gaṇa āila
prabhure kichu khāoyāite sabāra icchā haila

SYNONYMS

pūrve—formerly; *yadi*—when; *gauḍa ha-ite*—from Bengal; *bhakta-gaṇa āila*—the devotees arrived; *prabhure*—to Śrī Caitanya Mahāprabhu; *kichu*—something; *khāoyāite*—to feed; *sabāra icchā haila*—everyone desired.

TRANSLATION

Formerly, when all the devotees had arrived from Bengal, they all desired to give Śrī Caitanya Mahāprabhu something to eat.

TEXT 108

কেহ কোন প্রসাদ আনি' দেয় গোবিন্দ-ঠাঞি ।
'ইহা যেন অবশ্য ভক্ষণ করেন গোসাঞি' ॥ ১০৮ ॥

keha kona prasāda āni' deya govinda-ṭhāñi
'ihā yena avaśya bhakṣaṇa karena gosāñi'

SYNONYMS

keha—someone; *kona prasāda*—some variety of *prasāda; āni'*—bringing; *deya*—delivers; *govinda-ṭhāñi*—to Govinda; *ihā*—this; *yena*—that; *avaśya*—certainly; *bhakṣaṇa karena*—eats; *gosāñi*—Śrī Caitanya Mahāprabhu.

TRANSLATION

Each devotee would bring a certain type of prasāda. He would entrust it to Govinda and request him, "Please arrange that the Lord will surely eat this prasāda."

TEXT 109

কেহ পৈড়, কেহ নাড়ু, কেহ পিঠাপানা ।
বহুমূল্য উত্তম-প্রসাদ-প্রকার যার নানা ॥ ১০৯ ॥

keha paiḍa, keha nāḍu, keha piṭhā-pānā
bahu-mūlya uttama-prasāda-prakāra yāra nānā

SYNONYMS

keha—someone; *paiḍa*—a coconut preparation; *keha*—someone; *nāḍu*—sweetballs; *keha*—someone; *piṭhā*—cakes; *pānā*—sweet rice; *bahu-mūlya*—costly; *uttama-prasāda*—very palatable food; *prakāra yāra nānā*—of different varieties.

TRANSLATION

Some brought paiḍa [a coconut preparation], some brought sweetballs, and some brought cakes and sweet rice. The prasāda was of different varieties, all very costly.

TEXT 110

'অমুক্ এই দিয়াছে' গোবিন্দ করে নিবেদন ।
'ধরি' রাখ' বলি' প্রভু না করেন ভক্ষণ ॥ ১১০ ॥

'amuk ei diyāche' govinda kare nivedana
'dhari' rākha' bali' prabhu nā karena bhakṣaṇa

SYNONYMS

amuk—such and such devotee; *ei*—this; *diyāche*—has given; *govinda*—Govinda; *kare nivedana*—informs; *dhari' rākha*—please keep them; *bali'*—saying; *prabhu*—Śrī Caitanya Mahāprabhu; *nā karena bhakṣaṇa*—does not eat.

TRANSLATION

Govinda would present the prasāda and say to Śrī Caitanya Mahāprabhu, "This has been given by such and such devotee." The Lord, however, would not actually eat it. He would simply say, "Keep it in storage."

TEXT 111

ধরিতে ধরিতে ঘরের ভরিল এক কোণ ।
শত-জনের ভক্ষ্য যত হৈল সঞ্চয়ন ॥ ১১১ ॥

dharite dharite gharera bharila eka koṇa
śata-janera bhakṣya yata haila sañcayana

SYNONYMS

dharite dharite—keeping and keeping; *gharera*—of the room; *bharila*—filled up; *eka koṇa*—one corner; *śata-janera*—of one hundred people; *bhakṣya*—sufficient for feeding; *yata*—all; *haila*—there was; *sañcayana*—accumulation.

TRANSLATION

Govinda kept accumulating the food, and soon it filled a corner of the room. There was quite enough to feed at least a hundred people.

TEXT 112

গোবিন্দেরে সবে পুছে করিয়া যতন।
'আমা-দত্ত প্রসাদ প্রভুরে কি করাইলা ভক্ষণ ?১১২॥

govindere sabe puche kariyā yatana
'āmā-datta prasāda prabhure ki karāilā bhakṣaṇa?

SYNONYMS

govindere—unto Govinda; *sabe*—all the devotees; *puche*—inquired; *kariyā yatana*—with great eagerness; *āmā-datta prasāda*—the *prasāda* given by me; *prabhure*—unto Śrī Caitanya Mahāprabhu; *ki karāilā bhakṣaṇa*—have you given for eating.

TRANSLATION

All the devotees asked Govinda with great eagerness, "Have you given Śrī Caitanya Mahāprabhu the prasāda brought by me?"

TEXT 113

কাহাঁ কিছু কহি' গোবিন্দ করে বঞ্চন।
আর দিন প্রভুরে কহে নির্বেদ-বচন॥ ১১৩॥

kāhāṅ kichu kahi' govinda kare vañcana
āra dina prabhure kahe nirveda-vacana

SYNONYMS

kāhāṅ—to someone; *kichu*—something; *kahi'*—saying; *govinda*—Govinda; *kare vañcana*—told lies; *āra dina*—one day; *prabhure*—unto Śrī Caitanya Mahāprabhu; *kahe*—said; *nirveda-vacana*—a statement of disappointment.

TRANSLATION

When the devotees questioned Govinda, he had to tell them lies. Therefore one day he spoke to the Lord in disappointment.

TEXT 114

"আচার্যাদি মহাশয় করিয়া যতনে।
তোমারে খাওয়াইতে বস্তু দেন মোর স্থানে॥ ১১৪॥

"ācāryādi mahāśaya kariyā yatane
tomāre khāoyāite vastu dena mora sthāne

SYNONYMS

ācārya-ādi—headed by Advaita Ācārya; *mahāśaya*—respectable gentlemen; *kariyā yatane*—with great endeavor; *tomāre khāoyāite*—to feed You; *vastu dena*—deliver varieties of food; *mora sthāne*—to me.

TRANSLATION

"Many respectable devotees, headed by Advaita Ācārya, make a great endeavor to entrust me with varieties of food for You.

TEXT 115

তুমি সে না খাও, তাঁরা পুছে বার বার।
কত বঞ্চনা করিমু, কেমনে আমার নিস্তার ?"১১৫ ॥

tumi se nā khāo, tāṅrā puche bāra bāra
kata vañcanā karimu, kemane āmāra nistāra?"

SYNONYMS

tumi—You; *se*—that; *nā khāo*—do not eat; *tāṅrā*—they; *puche*—inquire; *bāra bāra*—again and again; *kata vañcanā karimu*—how long shall I cheat; *kemane*—how; *āmāra*—my; *nistāra*—deliverance.

TRANSLATION

"You do not eat it, but they ask me again and again. How long shall I go on cheating them? How shall I be freed from this responsibility?"

TEXT 116

প্রভু কহে,—'আদিবস্যা' দুঃখ কাঁহে মানে ?
কেবা কি দিয়াছে, তাহা আনহ এখানে ॥'১১৬ ॥

prabhu kahe,——'ādi-vasyā' duḥkha kāṅhe māne?
kebā ki diyāche, tāhā ānaha ekhāne'

SYNONYMS

prabhu kahe—the Lord replied; *ādi-vasyā*—you who have been residing with Me for a very long time; *duḥkha kāṅhe māne*—why are you unhappy about this; *kebā ki diyāche*—whatever they have delivered; *tāhā*—all that; *ānaha ekhāne*—bring here.

TRANSLATION

Śrī Caitanya Mahāprabhu replied, "Why are you so foolishly unhappy? Bring here to Me whatever they have given you."

PURPORT

Śrīla Bhaktivinoda Ṭhākura explains that the word *ādi-vasyā* refers to one who has been living with another for a very long time. Govinda was addressed as *ādi-vasyā* because he had been living with Śrī Caitanya Mahāprabhu for a very long time, whereas other devotees, who were mostly new, would come and go. In effect, the Lord told Govinda, "Since you have been living with Me for a long time, you should not be foolishly disappointed in this situation. Bring all the food to Me, and you will see that I can eat it."

TEXT 117

এত বলি' মহাপ্রভু বসিলা ভোজনে।
নাম ধরি' ধরি' গোবিন্দ করে নিবেদনে ॥ ১১৭ ॥

eta bali' mahāprabhu vasilā bhojane
nāma dhari' dhari' govinda kare nivedane

SYNONYMS

eta bali'—saying this; *mahāprabhu*—Śrī Caitanya Mahāprabhu; *vasilā bhojane*—sat down for eating; *nāma*—the name; *dhari' dhari'*—speaking; *govinda*—Govinda; *kare nivedane*—offers.

TRANSLATION

Śrī Caitanya Mahāprabhu sat down to eat. Then Govinda offered Him the preparations one after another, and as he did so he spoke the name of the person who had given each one.

TEXT 118

"আচার্যের এই পৈড়, পানা-সর-পূপী।
এই অমৃত-গুটিকা, মণ্ডা, কর্পূর-কূপী ॥ ১১৮ ॥

"ācāryera ei paiḍa, pānā-sara-pūpī
ei amṛta-guṭikā, maṇḍā, karpūra-kūpī

SYNONYMS

ācāryera—of Advaita Ācārya; *ei*—these; *paiḍa*—coconut preparation; *pānā*—sweet rice; *sara-pūpī*—cakes made with cream; *ei*—these; *amṛta-guṭikā*—sweetballs; *maṇḍā*—a type of round sweetmeat; *karpūra-kūpī*—a pot of camphor.

TRANSLATION

"These preparations—paiḍa, sweet rice, cakes made with cream, and also amṛta-guṭikā, maṇḍā and a pot of camphor—have been given by Advaita Ācārya.

TEXT 119

শ্রীবাস-পণ্ডিতের এই অনেক প্রকার।
পিঠা, পানা, অমৃতমণ্ডা, পদ্ম-চিনি আর ॥ ১১৯ ॥

śrīvāsa-paṇḍitera ei aneka prakāra
piṭhā, pānā, amṛta-maṇḍā padma-cini āra

SYNONYMS

śrīvāsa-paṇḍitera—of Śrīvāsa Paṇḍita; *ei*—these; *aneka prakāra*—many varieties; *piṭhā*—cakes; *pānā*—cream; *amṛta-maṇḍā*—another type of sweetball; *padma-cini*—*padma-cini; āra*—and.

TRANSLATION

"Next there are varieties of food—cakes, cream, amṛta-maṇḍā and padma-cini—given by Śrīvāsa Paṇḍita.

TEXT 120

আচার্যরত্নের এই সব উপহার।
আচার্যনিধির এই, অনেক প্রকার॥ ১২০ ॥

ācāryaratnera ei saba upahāra
ācāryanidhira ei, aneka prakāra

SYNONYMS

ācāryaratnera—of Candraśekhara; *ei*—these; *saba*—all; *upahāra*—presentations; *ācāryanidhira*—of Ācāryanidhi; *ei*—these; *aneka prakāra*—of different varieties.

TRANSLATION

"All these are gifts of Ācāryaratna, and these varieties of gifts are from Ācāryanidhi.

TEXT 121

বাসুদেব-দত্তের এই মুরারি-গুপ্তের আর ।
বুদ্ধিমন্ত-খাঁনের এই বিবিধ প্রকার ॥ ১২১ ॥

vāsudeva-dattera ei murāri-guptera āra
buddhimanta-khāṅnera ei vividha prakāra

SYNONYMS

vāsudeva-dattera—of Vāsudeva Datta; *ei*—these; *murāri-guptera*—of Murāri Gupta; *āra*—and; *buddhimanta-khāṅnera*—of Buddhimanta Khān; *ei*—these; *vividha prakāra*—of different varieties.

TRANSLATION

"And all these varieties of food have been given by Vāsudeva Datta, Murāri Gupta and Buddhimanta Khān.

TEXT 122

শ্রীমান্-সেন, শ্রীমান্-পণ্ডিত, আচার্যনন্দন ।
তাঁ-সবার দত্ত এই করহ ভোজন ॥ ১২২ ॥

śrīmān-sena, śrīmān-paṇḍita, ācārya-nandana
tāṅ-sabāra datta ei karaha bhojana

SYNONYMS

śrīmān-sena—Śivānanda Sena; *śrīmān-paṇḍita*—Śrīmān Paṇḍita; *ācārya-nandana*—Ācārya Nandana; *tāṅ-sabāra*—of all of them; *datta*—given; *ei*—these; *karaha bhojana*—please eat.

TRANSLATION

"These are gifts given by Śrīmān Sena, Śrīmān Paṇḍita and Ācārya Nandana. Please eat them all.

TEXT 123

কুলীনগ্রামের এই আগে দেখ যত ।
খণ্ডবাসী লোকের এই দেখ তত ॥" ১২৩ ॥

kulīna-grāmera ei āge dekha yata
khaṇḍa-vāsī lokera ei dekha tata"

SYNONYMS

kulīna-grāmera—of the residents of Kulīna-grāma; *ei*—these; *āge*—before; *dekha*—see; *yata*—all; *khaṇḍa-vāsī lokera*—of the residents of Khaṇḍa; *ei*—these; *dekha*—see; *tata*—so many.

TRANSLATION

"Here are the preparations made by the inhabitants of Kulīna-grāma, and these have been made by the inhabitants of Khaṇḍa."

TEXT 124

ঐছে সবার নাম লঞা প্রভুর আগে ধরে ।
সন্তুষ্ট হঞা প্রভু সব ভোজন করে ॥ ১২৪ ॥

aiche sabāra nāma lañā prabhura āge dhare
santuṣṭa hañā prabhu saba bhojana kare

SYNONYMS

aiche—in this way; *sabāra nāma*—everyone's name; *lañā*—taking; *prabhura āge*—before the Lord; *dhare*—he places; *santuṣṭa hañā*—being very satisfied; *prabhu*—the Lord; *saba*—all; *bhojana kare*—began to eat.

TRANSLATION

In this way, Govinda gave everyone's name as he put the food before the Lord. Being very satisfied, the Lord began to eat it all.

TEXTS 125-126

যদ্যপি মাসেকের বাসি মুকুতা নারিকেল ।
অমৃত-গুটিকাদি, পানাদি সকল ॥ ১২৫ ॥
তথাপি নূতনপ্রায় সব দ্রব্যের স্বাদ ।
'বাসি' বিস্বাদ নহে সেই প্রভুর প্রসাদ ॥ ১২৬ ॥

yadyapi māsekera vāsi mukuta nārikela
amṛta-guṭikādi, pānādi sakala

tathāpi nūtana-prāya saba dravyera svāda
'vāsi' visvāda nahe sei prabhura prasāda

SYNONYMS

yadyapi—although; *māsekera*—one month; *vāsi*—remaining; *mukuta nārikela*—a very hard sweet preparation of coconut; *amṛta-guṭikā*—*amṛta-guṭikā* sweetballs; *ādi*—etc.; *pānā*—sweet drinks; *ādi*—and so on; *sakala*—all; *tathāpi*—still; *nūtana-prāya*—as if fresh; *saba dravyera*—of every preparation; *svāda*—the taste; *vāsi*—stale; *visvāda*—tasteless; *nahe*—were not; *sei*—that; *prabhura prasāda*—the mercy of the Lord.

TRANSLATION

The hard sweets made of coconut, mukuta nārikela, the sweetballs, the many kinds of sweet drinks and all the other preparations were at least a month old, but although they were old, they had not become tasteless or stale. Indeed, they had all stayed fresh. That is the mercy of Śrī Caitanya Mahāprabhu.

TEXT 127

শত-জনের ভক্ষ্য প্রভু দণ্ডেকে খাইলা !
'আর কিছু আছে ?' বলি' গোবিন্দে পুছিলা ॥ ১২৭ ॥

śata-janera bhakṣya prabhu daṇḍeke khāilā!
'āra kichu āche?' bali' govinde puchilā

SYNONYMS

śata-janera—of one hundred persons; *bhakṣya*—eatables; *prabhu*—Śrī Caitanya Mahāprabhu; *daṇḍeke khāilā*—ate within twenty-four minutes; *āra kichu āche*—is there anything more; *bali'*—saying; *govinde*—unto Govinda; *puchilā*—inquired.

TRANSLATION

Within a very short time, Śrī Caitanya Mahāprabhu ate enough for a hundred people. Then He asked Govinda, "Is there anything more left?"

TEXT 128

গোবিন্দ বলে,—'রাঘবের ঝালি মাত্র আছে'।
প্রভু কহে,—'আজি রহু, তাহা দেখিমু পাছে' ॥১২৮

govinda bale,—'rāghavera jhāli mātra āche'
prabhu kahe,—'āji rahu, tāhā dekhimu pāche'

SYNONYMS

govinda bale—Govinda replied; *rāghavera jhāli* —the bags given by Rāghava; *mātra*—only; *āche*—there is; *prabhu kahe*—Śrī Caitanya Mahāprabhu said; *āji*—today; *rahu*—let remain; *tāhā*—that; *dekhimu*—I shall see; *pāche*—later.

TRANSLATION

Govinda replied, "Now there are only the bags of Rāghava." The Lord said, "Let them remain today. I shall see them later."

TEXT 129

আর দিন প্রভু যদি নিভৃতে ভোজন কৈলা।
রাঘবের ঝালি খুলি' সকল দেখিলা ॥ ১২৯ ॥

āra dina prabhu yadi nibhṛte bhojana kailā
rāghavera jhāli khuli' sakala dekhilā

SYNONYMS

āra dina—the next day; *prabhu*—Śrī Caitanya Mahāprabhu; *yadi*—when; *nibhṛte*—in a secluded place; *bhojana kailā*—took His lunch; *rāghavera*—of Rāghava Paṇḍita; *jhāli*—the bags; *khuli'*—opening; *sakala dekhilā*—saw everything.

TRANSLATION

The next day, while taking His lunch in a secluded place, Śrī Caitanya Mahāprabhu opened the bags of Rāghava and inspected their contents one after another.

TEXT 130

সব দ্রব্যের কিছু কিছু উপযোগ কৈলা।
স্বাদু, সুগন্ধি দেখি' বহু প্রশংসিলা ॥ ১৩০ ॥

saba dravyera kichu kichu upayoga kailā
svādu, sugandhi dekhi' bahu praśaṁsilā

SYNONYMS

saba dravyera—of all the articles; *kichu kichu*—something; *upayoga kailā*—used; *svādu*—tasteful; *su-gandhi*—aromatic; *dekhi'*—seeing; *bahu*—very much; *praśaṁsilā*—He praised.

TRANSLATION

He tasted a little of everything they contained and praised it all for its flavor and aroma.

TEXT 131

বৎসরেক তরে আর রাখিলা ধরিয়া ।
ভোজন-কালে স্বরূপ পরিবেশে খসাঞা ॥ ১৩১ ॥

vatsareka tare āra rākhilā dhariyā
bhojana-kāle svarūpa pariveśe khasāñā

SYNONYMS

vatsareka—one year; *tare*—for; *āra*—balance; *rākhilā dhariyā*—kept in stock; *bhojana-kāle*—at the time of lunch; *svarūpa*—Svarūpa Dāmodara Gosvāmī; *pariveśe*—administered; *khasāñā*—taking out little by little.

TRANSLATION

All the varieties of the remaining prasāda were kept to eat throughout the year. When Śrī Caitanya Mahāprabhu ate His lunch, Svarūpa Dāmodara Gosvāmī would serve it little by little.

TEXT 132

কভু রাত্রিকালে কিছু করেন উপযোগ ।
ভক্তের শ্রদ্ধার দ্রব্য অবশ্য করেন উপভোগ ॥১৩২॥

kabhu rātri-kāle kichu karena upayoga
bhaktera śraddhāra dravya avaśya karena upabhoga

SYNONYMS

kabhu—sometimes; *rātri-kāle*—at night; *kichu*—some; *karena upayoga*—used; *bhaktera*—of the devotees; *śraddhāra*—with faith and love; *dravya*—preparations; *avaśya*—certainly; *karena upabhoga*—enjoys.

TRANSLATION

Sometimes Śrī Caitanya Mahāprabhu would take some of it at night. The Lord certainly enjoys preparations made with faith and love by His devotees.

PURPORT

Kṛṣṇa is very pleased with His devotees and their offerings. Therefore in *Bhagavad-gītā* the Lord says:

patraṁ puṣpaṁ phalaṁ toyaṁ
yo me bhaktyā prayacchati
tad ahaṁ bhakty-upahṛtam
aśnāmi prayatātmanaḥ

"If one offers Me with love and devotion a leaf, a flower, fruit or water, I will accept it." (Bg. 9.26) Herein also we find that Śrī Caitanya Mahāprabhu accepted all this food because it had been offered by His devotees. Sometimes He would eat it during lunch and sometimes at night, but He would always think that since His devotees had offered it with great love and affection, He must eat it.

TEXT 133

এইমত মহাপ্রভু ভক্তগণ-সঙ্গে ।
চাতুর্মাস্য গোঙাইলা কৃষ্ণকথা-রঙ্গে ॥ ১৩৩ ॥

ei-mata mahāprabhu bhakta-gaṇa-saṅge
cāturmāsya goṅāilā kṛṣṇa-kathā-raṅge

SYNONYMS

ei-mata—in this way; *mahāprabhu*—Śrī Caitanya Mahāprabhu; *bhakta-gaṇa-saṅge*—with His personal devotees; *cāturmāsya goṅāilā*—passed the four months of the rainy season; *kṛṣṇa-kathā-raṅge*—in the happiness of discussing topics about Kṛṣṇa.

TRANSLATION

Thus Śrī Caitanya Mahāprabhu spent the entire period of Cāturmāsya [the four months of the rainy season] in the happiness of discussing topics of Kṛṣṇa with His devotees.

TEXT 134

মধ্যে মধ্যে আচার্যাদি করে নিমন্ত্রণ ।
ঘরে ভাত রান্ধে আর বিবিধ ব্যঞ্জন ॥ ১৩৪ ॥

madhye madhye ācāryādi kare nimantraṇa
ghare bhāta rāndhe āra vividha vyañjana

SYNONYMS

madhye madhye—at intervals; *ācārya-ādi*—Advaita Ācārya and others; *kare nimantraṇa*—invite; *ghare*—at home; *bhāta*—rice; *rāndhe*—cook; *āra*—and; *vividha vyañjana*—varieties of vegetables.

TRANSLATION

From time to time, Advaita Ācārya and others would invite Śrī Caitanya Mahāprabhu for home-cooked rice and varieties of vegetables.

TEXTS 135-136

মরিচের ঝাল, আর মধুরাম্ল আর ।
আদা, লবণ, লেম্বু, দুগ্ধ, দধি, খণ্ডসার ॥ ১৩৫ ॥
শাক দুই-চারি, আর সুকুতার ঝোল ।
নিম্ব-বার্তাকী, আর ভৃষ্ট-পটোল ॥ ১৩৬ ॥

maricera jhāla, āra madhurāmla āra
ādā, lavaṇa, lembu, dugdha, dadhi, khaṇḍa-sāra

śāka dui-cāri, āra sukutāra jhola
nimba-vārtākī, āra bhṛṣṭa-paṭola

SYNONYMS

maricera jhāla—a pungent preparation with black pepper; *āra*—as well as; *madhurāmla*—a sweet-and-sour preparation; *āra*—also; *ādā*—ginger; *lavaṇa*—salted preparations; *lembu*—lime; *dugdha*—milk; *dadhi*—yogurt; *khaṇḍa-sāra*—cheese; *śāka dui-cāri*—spinach of two to four kinds; *āra*—and; *sukutāra jhola*—a soup made of bitter melon; *nimba-vārtākī*—eggplant mixed with *nimba* leaves; *āra*—and; *bhṛṣṭa-paṭola*—fried *paṭola.*

TRANSLATION

They offered pungent preparations made with black pepper, sweet-and-sour preparations, ginger, salty preparations, limes, milk, yogurt, cheese, two or four kinds of spinach, soup made with bitter melon, eggplant mixed with nimba flowers, and fried paṭola.

TEXT 137

ভৃষ্ট ফুলবড়ী, আর মুদ্গ-ডালি-সূপ ।
বিবিধ ব্যঞ্জন রান্ধে প্রভুর রুচি-অনুরূপ ॥ ১৩৭ ॥

bhṛṣṭa phula-baḍī, āra mudga-ḍāli-sūpa
vividha vyañjana rāndhe prabhura ruci-anurūpa

SYNONYMS

bhṛṣṭa—fried; *phula-baḍī*—a hot *dahl* preparation; *āra*—and; *mudga-ḍāli-sūpa*—a liquid preparation made from mung *dahl; vividha vyañjana*—varieties of vegetables; *rāndhe*—used to cook; *prabhura ruci-anurūpa*—very tasteful for Śrī Caitanya Mahāprabhu.

TRANSLATION

They also offered phula-baḍī, liquid mung dahl and many vegetables, all cooked according to the Lord's taste.

TEXT 138

জগন্নাথের প্রসাদ আনে করিতে মিশ্রিত ।
কাহাঁ একা যায়েন, কাহাঁ গণের সহিত ॥ ১৩৮ ॥

jagannāthera prasāda āne karite miśrita
kāhāṅ ekā yāyena, kāhāṅ gaṇera sahita

SYNONYMS

jagannāthera—of Lord Jagannātha; *prasāda*—remnants of food; *āne*—bring; *karite miśrita*—mixing; *kāhāṅ*—somewhere; *ekā yāyena*—goes alone; *kāhāṅ*—somewhere; *gaṇera sahita*—with associates.

TRANSLATION

They would mix these preparations with the remnants of food from Lord Jagannātha. When Śrī Caitanya Mahāprabhu accepted the invitations, He went sometimes alone and sometimes with His associates.

TEXT 139

আচার্যরত্ন, আচার্যনিধি, নন্দন, রাঘব ।
শ্রীবাস-আদি যত ভক্ত, বিপ্র সব ॥ ১৩৯ ॥

ācāryaratna, ācāryanidhi, nandana, rāghava
śrīvāsa-ādi yata bhakta, vipra saba

SYNONYMS

ācāryaratna—Ācāryaratna; *ācāryanidhi*—Ācāryanidhi; *nandana*—Nandana Ācārya; *rāghava*—Rāghava Paṇḍita; *śrīvāsa-ādi*—headed by Śrīvāsa; *yata bhakta*—all devotees; *vipra saba*—all *brāhmaṇas.*

TRANSLATION

Devotees like Ācāryaratna, Ācāryanidhi, Nandana Ācārya, Rāghava Paṇḍita and Śrīvāsa were all of the brāhmaṇa caste.

TEXTS 140-141

এইমত নিমন্ত্রণ করেন যত্ন করি ।
বাসুদেব, গদাধর-দাস, গুপ্ত-মুরারি ॥ ১৪০ ॥
কুলীনগ্রামী, খণ্ডবাসী, আর যত জন ।
জগন্নাথের প্রসাদ আনি' করে নিমন্ত্রণ ॥ ১৪১ ॥

ei-mata nimantraṇa karena yatna kari
vāsudeva, gadādhara-dāsa, gupta-murāri

kulīna-grāmī, khaṇḍa-vāsī, āra yata jana
jagannāthera prasāda āni' kare nimantraṇa

SYNONYMS

ei-mata—like this; *nimantraṇa*—invitation; *karena*—execute; *yatna kari*—with devotion; *vāsudeva*—Vāsudeva; *gadādhara-dāsa*—Gadādhara dāsa; *gupta-murāri*—Murāri Gupta; *kulīna-grāmī*—the inhabitants of Kulīna-grāma; *khaṇḍa-vāsī*—the inhabitants of Khaṇḍa; *āra*—and; *yata jana*—many other persons; *jagannāthera prasāda*—remnants of the food of Jagannātha; *āni'*—bringing; *kare nimantraṇa*—invite.

TRANSLATION

They would extend invitations to the Lord. Vāsudeva Datta, Gadādhara dāsa, Murāri Gupta, the inhabitants of Kulīna-grāma and Khaṇḍa and many other devotees who were not brāhmaṇas by caste would purchase food offered to Lord Jagannātha and then extend invitations to Śrī Caitanya Mahāprabhu.

PURPORT

The inhabitants of Kulīna-grāma, such as Satyarāja Khān and Rāmānanda Vasu, were not *brāhmaṇas* by caste, nor were the inhabitants of Khaṇḍa, such as Mukunda dāsa, Narahari dāsa and Raghunandana. Therefore they would purchase *prasāda* from the market where the remnants of Lord Jagannātha's food was sold and then extend invitations to Śrī Caitanya Mahāprabhu, whereas Ācāryaratna, Ācāryanidhi and others who were *brāhmaṇas* by caste would cook at home when they invited the Lord. Caitanya Mahāprabhu observed the etiquette then current in society by accepting only *prasāda* cooked by members of the *brāhmaṇa* caste, but on principle He accepted invitations from His devotees, regardless of whether they were *brāhmaṇas* by caste.

TEXT 142

শিবানন্দ-সেনের শুন নিমন্ত্রণাখ্যান ।
শিবানন্দের বড়-পুত্রের 'চৈতন্যদাস' নাম ॥ ১৪২ ॥

śivānanda-senera śuna nimantraṇākhyāna
śivānandera baḍa-putrera 'caitanya-dāsa' nāma

SYNONYMS

śivānanda-senera—of Śivānanda Sena; *śuna*—hear; *nimantraṇa-ākhyāna*—the story of the invitation; *śivānandera*—of Śivānanda Sena; *baḍa-putrera*—of the eldest son; *caitanya-dāsa nāma*—the name is Caitanya dāsa.

TRANSLATION

Now hear about the invitation Śivānanda Sena extended to the Lord. His eldest son was named Caitanya dāsa.

TEXT 143

প্রভুরে মিলাইতে তাঁরে সঙ্গেই আনিলা ।
মিলাইলে, প্রভু তাঁর নাম ত' পুছিলা ॥ ১৪৩ ॥

prabhure milāite tāṅre saṅgei ānilā
milāile, prabhu tāṅra nāma ta' puchilā

SYNONYMS

prabhure milāite—to introduce to the Lord; *tāṅre*—him, Caitanya dāsa; *saṅgei*—along; *ānilā*—brought; *milāile*—when he introduced him; *prabhu*—Śrī Caitanya Mahāprabhu; *tāṅra*—his; *nāma*—name; *ta'*—thereupon; *puchilā*—inquired.

TRANSLATION

When Śivānanda brought his son, Caitanya dāsa, to be introduced to the Lord, Śrī Caitanya Mahāprabhu inquired about his name.

TEXT 144

'চৈতন্যদাস' নাম শুনি' কহে গৌররায়।
'কিবা নাম ধরাঞাছ, বুঝন না যায়' ॥ ১৪৪ ॥

'caitanya-dāsa' nāma śuni' kahe gaura-rāya
'kibā nāma dharāñācha, bujhana nā yāya'

SYNONYMS

caitanya-dāsa—Caitanya dāsa; *nāma*—name; *śuni'*—hearing; *kahe gaura-rāya*—Śrī Caitanya Mahāprabhu said; *kibā*—what; *nāma*—name; *dharāñācha*—you have given; *bujhana nā yāya*—it cannot be understood.

TRANSLATION

When the Lord heard that his name was Caitanya dāsa, He said, "What kind of name have you given him? It is very difficult to understand."

TEXT 145

সেন কহে,—'যে জানিলুঁ, সেই নাম ধরিল'।
এত বলি' মহাপ্রভুরে নিমন্ত্রণ কৈল ॥ ১৪৫ ॥

sena kahe,——'ye jāniluṅ, sei nāma dharila'
eta bali' mahāprabhure nimantraṇa kaila

SYNONYMS

sena kahe—Śivānanda Sena replied; *ye jāniluṅ*—whatever I know; *sei nāma*—that name; *dharila*—he has kept; *eta bali'*—saying this; *mahāprabhure*—unto Śrī Caitanya Mahāprabhu; *nimantraṇa kaila*—gave an invitation.

TRANSLATION

Śivānanda Sena replied, "He has kept the name that appeared to me from within." Then he invited Śrī Caitanya Mahāprabhu for lunch.

TEXT 146

জগন্নাথের বহুমূল্য প্রসাদ আনাইলা।
ভক্তগণে লঞা প্রভু ভোজনে বসিলা ॥ ১৪৬ ॥

jagannāthera bahu-mūlya prasāda ānāilā
bhakta-gaṇe lañā prabhu bhojane vasilā

SYNONYMS

jagannāthera—of Lord Jagannātha; *bahu-mūlya*—very costly; *prasāda*—remnants of food; *ānāilā*—brought; *bhakta-gaṇe*—the devotees; *lañā*—taking along; *prabhu*—Śrī Caitanya Mahāprabhu; *bhojane vasilā*—sat down to accept *prasāda.*

TRANSLATION

Śivānanda Sena had bought very costly remnants of Lord Jagannātha's food. He brought it in and offered it to Śrī Caitanya Mahāprabhu, who sat down to accept the prasāda with His associates.

TEXT 147

শিবানন্দের গৌরবে প্রভু করিলা ভোজন ।
অতিগুরু-ভোজনে প্রভুর প্রসন্ন নহে মন ॥ ১৪৭ ॥

śivānandera gaurave prabhu karilā bhojana
ati-guru-bhojane prabhura prasanna nahe mana

SYNONYMS

śivānandera—of Śivānanda Sena; *gaurave*—out of honor; *prabhu*—Śrī Caitanya Mahāprabhu; *karilā bhojana*—ate; *ati-guru-bhojane*—because of eating too much; *prabhura*—of Śrī Caitanya Mahāprabhu; *prasanna nahe mana*—the mind was not satisfied.

TRANSLATION

Because of Śivānanda Sena's glories, Śrī Caitanya Mahāprabhu ate all kinds of prasāda to honor his request. However, the Lord ate more than necessary, and therefore His mind was dissatisfied.

TEXT 148

আর দিন চৈতন্যদাস কৈলা নিমন্ত্রণ ।
প্রভুর 'অভীষ্ট' বুঝি' আনিলা ব্যঞ্জন ॥ ১৪৮ ॥

āra dina caitanya-dāsa kailā nimantraṇa
prabhura 'abhīṣṭa' bujhi' ānilā vyañjana

SYNONYMS

āra dina—next day; *caitanya-dāsa*—the son of Śivānanda Sena; *kailā nimantraṇa*—invited; *prabhura*—of Śrī Caitanya Mahāprabhu; *abhīṣṭa*—desire; *bujhi'*—understanding; *ānilā vyañjana*—bought different vegetables.

TRANSLATION

The next day, Caitanya dāsa, the son of Śivānanda Sena, extended an invitation to the Lord. He could understand the Lord's mind, however, and therefore he arranged for a different kind of food.

TEXT 149

দধি, লেম্বু, আদা, আর ফুলবড়া, লবণ ।
সামগ্রী দেখিয়া প্রভুর প্রসন্ন হৈল মন ॥ ১৪৯ ॥

dadhi, lembu, ādā, āra phula-baḍā, lavaṇa
sāmagrī dekhiyā prabhura prasanna haila mana

SYNONYMS

dadhi—yogurt; *lembu*—lime; *ādā*—ginger; *āra*—and; *phula-baḍā*—soft cake made of *dahl; lavaṇa*—salt; *sāmagrī dekhiyā*—seeing these ingredients; *prabhura*—of Śrī Caitanya Mahāprabhu; *prasanna*—satisfied; *haila*—became; *mana*—the mind.

TRANSLATION

He offered yogurt, limes, ginger, soft baḍā and salt. Seeing all these arrangements, Śrī Caitanya Mahāprabhu was very pleased.

PURPORT

By the grace of Śrī Caitanya Mahāprabhu, Caitanya dāsa understood the Lord's mind. Therefore he arranged for food that would counteract the heavy meal the Lord had eaten the previous day.

Later in life, Caitanya dāsa became a very learned Sanskrit scholar and wrote many books. Among these books, his commentary on *Kṛṣṇa-karṇāmṛta* is very famous. There is another book called *Caitanya-caritāmṛta,* which is a work of Sanskrit poetry. It is said that this was also composed by him.

TEXT 150

প্রভু কহে,—"এ বালক আমার মত জানে ।
সন্তুষ্ট হইলাঙ আমি ইহার নিমন্ত্রণে ॥" ১৫০ ॥

prabhu kahe,—"ei bālaka āmāra mata jāne
santuṣṭa ha-ilāṅ āmi ihāra nimantraṇe"

SYNONYMS

prabhu kahe—Śrī Caitanya Mahāprabhu said; *ei bālaka*—this boy; *āmāra mata*—My mind; *jāne*—can understand; *santuṣṭa ha-ilāṅ*—am very satisfied; *āmi*—I; *ihāra nimantraṇe*—by his invitation.

TRANSLATION

Śrī Caitanya Mahāprabhu said, "This boy knows My mind. Therefore I am very satisfied to keep his invitation."

TEXT 151

এত বলি' দধি-ভাত করিলা ভোজন ।
চৈতন্যদাসেরে দিলা উচ্ছিষ্ট-ভাজন ॥ ১৫১ ॥

eta bali' dadhi-bhāta karilā bhojana
caitanya-dāsere dilā ucchiṣṭa-bhājana

SYNONYMS

eta bali'—saying this; *dadhi-bhāta*—yogurt with rice; *karilā bhojana*—ate; *caitanya-dāsere*—unto Caitanya dāsa; *dilā*—He offered; *ucchiṣṭa-bhājana*—the remnants of His food.

TRANSLATION

After saying this, the Lord ate the rice mixed with yogurt and offered Caitanya dāsa the remnants of His food.

TEXT 152

চারিমাস এইমত নিমন্ত্রণে যায় ।
কোন কোন বৈষ্ণব 'দিবস' নাহি পায় ॥ ১৫২ ॥

cāri-māsa ei-mata nimantraṇe yāya
kona kona vaiṣṇava 'divasa' nāhi pāya

SYNONYMS

cāri-māsa—for four months; *ei-mata*—in this way; *nimantraṇe yāya*—Śrī Caitanya Mahāprabhu keeps His invitations; *kona kona vaiṣṇava*—some of the Vaiṣṇava devotees; *divasa*—day; *nāhi pāya*—could not get.

TRANSLATION

The four months of Cāturmāsya passed in this manner, with the Lord accepting invitations from His devotees. Because of a heavy schedule of invitations, however, some of the Vaiṣṇavas could not get an open day on which to invite the Lord.

TEXT 153

গদাধর-পণ্ডিত, ভট্টাচার্য সার্বভৌম ।
ইঁহা সবার আছে ভিক্ষার দিবস-নিয়ম ॥ ১৫৩ ॥

gadādhara-paṇḍita, bhaṭṭācārya sārvabhauma
iṅhā sabāra āche bhikṣāra divasa-niyama

SYNONYMS

gadādhara-paṇḍita—Paṇḍita Gadādhara; *bhaṭṭācārya sārvabhauma*—Sārvabhauma Bhaṭṭācārya; *iṅhā sabāra*—of all these persons; *āche*—there is; *bhikṣāra*—for accepting invitations; *divasa-niyama*—a fixed date in every month.

TRANSLATION

Gadādhara Paṇḍita and Sārvabhauma Bhaṭṭācārya had fixed dates on which Śrī Caitanya Mahāprabhu would accept their invitations every month.

TEXTS 154-155

গোপীনাথাচার্য, জগদানন্দ, কাশীশ্বর ।
ভগবান্, রামভদ্রাচার্য, শঙ্কর, বক্রেশ্বর ॥ ১৫৪ ॥
মধ্যে মধ্যে ঘর-ভাতে করে নিমন্ত্রণ ।
অন্যের নিমন্ত্রণে প্রসাদে কৌড়ি দুইপণ ॥ ১৫৫ ॥

gopīnāthācārya, jagadānanda, kāśīśvara
bhagavān, rāmabhadrācārya, śaṅkara, vakreśvara

madhye madhye ghara-bhāte kare nimantraṇa
anyera nimantraṇe prasāde kauḍi dui-paṇa

SYNONYMS

gopīnātha-ācārya—Gopīnātha Ācārya; *jagadānanda*—Jagadānanda Paṇḍita; *kāśīśvara*—Kāśīśvara; *bhagavān*—Bhagavān; *rāmabhadra-ācārya*—Rāma bhadrācārya; *śaṅkara*—Śaṅkara; *vakreśvara*—Vakreśvara; *madhye madhye*—at intervals; *ghara-bhāte*—with rice at home; *kare nimantraṇa*—invite; *anyera nimantraṇa*—for others' invitations; *prasāde*—*prasāda; kauḍi dui-paṇa*—two *panas* of conchshells (160 conchshells).

TRANSLATION

Gopīnātha Ācārya, Jagadānanda, Kāśīśvara, Bhagavān, Rāmabhadrācārya, Śaṅkara and Vakreśvara, who were all brāhmaṇas, extended invitations to Śrī Caitanya Mahāprabhu and offered Him food cooked at home, whereas other devotees would pay two paṇas of small conchshells to purchase Jagannātha's prasāda and then invite the Lord.

TEXT 156

প্রথমে আছিল 'নির্বন্ধ' কৌড়ি চারিপণ ।
রামচন্দ্রপুরী-ভয়ে ঘাটাইলা নিমন্ত্রণ ॥ ১৫৬ ॥

prathame āchila 'nirbandha' kauḍi cāri-paṇa
rāmacandra-purī-bhaye ghāṭāilā nimantraṇa

SYNONYMS

prathame—in the beginning; *āchila*—it was; *nirbandha*—fixed; *kauḍi cāri-paṇa*—four *paṇas* of conchshells; *rāmacandra-purī-bhaye*—because of the restriction of Rāmacandra Purī; *ghāṭāilā*—decreased; *nimantraṇa*—the price of an invitation.

TRANSLATION

At first the cost of Jagannātha prasāda for an invitation was four paṇas of conchshells, but when Rāmacandra Purī was there, the price was cut in half.

TEXT 157

চারিমাস রহি' গৌড়ের ভক্তে বিদায় দিলা ।
নীলাচলের সঙ্গী ভক্ত সঙ্গেই রহিলা ॥ ১৫৭ ॥

cāri-māsa rahi' gauḍera bhakte vidāya dilā
nīlācalera saṅgī bhakta saṅgei rahilā

SYNONYMS

cāri-māsa rahi'—remaining for four months; *gauḍera bhakte*—to the devotees coming from Bengal; *vidāya dilā*—bade farewell; *nīlācalera saṅgī*—associates at Jagannātha Purī; *bhakta*—devotees; *saṅgei*—with; *rahilā*—remained.

TRANSLATION

The devotees who came from Bengal stayed with Śrī Caitanya Mahāprabhu for four consecutive months, and then the Lord bade them farewell. After the Bengali devotees departed, the devotees who were the Lord's constant companions at Jagannātha Purī stayed with the Lord.

TEXT 158

এই ত' কহিলুঁ প্রভুর ভিক্ষা-নিমন্ত্রণ ।
ভক্ত-দত্ত বস্তু যৈছে কৈলা আস্বাদন ॥ ১৫৮ ॥

ei ta' kahiluṅ prabhura bhikṣā-nimantraṇa
bhakta-datta vastu yaiche kailā āsvādana

SYNONYMS

ei ta'—thus; *kahiluṅ*—I have described; *prabhura*—of Śrī Caitanya Mahāprabhu; *bhikṣā-nimantraṇa*—the invitation to dine; *bhakta-datta*—offered by the devotees; *vastu*—things; *yaiche*—as; *kailā āsvādana*—He tasted.

TRANSLATION

Thus I have described how Śrī Caitanya Mahāprabhu accepted invitations and how He accepted and tasted the prasāda offered by His devotees.

TEXT 159

তার মধ্যে রাঘবের ঝালি-বিবরণ ।
তার মধ্যে পরিমুণ্ডা-নৃত্য-কথন ॥ ১৫৯ ॥

tāra madhye rāghavera jhāli-vivaraṇa
tāra madhye pari-muṇḍā-nṛtya-kathana

SYNONYMS

tāra madhye—in the midst of that; *rāghavera*—of Rāghava Paṇḍita; *jhāli-vivaraṇa*—description of the bags of food; *tāra madhye*—along with that; *pari-muṇḍā-nṛtya-kathana*—the description of dancing in the temple of Jagannātha.

TRANSLATION

In the midst of that narration are descriptions of Rāghava Paṇḍita's bags of food and the dancing in the temple of Jagannātha.

TEXT 160

শ্রদ্ধা করি' শুনে যেই চৈতন্যের কথা।
চৈতন্যচরণে প্রেম পাইবে সর্বথা ॥ ১৬০ ॥

śraddhā kari' śune yei caitanyera kathā
caitanya-caraṇe prema pāibe sarvathā

SYNONYMS

śraddhā kari'—with great faith and love; *śune*—hears; *yei*—anyone who; *caitanyera kathā*—the narration of the activities of Śrī Caitanya Mahāprabhu; *caitanya-caraṇe*—at the lotus feet of Śrī Caitanya Mahāprabhu; *prema*—love; *pāibe*—must achieve; *sarvathā*—without fail.

TRANSLATION

One who hears about the pastimes of Śrī Caitanya Mahāprabhu with faith and love will certainly attain ecstatic love for the lotus feet of Śrī Caitanya Mahāprabhu without fail.

TEXT 161

শুনিতে অমৃত-সম জুড়ায় কর্ণ-মন।
সেই ভাগ্যবান্, যেই করে আস্বাদন ॥ ১৬১ ॥

śunite amṛta-sama juḍāya karṇa-mana
sei bhāgyavān, yei kare āsvādana

SYNONYMS

śunite—to hear; *amṛta-sama*—just like nectar; *juḍāya karṇa-mana*—satisfies the ears and mind; *sei bhāgyavān*—he is very fortunate; *yei*—who; *kare āsvādana*—tastes.

TRANSLATION

Narrations of Śrī Caitanya Mahāprabhu's activities are just like nectar to hear. Indeed, they satisfy both the ears and mind. One who tastes the nectar of these activities is certainly very fortunate.

TEXT 162

শ্রীরূপ-রঘুনাথ-পদে যার আশ।
চৈতন্যচরিতামৃত কহে কৃষ্ণদাস ॥ ১৬২ ॥

śrī-rūpa-raghunātha-pade yāra āśa
caitanya-caritāmṛta kahe kṛṣṇadāsa

SYNONYMS

śrī-rūpa—Śrīla Rūpa Gosvāmī; *raghunātha*—Śrīla Raghunātha dāsa Gosvāmī; *pade*—at the lotus feet; *yāra*—whose; *āśa*—expectation; *caitanya-caritāmṛta*—the book named *Caitanya-caritāmṛta; kahe*—describes; *kṛṣṇadāsa*—Śrīla Kṛṣṇadāsa Kavirāja Gosvāmī.

TRANSLATION

Praying at the lotus feet of Śrī Rūpa and Śrī Raghunātha, always desiring their mercy, I, Kṛṣṇadāsa, narrate Śrī Caitanya-caritāmṛta, following in their footsteps.

Thus end the Bhaktivedanta purports to the Śrī Caitanya-caritāmṛta, Antya-līlā, *Tenth Chapter, describing how Lord Śrī Caitanya Mahāprabhu tasted the* prasāda *offered by His devotees.*

References

The statements of *Śrī Caitanya-caritāmṛta* are all confirmed by standard Vedic authorities. The following authentic scriptures are quoted in this book on the pages listed. Numerals in bold type refer the reader to *Śrī Caitanya-caritāmṛta's* translations. Numerals in regular type are references to its purports.

Amṛta-pravāha-bhāṣya (Bhaktivinoda Ṭhākura), 1, 83, 203

Anubhāṣya (Bhaktisiddhānta Sarasvatī), 96

Bhagavad-gītā, 92, 114, 160, 260

Bhakti-sandarbha (Jīva Gosvāmī), 95

Laghu-bhāgavatāmṛta (Rūpa Gosvāmī), **8**

Laghu-toṣaṇī (Jīva Gosvāmī), 95

Nāma-kaumudī, **43**

Nārāyaṇa-saṁhitā, 7

Śrīmad-Bhāgavatam, **5, 14-15, 16, 23, 25, 26,** 95, 118-119, 162, **167,** 194

Viṣṇu-bhakti-candrodaya, 96

Glossary

A

Ācārya—a spiritual master who teaches by his own example.
Acintya-bhedābheda-tattva—Lord Caitanya's "simultaneously one and different" doctrine, which establishes the inconceivable simultaneous existence of the Absolute Truth as both personal and impersonal.
Aiśvarya-jñāna-yukta—emotion with an understanding of the Lord's full opulences.
Artha—economic development.
Āśrama—four orders of spiritual life.
Avatāra—(literally, one who descends) an incarnation of the Lord who descends from the spiritual sky to the material universe with a particular mission described in the scriptures.

B

Bāla-gopāla—the child Kṛṣṇa.
Bhagavān—a name of Kṛṣṇa which means one who possesses all opulences.
Bhāva—the stage of transcendental ecstasy experienced after transcendental affection.
Brahmacarya—student life of celibacy and study under a spiritual master.
Brāhmaṇa—the intelligent class of men.

D

Dāsya-rasa—loving relationship with Kṛṣṇa in servitorship.
Dharma—religiosity.

G

Gadādhara-prāṇanātha—Lord Caitanya, the life and soul of Gadādhara Paṇḍita.
Gadāira Gaura—Lord Caitanya, the Lord Gaurāṅga of Gadādhara Paṇḍita.
Gosvāmī—one who controls his senses.
Gṛhastha—regulated married life.

J

Jagad-guru—spiritual master of the entire world.

K

Kali-yuga—the age of quarrel, the fourth and last age in the cycle of a *mahā-yuga*.
Kāma—lust.

Karma—fruitive work.
Karma-kāṇḍa—the section of the *Vedas* dealing with fruitive work.
Karmīs—fruitive workers.
Kauḍis—small conchshells.
Kevala—pure, uncontaminated emotion.
Kiśora-gopāla—Kṛṣṇa as a young boy.
Kṛṣṇa-bhakti—loving devotional service to Kṛṣṇa.
Kṣatriya—the administrative and warrior class of men.

M

Mahā-mantra—the great chanting for deliverance: Hare Kṛṣṇa, Hare Kṛṣṇa, Kṛṣṇa Kṛṣṇa, Hare Hare/ Hare Rāma, Hare Rāma, Rāma Rāma, Hare Hare.
Māyāvādī—impersonalist or voidist adhering to the belief that ultimately God is formless and without personality.
Mlecchas—meateaters.
Mokṣa—liberation.
Mukunda—Kṛṣṇa, the bestower of liberation.

P

Paramahaṁsa-ṭhākura—one who acts as an *ācārya* directly presenting Lord Kṛṣṇa by spreading His name and fame.
Parama-puruṣārtha—the supreme goal of life.
Paramātmā—the Supreme, the localized aspect of the Supreme Lord within the heart of all living entities.
Paramparā—disciplic succession.
Para-vidhi—*Bhāgavatam* injunction against criticizing characteristics or activities of others.
Pati—a husband.
Prākṛta-sahajiyās—so-called Vaiṣṇavas who take everything very lightly.
Prakṛti—material nature.
Purāṇas—the eighteen very old books which are histories of this and other planets.
Puruṣārtha—the goal of life.
Pūrva-vidhi—*Bhāgavatam* injunction against praising characteristics or activities of others.

S

Sakhya-rasa—loving relationships with Kṛṣṇa in friendship.
Sannyāsa—the renounced order of spiritual life.
Śleṣokti—a statement having two meanings.
Śṛṅgāra—an array of garments worn for amorous purposes.
Śuddha-bhāva—pure consciousness.
Śūdra—the laboring and servant class of men.

T

Ṭīkās—commentaries.

V

Vaiṣṇava—a devotee of the Supreme Lord Viṣṇu, or Kṛṣṇa.
Vaiśya—the mercantile and agricultural class of men.
Vānaprastha—the retired order of spiritual life.
Varṇas—the four orders of social life.
Vāsanā—a wish or desire.
Vātsalya-rasa—loving relationship with Kṛṣṇa in parenthood.
Viṣayī—a person engaged in material activities.
Vṛndāvana—the site of Kṛṣṇa's transcendental village pastimes, exhibited when He was present on earth about 5,000 years ago.

Bengali Pronunciation Guide

BENGALI DIACRITICAL EQUIVALENTS AND PRONUNCIATION

Vowels

অ a আ ā ই i ঈ ī উ u ঊ ū ঋ ṛ

ৠ ṝ এ e ঐ ai ও o ঔ au

ং ṁ *(anusvāra)* ঁ ṅ *(candra-bindu)* ঃ ḥ *(visarga)*

Consonants

Gutterals:	ক ka	খ kha	গ ga	ঘ gha	ঙ ṅa
Palatals:	চ ca	ছ cha	জ ja	ঝ jha	ঞ ña
Cerebrals:	ট ṭa	ঠ ṭha	ড ḍa	ঢ ḍha	ণ ṇa
Dentals:	ত ta	থ tha	দ da	ধ dha	ন na
Labials:	প pa	ফ pha	ব ba	ভ bha	ম ma
Semivowels:	য ya	র ra	ল la	ব va	
Sibilants:	শ śa	ষ ṣa	স sa	হ ha	

Vowel Symbols

The vowels are written as follows after a consonant:

া ā ি i ী ī ু u ূ ū ৃ ṛ ৄ ṝ ে e ৈ ai ো o ৌ au

For example: কা kā কি ki কী kī কু ku কূ kū কৃ kṛ

কৄ kṝ কে ke কৈ kai কো ko কৌ kau

The letter *a* is implied after a consonant with no vowel symbol.

The symbol *virāma* (্) indicates that there is no final vowel. ক্ k

The letters above should be pronounced as follows:

a –like the *o* in h*o*t; sometimes like the *o* in go; final *a* is usually silent.
ā –like the *a* in f*a*r.
i, ī –like the *ee* in m*ee*t.
u, ū –like the *u* in r*u*le.
ṛ –like the *ri* in *ri*m.
ṝ –like the *ree* in *ree*d.
e –like the *ai* in p*ai*n; rarely like *e* in b*e*t.
ai –like the *oi* in b*oi*l.
o –like the *o* in g*o*.
au –like the *ow* in *ow*l.
ṁ –*(anusvāra)* like the *ng* in so*ng*.
ḥ –*(visarga)* a final *h* sound like in Ah.
ṅ –*(candra-bindu)* a nasal *n* sound like in the French word *bon*.
k –like the *k* in *k*ite.
kh –like the *kh* in Ec*kh*art.
g –like the *g* in *g*ot.
gh –like the *gh* in bi*g-h*ouse.
ṅ –like the *n* in ba*n*k.
c –like the *ch* in *ch*alk.
ch –like the *chh* in mu*ch-h*aste.
j –like the *j* in *j*oy.
jh –like the *geh* in colle*ge-h*all.
ñ –like the *n* in bu*n*ch.
ṭ –like the *t* in *t*alk.
ṭh –like the *th* in ho*t-h*ouse.
ḍ –like the *d* in *d*awn.
ḍh –like the *dh* in goo*d-h*ouse.
ṇ –like the *n* in *g*naw.
t–as in *t*alk but with the tongue against the the teeth.
th–as in ho*t-h*ouse but with the tongue against the teeth.
d–as in *d*awn but with the tongue against the teeth.
dh–as in goo*d-h*ouse but with the tongue against the teeth.
n–as in *n*or but with the tongue against the teeth.
p –like the *p* in *p*ine.
ph –like the *ph* in *ph*ilosopher.
b –like the *b* in *b*ird.
bh –like the *bh* in ru*b-h*ard.
m –like the *m* in *m*other.
y –like the *j* in *j*aw. য
y –like the *y* in *y*ear. য়
r –like the *r* in *r*un.
l –like the *l* in *l*aw.
v –like the *b* in *b*ird or like the *w* in d*w*arf.
ś, ṣ –like the *sh* in *sh*op.
s –like the *s* in *s*un.
h–like the *h* in *h*ome.

This is a general guide to Bengali pronunciation. The Bengali transliterations in this book accurately show the original Bengali spelling of the text. One should note, however, that in Bengali, as in English, spelling is not always a true indication of how a word is pronounced. Tape recordings of His Divine Grace A. C. Bhaktivedanta Swami Prabhupāda chanting the original Bengali verses are available from the International Society for Krishna Consciousness, 3764 Watseka Ave., Los Angeles, California 90034.

Index of Bengali and Sanskrit Verses

This index constitutes a complete alphabetical listing of the first and third line of each four-line verse and both lines of each two-line verse in *Śrī Caitanya-caritāmṛta*. In the first column the transliteration is given, and in the second and third columns respectively the chapter-verse references and page number for each verse are to be found.

B

J

K

L

M

N

P

R

General Index

Numerals in bold type indicate references to *Śrī Caitanya-caritāmṛta's* verses. Numerals in regular type are references to its purports.

A

Ācārya
 See: Spiritual master
Ācāryanidhi
 descended in Bengal, **28**
Ācāryaratna
 descended in Bengal, **28**
Activities
 of Caitanya as beautiful, **126**
 two kinds rejected in revealed scriptures, **118**
Advaita Ācārya
 as dancer at car festival, **38**
 as directly the Supreme Lord, **9**
 as incarnation of Supreme Lord, **85**
 induces Kṛṣṇa to descend, **85**
 led devotees from Bengal to Jagannātha Purī, **205**
 qualities of, **10**
 took *prasāda* with Caitanya, **34**
 Vallabha Bhaṭṭa argued with, **50**-52
Akiñcana Kṛṣṇadāsa
 went to Jagannātha Purī, **208**
Ālālanātha
 Caitanya desires to go to, **157**
Amṛta-pravāha-bhāṣya
 summary of Eighth Chapter given in, 83
 summary of Chapter Ten in, 203
 summary of Chapter Seven in, 1
Anubhāṣya
 cited on *nirbandha*, 96
Anyābhilāṣitā-śūnyaṁ
 verses quoted, 162
Api cet sudurācāro
 verses quoted, 160
Arjuna
 addressed by Kṛṣṇa, **114**
Āruhya kṛcchreṇa paraṁ padaṁ
 verses quoted, 162
Āśramas
 ācārya is spiritual master of all, 7
Attachment
 to speculation precludes relationship with Kṛṣṇa, **96**
Austerity
 Kṛṣṇa inaccessible merely by, **14-15**

B

Bali Mahārāja
 as great devotee of Vāmana, 136
 came to visit Caitanya, **135**
Bengal
 Advaita led devotees from, **205**
 devotees of go to see Caitanya, **2**
 list of devotees who descended in, **28**
Bhagavad-gītā
 quoted, 114
 quoted on happiness of Brahman realized soul, 92
 quoted on offerings accepted by Kṛṣṇa, 260
 quoted on proper situation of devotee, 160
Bhagavān Ācārya
 Caitanya accepts dinner invitation of, **124**
 offered Caitanya home-cooked food, **270**
Bhagavān Paṇḍita
 went to Jagannātha Purī, **208**
Bhakti
 See: Devotional service
Bhakti-sandarbha
 quoted on mental speculation, 95
Bhaktisiddhānta Sarasvatī
 cited on becoming *jagad-guru,* 7

D

Damayantī
considered Caitanya an ordinary human, 211
cooked many things for Caitanya, **209-219**
Dāmodara
descended in Bengal, **28**
Death
Mādhavendra Purī remembers Kṛṣṇa at, **97-101**
Demigods
visited Caitanya, **134**
Desires
Offenses cause material, **95-**96
Devotees
Caitanya life and soul of, **85**
condemn Rāmacandra Purī, **109**
gave up eating, **111**
of Caitanya overeat, **90**
of Caitanya reduced eating, **115**
protected from reactions to sin, **160**
showbottle, **161-**162
Uddhava as greatest of, **25-27**
Devotional service
as essence of all mystic *yoga*, **12**
conjugal love of *gopīs* as highest, **24**
finer points of etiquette in, **245**
learned from pure Vaiṣṇava, 29
pure described, 162
the true result of, 194
Dharmaḥ projjhita-kaitavo 'tra
quoted, 194
Disciple
reprimanded by spiritual master, 93
Dreams
affect *yoga* practice, **114**
Duties
should be properly executed, **114**
Dvāpara-yuga
system of religion in, 7
Dvāparīyair janair viṣṇuḥ
verses quoted, 7

E

Ecstatic symptoms
manifested by Caitanya, **133**
of Caitanya, **233-235**

F

Fasting
unnecessarily precludes *yoga* practice, **114**
Food
cost of Caitanya's, **123**
eating sweets affects sense control, **104**

G

Gadādhara Paṇḍita
as dancer at car festival, **38**
Caitanya accepts dinner invitation of, **124**
converted Vallabha Bhaṭṭa to worship of Kiśora-gopāla, **71**
descended in Bengal, **28**
heard explanations of Vallabha Bhaṭṭa, **47-48**
love of compared to Rukmiṇīdevī's, **69-**70
refused to act as spiritual master, **72**
Vallabha Bhaṭṭa initiated by, **81**
Gadādhara-prāṇanātha
as name of Caitanya, **77**
Gadāira Gaura
Caitanya known as, **78**
Gandharvas
visited Caitanya, **134**
Gaṅgādāsa
went to Jagannātha Purī, **208**
Ganges
pastimes of Caitanya compared to, **78**
Garuḍa Paṇḍita
went to Jagannātha Purī, **208**
Gauḍīya-sampradāya
congregational chanting of, **223**

J

K

Q

R

S

Supersoul
yogīs know the Lord as, **19**
Supreme Lord
acts for everyone's welfare, **59**
Svarūpa Dāmodara
Caitanya tasted bliss in company of, **134**
ecstatic love personified by, **21**
sang to Caitanya, **232**
served *prasāda* to devotees, **36**
Vallabha Bhaṭṭa argued with, **50**
Śyāmasundara
as name of Kṛṣṇa, **43-44**

U

Uddhava
as greatest devotee, **25-**27

V

Vaiṣṇavas
criticized by Māyāvādīs, 96-97
See also: Devotees
Vaiṣṇavism
power of Advaita's, **10**
Vakreśvara
as dancer at car festival, **38**
descended in Bengal, **28**
offered Caitanya home-cooked food, **270**
Vallabha Bhaṭṭa
accustomed to worshiping child Kṛṣṇa, **71**
converted to worship of Kiśora-gopāla, **71**
initiated by Gadādhara Paṇḍita, **81**
like duck in society of swans, **50**
pride of cut down by Caitanya, **29-**30, 57-66
seemed like glowworm compared to other Vaiṣṇavas, **33**
went to Jagannātha Purī to meet the Lord, **3**
Vallabha Bhaṭṭa
wrote commentary on *Bhāgavatam,* **41-42, 55**
Vāmana
Bali Mahārāja as great devotee of, 136
Vāṇīnātha Rāya
arrest of, **146**
Caitanya's mercy on, **194**
incessantly chanted *mahā-mantra,* **156**
Vedas
divided by Vyāsadeva, 136
Virocana
as son of Prahlāda Mahārāja, 136
Viṣṇu
regarded as *māya* by Māyāvādīs, 96-97
See also: Kṛṣṇa, Nārāyaṇa
Viṣṇu-bhakti-candrodaya
quoted on material desires, 96
Varṇas
ācārya is spiritual master of all, 7
Vāsudeva Datta
descended in Bengal, **28**
went to Jagannātha Purī, **208**
Vrajabhūmi
See: Vṛndāvana
Vṛndāvana
devotees in consider Kṛṣṇa an ordinary human, 211
devotees in enjoy association of Kṛṣṇa, 15
Vyāsadeva
as author of the *Vedas,* 136
praises attitude of pure devotees, **17**
visited Caitanya, **135**

W

World, material
seed of ecstatic love for Kṛṣṇa sowed in, **101**
Worship, temple
as system of religion in Dvāpara-yuga, 7

Y

The Author

His Divine Grace A. C. Bhaktivedanta Swami Prabhupāda appeared in this world in 1896 in Calcutta, India. He first met his spiritual master, Śrīla Bhaktisiddhānta Sarasvatī Gosvāmī, in Calcutta in 1922. Bhaktisiddhānta Sarasvatī, a prominent devotional scholar and the founder of sixty-four Gauḍīya Maṭhas (Vedic Institutes), liked this educated young man and convinced him to dedicate his life to teaching Vedic knowledge. Śrīla Prabhupāda became his student, and eleven years later (1933) at Allahabad he became his formally initiated disciple.

At their first meeting, in 1922, Śrīla Bhaktisiddhānta Sarasvatī Ṭhākura requested Śrīla Prabhupāda to broadcast Vedic knowledge through the English language. In the years that followed, Śrīla Prabhupāda wrote a commentary on the *Bhagavad-gītā,* assisted the Gauḍīya Maṭha in its work and, in 1944, without assistance, started an English fortnightly magazine, edited it, typed the manuscripts and checked the galley proofs. He even distributed the individual copies freely and struggled to maintain the publication. Once begun, the magazine never stopped; it is now being continued by his disciples in the West.

Recognizing Śrīla Prabhupāda's philosophical learning and devotion, the Gauḍīya Vaiṣṇava Society honored him in 1947 with the title "Bhaktivedanta." In 1950, at the age of fifty-four, Śrīla Prabhupāda retired from married life, and four years later he adopted the *vānaprastha* (retired) order to devote more time to his studies and writing. Śrīla Prabhupāda traveled to the holy city of Vṛndāvana, where he lived in very humble circumstances in the historic medieval temple of Rādhā-Dāmodara. There he engaged for several years in deep study and writing. He accepted the renounced order of life (*sannyāsa*) in 1959. At Rādhā-Dāmodara, Śrīla Prabhupāda began work on his life's masterpiece: a multivolume translation and commentary on the eighteen thousand verse *Śrīmad-Bhāgavatam* (*Bhāgavata Purāṇa*). He also wrote *Easy Journey to Other Planets.*

After publishing three volumes of *Bhāgavatam,* Śrīla Prabhupāda came to the United States, in 1965, to fulfill the mission of his spiritual master. Since that time, His Divine Grace has written over forty volumes of authoritative translations, commentaries and summary studies of the philosophical and religious classics of India.

In 1965, when he first arrived by freighter in New York City, Śrīla Prabhupāda was practically penniless. It was after almost a year of great difficulty that he established the International Society for Krishna Consciousness in July of 1966. Under his careful guidance, the Society has grown within a decade to a worldwide confederation of almost one hundred *āśramas,* schools, temples, institutes and farm communities.

In 1968, Śrīla Prabhupāda created New Vṛndāvana, an experimental Vedic community in the hills of West Virginia. Inspired by the success of New Vṛndāvana, now a thriving farm community of more than one thousand acres, his students have since founded several similar communities in the United States and abroad.

In 1972, His Divine Grace introduced the Vedic system of primary and secondary education in the West by founding the *Gurukula* school in Dallas, Texas. The school began with 3 children in 1972, and by the beginning of 1975 the enrollment had grown to 150.

Śrīla Prabhupāda has also inspired the construction of a large international center at Śrīdhāma Māyāpur in West Bengal, India, which is also the site for a planned Institute of Vedic Studies. A similar project is the magnificent Kṛṣṇa-Balarāma Temple and International Guest House in Vṛndāvana, India. These are centers where Westerners can live to gain firsthand experience of Vedic culture.

Śrīla Prabhupāda's most significant contribution, however, is his books. Highly respected by the academic community for their authoritativeness, depth and clarity, they are used as standard textbooks in numerous college courses. His writings have been translated into eleven languages. The Bhaktivedanta Book Trust, established in 1972 exclusively to publish the works of His Divine Grace, has thus become the world's largest publisher of books in the field of Indian religion and philosophy. Its latest project is the publishing of Śrīla Prabhupāda's most recent work: a seventeen-volume translation and commentary—completed by Śrīla Prabhupāda in only eighteen months—on the Bengali religious classic *Śrī Caitanya-caritāmṛta.*

In the past ten years, in spite of his advanced age, Śrīla Prabhupāda has circled the globe twelve times on lecture tours that have taken him to six continents. In spite of such a vigorous schedule, Śrīla Prabhupāda continues to write prolifically. His writings constitute a veritable library of Vedic philosophy, religion, literature and culture.